The National Kitchen & Bath Association

presents

U N I V E R S A L

B A T H R O O M

P L A N N I N G

Design That Adapts To People

Mary Jo Peterson, CKD, CBD, CHE

BOOK STORE

- **Publisher: Nick Geragi, CKD, CBD, NCIDQ**

- **Director of Communications: Donna M. Luzzo**

- **Director of Marketing: Nora DePalma**

- **Executive Director: Paul A. Kohmescher**

Copyright © 1996, by The National Kitchen & Bath Association. All rights reserved. No part of this publication may be reproduced, stored in a retrieval system or transmitted in any form or by any means, electronic, mechanical, photocopy, recording or otherwise without the express prior written permission of the copyright owner.

ISBN 1-887127-01-1

Information about this book and other NKBA publications, *Universal Kitchen Planning- Design That Adapts To People, The Enabling Products Sourcebook 2* and NKBA's design seminars may be obtained from The National Kitchen & Bath Association, 687 Willow Grove Street, Hackettstown, NJ, 07840, phone (800) THE-NKBA, fax (908) 852-1695.

This book is intended for professional use by residential bathroom designers. The procedures and advice herein have been shown to be appropriate for the applications described; however, no warranty (expressed or implied) is intended or given. Moreover, the user of this book is cautioned to be familiar with and to adhere to all manufacturers' planning, installation and use/care instructions. In addition, the user is urged to become familiar with and adhere to all applicable local, state and federal building codes, licensing and legislation requirements governing the user's ability to perform all tasks associated with design and installation standards, and to collaborate with licensed practitioners who offer professional services in the technical areas of mechanical, electrical and load bearing design as required for regulatory approval, as well as health and safety regulations.

Cover Bathroom designed by Annette DePaepe, CKD, CBD, ASID, AMD Designs, Hackettstown, NJ.

Cover Photos courtesy of Wilsonart International.

A Special Thanks

The author would like to thank Ron Mace, FAIA, and the Center for Universal Design, Ed Steinfeld and Abir Mullick, Center for Inclusive Design and Environmental Access, School of Architecture and Planning at SUNY Buffalo, for their continued reference and personal support.

NKBA would like to thank many other individuals and organizations that have contributed to the content and preparation of this book.

NKBA's Universal Design Committee; Margaret Wylde, Institute for Technology Development; Joan Eisenberg, CKD, CBD, CHE, JME Consulting Inc; James Krengel, CKD, CBD, Kitchens by Krengel; Abir Mullick, Dept. of Architecture, State University of NY at Buffalo; Ken Smith, CKD, CBD, National Kitchen & Bath Association; Doris LaCroix, CKD, CBD, Design First Kitchen & Bath Interiors; Ron Mace, FAIA, Center for Universal Design, North Carolina State University and Nick Geragi, CKD, CBD, NCIDQ, National Kitchen & Bath Association and Mary Jo Peterson, CKD, CBD, CHE, Mary Jo Peterson Design Consultants.

Other Contributors:

- **Subject Editor: Bill Partsch, Senior Editor - Kitchen and Bath Business Magazine**

- **Illustrations: Kate Erwin, CKD,**
  Design Services Unlimited, Syracuse, NY.

- **Electronic Publishing/Design: Beth A. Treen,**
  Computer Connection, West Winfield, NY.

- **Abir Mullick, Mark Eberle, Glenn Goatha, Sherry Altman - IDEA SUNY Buffalo, Bath Seat and Lift Ideas.**

- **American Standard Inc. - Heather Bathroom Project Photography.**

- **Annette DePaepe, CKD, CBD, ASID, AMD Designs, Hackettstown, NJ.**

- **Dee Reis-Braaten, MS Occupational Therapy, Ridgefield, CT.**

- **Gordon Beall, Dobkin Bathroom Project Photography**

- **Joy Myers-Piske, CKD, Winnipeg, Manitoba.**

- **Mary Seymour, Norwalk, CT.**

- **Ron Mace - Center For Accessible Housing, Raleigh, NC.**

- **Wilsonart International - Kline Bathroom Project Photography**

NATIONAL KITCHEN
NKBA
& BATH ASSOCIATION

From The Publisher

Dear Industry Professional,

Designing rooms that suit the needs of all users throughout their lifecycle is the purpose of universal design. The ability to create rooms that can be used by more types of people, including people with children, people with disabilities and people who are aging, is essential for success in today's marketplace. As the baby boomer generation, -- the largest segment of the population, -- grows older, these design concepts will become even more important.

The National Kitchen & Bath Association (NKBA) recognizes that universal design is a fact of life and that all members of the kitchen and bathroom industry need comprehensive, up-to-date information on this subject. Providing that information is the purpose of "Universal Bathroom Planning, Design That Adapts To People."

To create this book, NKBA teamed up with experts in the field of universal design. The collective knowledge, expertise and ideas of all the industry and design professionals involved ensure that the information found within this book is accurate, thorough and practical.

Every aspect of universal design as it applies to bathroom planning is covered in the following pages including: history, demographics, the definition of universal design; assisting the universal design client; design guidelines; cabinets, countertops, fixtures and equipment; safety; laws and standards; and marketing universal design services.

"Universal Bathroom Planning, Design That Adapts To People" is intended to help you understand universal design concepts. It will also help build your business by increasing your expertise, allowing you to provide greater value and superior service to all of your clients. With this book, you will learn how to create functional, universally designed bathrooms without sacrificing aesthetics.

We hope you embrace this publication by implementing the principles it promotes. You are encouraged to attend NKBA's Universal Design seminars which are conducted throughout the year.

Nick Geragi, CKD, CBD, NCIDQ
Publisher, NKBA Books
Director of Education and Product Development

FORWARD
by
Ed Steinfeld, AIA

Universal Design is receiving attention all over the world. It has sparked interest among advocates of disability rights and the aged. Corporations view it as a means to extend their market for products and services. Computer software and hardware designers are using it to insure that everyone will get ready access to the information highway.

Kitchen and bathroom designers will benefit from the practice of universal design. All clients will appreciate the added functionality and the attention to details that results. But, most importantly, universally designed kitchens and bathrooms will have lasting value because they meet the needs of individuals over their entire life span.

This book is a comprehensive presentation of the universal design idea in a form that kitchen and bathroom designers will find very useful. Not only does it communicate the concept of detail that a designer needs to do it right. It is filled with good ideas and information to design bathrooms that will fulfill the needs of the entire population.

Ed Steinfeld, AIA
Center for Inclusive Design & Environmental Access,
School of Architecture, SUNY Buffalo

TABLE OF CONTENTS

INTRODUCTION

INTRODUCTION

The bathroom is the one room in our home that is used by every person in the household and many who visit. Our lives and the makeup of our households are the subject of change, and our homes must respond to the corresponding change in needs. This book is a step toward designing bathrooms that are not only beautiful but flexible and adaptable, to meet those varied needs.

Traditional bathroom designs have accommodated products and the almost non-existent average user. As bathroom designers, we can and do break some of these molds and design spaces that suit users of varied sizes and abilities. Changing requirements of our clients due to age, physical abilities, stature, or lifestyle dictate that we expand on the process.

While there are several laws and standards that deal with universal or accessible design, the ANSI A117.1, *American National Standard for Accessible and Usable Buildings and Facilities*, will be the touchstone of this book. There are variations and differences in existing laws and standards, but there is a trend toward uniformity and the ANSI Standard is frequently referenced.

Designers must verify with appropriate authorities when a specific project falls under a local code. Keep in mind that these national standards are minimums needed and that the designer must plan for the individual client and go beyond these minimums whenever possible.

chapter 1

THE MOVE TOWARD UNIVERSAL DESIGN

The world is changing and it's time for designers to respond. Our growing awareness of changing life styles and diversity must change the way we design bathrooms.

Traditionally, the built environment has been designed for an idealized, able-bodied, non-elderly adult. Since that description fits less than 15% of our population, the result is environments, including bathrooms, which create handicaps or barriers for the rest of us.

Demographics, legislation, public awareness and personal experience are pressing us to examine the basic assumptions we have used in design. Through this examination and a growing appreciation for diversity, a trend has emerged that calls for more flexibility and adaptability in design, allowing for use by more kinds of people more often. This trend is towards universal design which, once incorporated, will be simply good design.

HISTORY

The history of universal design from the end of World War II to the present can be seen in legal changes and our ever-changing life-styles. The design implications of this history and the terminology relating to it are important to learn. Once understood, universal design will be at its best when not labeled or defined, but truly incorporated as an essential part of all good design.

Need For Universal Design

Awareness of the need for universal and accessible design has been growing since the end of World War II. Disabled veterans, polio epidemics and the booming population meant more people required specialized accessible design. In response to this, in 1961, the **American National Standards Institute** published the first design standard on accessibility, the *"Specifications for Making Buildings and Facilities Accessible to and Usable by the Physically Handicapped",* **(ANSI 117.1-1961).** Since then, the awareness of the need for accessibility has grown. Recognition of the rights of minorities, including children, the disabled and the elderly has grown as well. Following the **ANSI Standard of 1961**, other laws and standards were developed on the state, local and federal levels, creating problems with inconsistency and interpretation.

From the fifties to the eighties, awareness of the need for accessibility in all aspects of life grew. Recognition of minority rights also continued to grow. In 1980, ANSI published a revised standard to create some consistency. In the mid-80's, the **Uniform Federal Accessibility Standards (UFAS)**, used for all federally funded construction subject to the **Architectural Barriers Act**, incorporated the revised ANSI standard, creating a standard that, for the most part, was indeed uniform. In 1988, the **Fair Housing Amendment** to the **Civil Rights Act** of 1968 was passed into law, with guidelines published in 1991 that reference the ANSI standard to some extent. This law impacted multiple housing units with four or more units under one roof.

In 1990, the **Americans with Disabilities Act (ADA)** was passed, with guidelines passed in 1991, again referencing the ANSI standard to a great extent. This law stipulated mandatory conditions for public places and truly changed the way we view the built environment. The intent of all these regulations is not *"separate but equal."* It is to recognize and defend the diversity of our culture and to incorporate this diversity in all aspects of life, including design. In 1992, ANSI again revised the standard. Design standards are constantly under review and revision, moving toward uniformity and the goal of making universal design concepts an integral part of every space and product we develop.

Changing Lifestyles

In terms of lifestyle, from post-World War II to the present, we have become a country where everyone shares in the responsibilities and activities of home life. In the 1950's, the bathroom was typically not flexible or luxurious, but simply a place where one performed certain basic functions. The standard American bathroom was 5' x 7' (152cm x 213cm) with a 30" (72cm) high vanity and lavatory, a water closet at 15" (38cm) high, and a combination bathtub/shower that was 30" x 60" (72cm x 152cm), with a curtain or sliding door. If a person was other than ideal height and physical ability, he would need assistance to adapt to this environment.

Today, the bathroom needs to be as varied as the characteristics of the people using it. Household members may include the children of the 50's, now middle-aged, as well as their parents and children, all with varying physical abilities, all needing to use the space safely and independently.

Todays bathroom may be a place to dress, to workout, to hear the morning news, or to relax, possibly by more than one person at a time and probably by people with varying physical characteristics.

Further changes in the needs of our clients center around independence for people with disabilities. The largest segment of people with disabilities is the group with impaired mobility or dexterity (whether injury- or illness-related). *"This group includes 37 million Americans with arthritis, 21 million of whom are under the age of 65. An estimated 21 million Americans have hearing impairments, and 16 million Americans have visual impairments."*

The number of people with disabilities is growing. People born with a disability or having injury - or illness - related disabilities are surviving at a greater rate. Life expectancies are longer, especially for women.

A major force in changing the needs of our clients is the aging process. **By the year 2020, over 20% of our population will be over 65.** According to an **American Association of Retired Persons (AARP)** survey, 84% of these people wish to stay in their homes and *"age in place."* Exploration of residential design options relating to independent living is part of the national health care reform movement.

These statistics become more real as we reflect on our own lifestyles and circumstances.

We can think of parents or grandparents who have moved out of their homes, perhaps into ours or into a group setting. We want to see them leading independent and dignified lives. We can recognize the roles of those elders and children in our daily household responsibilities. We can acknowledge the difficult or impossible barriers in our homes that become apparent only when we experience physical disabilities. Best of all, we can create bathrooms that are beautiful and flexible and allow for these differences in the lives of our home community.

DESIGN TERMS DEFINED

The following definitions of terms relating to universal design, adapted from the **Center for Universal Design**, should increase understanding and awareness. As universal design becomes incorporated into all good design, the need for labels will be eliminated.

Universal Design

Items that most people can use, regardless of their level of ability or disability, are considered universally usable. Many accessible and adaptable features are universally usable. *For example*, round door knobs are not usable by people with limited use of their hands, but lever handles, available in all price ranges, styles and colors, are usable by almost everyone, even people who have no hands.

Some items are made more universally usable by their placement. Light switches at lower heights and electrical receptacles raised to 15" - 48" (38cm - 122cm) above the floor are within reach of most people without requiring bending or stretching. Bathtub controls located off center, toward the outside of the tub, provide the same benefit.

Universal design addresses the scope of accessibility and suggests making all elements and spaces accessible to and usable by all people as much as possible. This is accomplished through thoughtful planning and design at all stages of any design project. It need not increase costs or result in special, clinical or *"different"* looking facilities.

Universal design requires an understanding and consideration of the broad range of human abilities throughout life. Creative application of that knowledge results in products, buildings and facilities that are usable by more people, regardless of their level of ability or disability.

By considering the needs of people with physical limitations in the design of products and spaces, we can make them not only easier and safer to use, but also more marketable and profitable. This universal design approach goes beyond the minimum requirements of accessibility law.

Accessible Design

Accessible generally means that the dwelling meets prescribed requirements for accessible housing.

Accessible features in homes include wide doors, sufficient clear floor space for wheelchairs, lower countertop segments, lever- and loop-type hardware, seats at bathing fixtures, grab bars in bathrooms, knee spaces under sinks and counters, audible and visual signals, switches and controls in easily reached locations, entrances free of steps and stairs, and an accessible route throughout the house. Most *"accessible"* features are permanently fixed in place.

Adaptable Design

Adaptable features are either adjustable or capable of being easily and immediately added or removed to *"adapt"* the unit to individual needs or preferences.

In an adaptable home, wide doors, no steps, knee spaces, control and switch locations, grab bar reinforcing and other access features must be built in. Grab bars, however, can be omitted and installed when needed. Because the necessary backing is already provided, the bars can simply be screwed in place without opening the existing walls to install reinforcing. Knee spaces can be concealed by installing a removable base cabinet that can simply be unscrewed from adjacent cabinets and slipped out when needed or by installing self-storing cabinet doors that fold and slide back. Countertops and closet rods can be placed on adjustable supports rather than fixed at lower heights as required for some wheelchair users.

Adaptable design means readily adjusted. It is best to remember adaptable features as those that can be adjusted in a short time by unskilled labor without involving structural or finish-material changes.

In addition, the following terms are frequently used.

Barrier-Free Design

Design that eliminates the obstacles in a space or product, making it fully usable by people of varying size and abilities.

Intergenerational or Lifespan Design

Design that allows people full function, regardless of changes due to age or current physical abilities.

At the time that the 1992 NKBA first edition **Bathroom Industry Technical Manuals** were going to press, the concept of universal design was gaining momentum. Recognition of the facts that we are aging and people with or without disabling conditions are living longer has precipitated this momentum. Changes in our lifestyles and Lifespan have created a growing need for changes in the way we design bathrooms for everyone. Increased awareness and improved standards have provided for the expansion of universal design principles in the newly revised **NKBA Bathroom Guidelines** as presented in this publication.

chapter 2

41
DESIGN
GUIDELINES
OF
BATHROOM
PLANNING

Universal bathroom design requires an understanding and consideration of the broad range of human abilities as well as the other parameters of a design project. It is intended that a bathroom designed around these guidelines will be functional, safe and universal. It is also likely that when the guidelines are applied, along with the other constraints of a particular situation, some things will be compromised.

Because every guideline cannot be followed everytime and no design can be all things to all people, judgments must frequently be made to achieve an optimum balance.

- The window that can be easily opened by arthritic hands may also provide easy access to a burglar.

- The shower control that is easily accessed by a seated person may also be within the reach of a toddler.

- The clear floor space required for transfer from a wheelchair

---

to a toilet may not be feasible given cost and space constraints.

Because there are over 40 million pre-existing homes in the United States alone, designers may often have to work with the typical 5' x 7' (152cm x 213cm) bathroom space. Designers are encouraged to expand this space as necessary to provide universal access. When this is not possible, designers will need to make judgements based on the scope of the project, the space available and the needs and budget of the client. Particularly in these instances, job parameters must be weighted against the guidelines.

These guidelines are provided to be the basis for that judgment.

The diversities in population which make up our society dictate that these guidelines be revised to more fully incorporate universal design as clarified in the **Uniform Federal Accessibility Standards (UFAS)** and the **American National Standard for Accessible and Usable Buildings and Facilities (ANSI A117.1-1992)**. The dimensions included in these NKBA Guidelines are based on ANSI and UFAS, but they are not intended to replace them.

To date, most single-family residential projects do not fall under any standard for accessibility, but this is changing. If a particular project is subject to local, state or national laws or codes, the designer must comply with those requirements. These guidelines and the space planning provided here are intended to be useful design standards, supplemental to the applicable codes. Not rules, but guidelines, they will help you in planning bathrooms that are functional and flexible or universal to better meet the needs of today's varied lifestyles.

NKBA's 41 Guidelines of Bathroom Planning

SECTION I: Clear Floor Spaces and Door Openings
Guideline 1 to Guideline 10

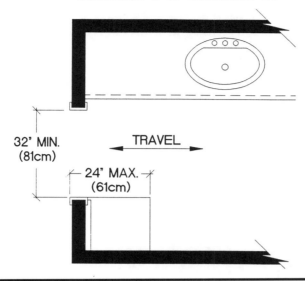

Guideline 1a - The clear space at doorways should be at least 32" (81cm) wide and not more than 24" (61cm) deep in the direction of travel.

Guideline 1a Clarification - While a designer should always try to meet this goal, physical constraints of a job site may require deviation from the guideline. Be aware that a lesser clearance may not allow for full use by all people.

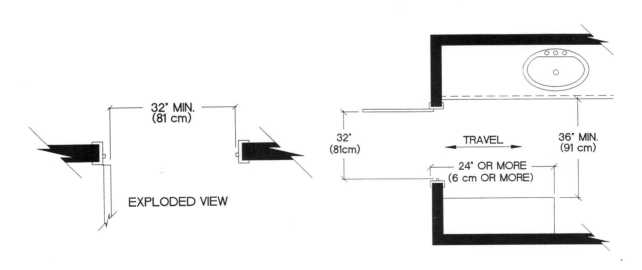

Guideline 1b - The clear space at a doorway must be measured at the narrowest point.

Guideline 1c - Walkways (passages between vertical objects greater than 24" (61cm) deep in the direction of travel), should be a minimum of 36" (91cm) wide.

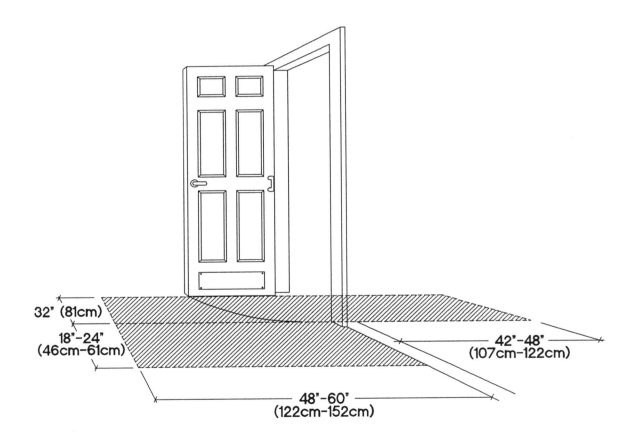

32" (81cm)

18"-24"
(46cm-61cm)

42"-48"
(107cm-122cm)

48"-60"
(122cm-152cm)

Guideline 2 - A clear floor space at least the width of the door on the push side and a larger clear floor space on the pull side should be planned at doors for maneuvering to open, close, and pass through the doorway. The exact amount needed will depend on the type of door and the approach.

UNIVERSAL BATHROOM PLANNING

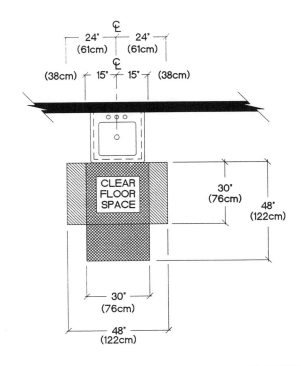

Guideline 3 - A minimum clear floor space of 30" x 48" (76cm x 122cm) either parallel or perpendicular should be provided at the lavatory.

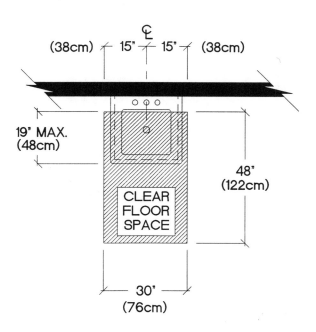

Guideline 3 Clarification - Up to 19" (48cm) of the 48" (122cm) clear floor space dimension can extend under the lavatory when a knee space is provided.

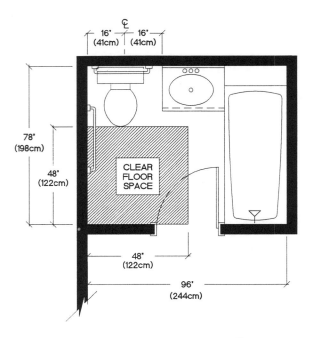

Guideline 4a - A minimum clear floor space of 48" x 48" (122cm x 122cm) should be provided in front of the toilet. A minimum of 16" (41cm) of that clear floor space must extend to each side of the centerline of the fixture.

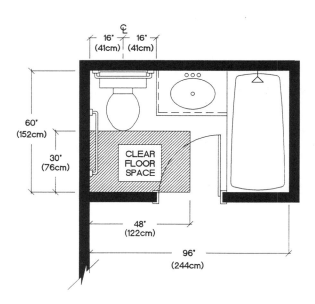

Guideline 4a Clarification - While a designer should always try to meet this goal, physical constraints of a job site may require deviation from the guideline. If a 48" x 48" (122cm x 122cm) clear floor space is unavailable, this space may be reduced to 30" x 48" (76cm x 122cm). This compromise may not allow for full use by all people.

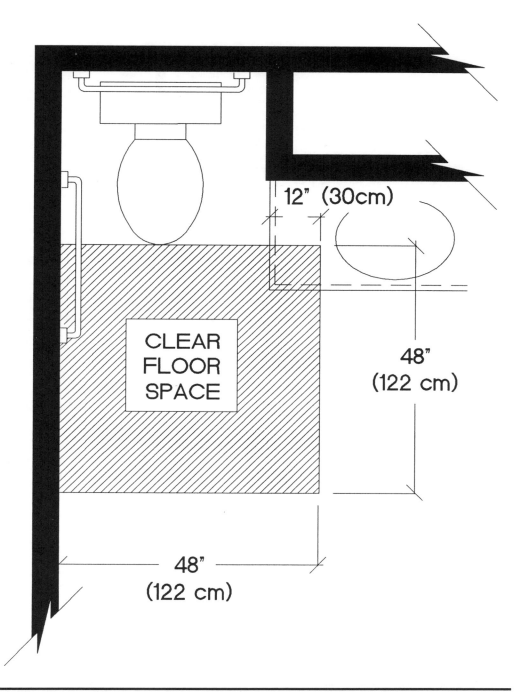

12" (30cm)

CLEAR
FLOOR
SPACE

48"
(122 cm)

48"
(122 cm)

Guideline 4b - Up to 12" (30cm) of the 48" x 48" (122cm x 122cm) clear floor space can extend under the lavatory when total access to a knee space is provided.

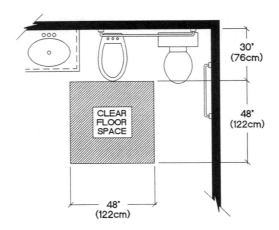

Guideline 5 - A minimum clear floor space of 48" x 48" (122cm x 122cm) from the front of the bidet should be provided.

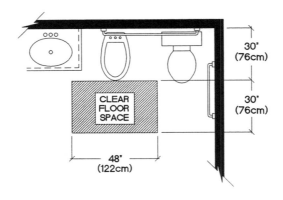

Guideline 5 Clarification 1 - While a designer should always try to meet this goal, physical constraints of a job site may require deviation from the guideline. If a 48" x 48" (122cm x 122cm) clear floor space is not available, this space may be reduced to 30" x 48" (76cm x 122cm). This compromise may not allow for full use by all people.

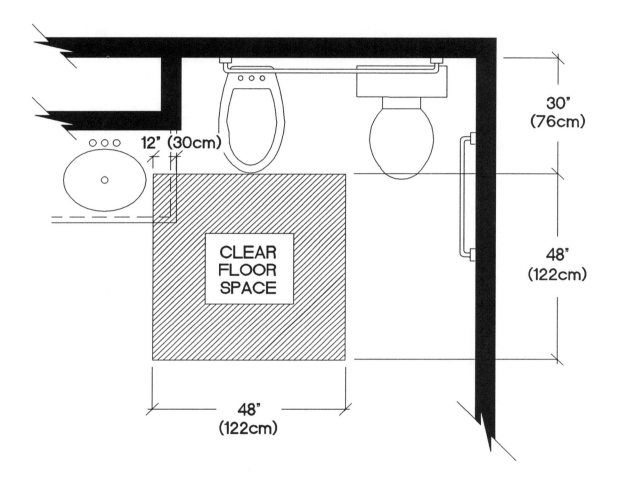

12" (30cm)

**30"
(76cm)**

**CLEAR
FLOOR
SPACE**

**48"
(122cm)**

**48"
(122cm)**

Guideline 5 Clarification 2 - Up to 12" (30cm) of the 48" x 48" (122cm x 122cm) of the clear floor space can extend under the lavatory when total access to a knee space is provided.

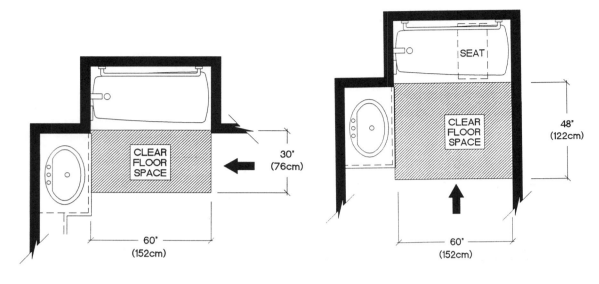

PARALLEL APPROACH

PERPENDICULAR APPROACH

Guideline 6a - The minimum clear floor space at a bathtub is 60" (152cm) wide by 30" (76cm) deep for a parallel approach, even with the length of the bathtub.

Guideline 6b - The minimum clear floor space at a bathtub is 60" (152cm) wide x 48" (122cm) deep for a perpendicular approach.

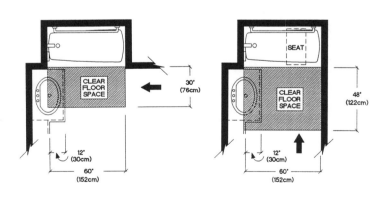

PARALLEL APPROACH

PERPENDICULAR APPROACH

Guideline 6a, 6b Clarification 1 - Up to 12" (30cm) of the 60" (152cm) clear floor space required for parallel or perpendicular approach can extend under the lavatory when total access to a kneespace is provided.

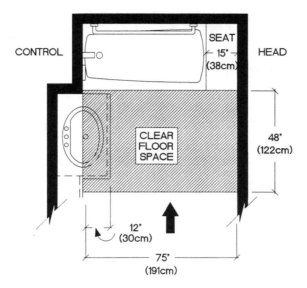

Guideline 6a, 6b Clarification 2 - If a built-in seat is planned, increase the width of the clear floor space by the depth of the seat, a minimum 15" (38cm).

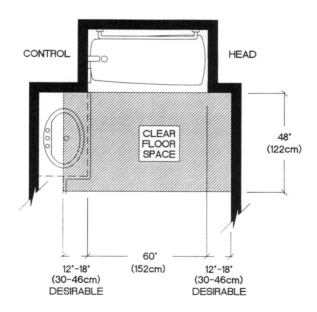

Guideline 6a, 6b Clarification 3 - An additional 12"-18" (30cm-46cm) of clear floor space beyond the control wall is desirable to ease access to controls. The same 12"-18" (30cm-46cm) of clear floor space is desirable beyond the head of the bathtub for maneuvering mobility aids for transfer.

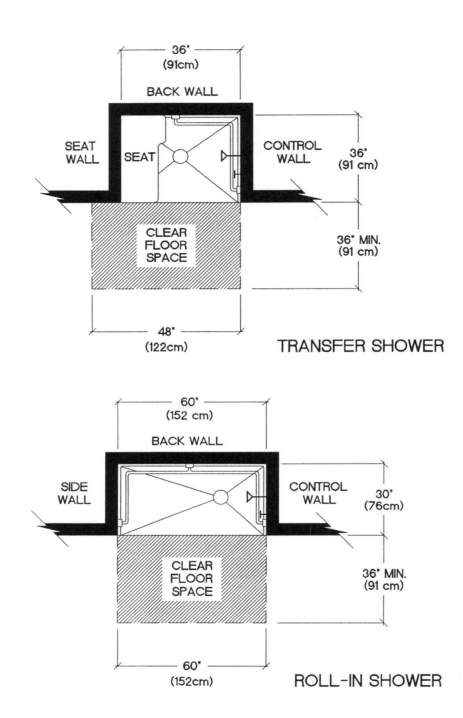

TRANSFER SHOWER

36"
(91cm)

BACK WALL

SEAT WALL

SEAT

CONTROL WALL

36"
(91 cm)

CLEAR FLOOR SPACE

36" MIN.
(91 cm)

48"
(122cm)

ROLL-IN SHOWER

60"
(152 cm)

BACK WALL

SIDE WALL

CONTROL WALL

30"
(76cm)

CLEAR FLOOR SPACE

36" MIN.
(91 cm)

60"
(152cm)

Guideline 7 - The minimum clear floor space at showers less than 60" (152cm) wide should be 36" (91cm) deep by the width of the shower plus 12" (30cm). The 12" (30cm) should extend beyond the seat wall. At a shower that is 60" (152cm) wide or greater, clear floor space should be 36" (91cm) deep by the width of the shower.

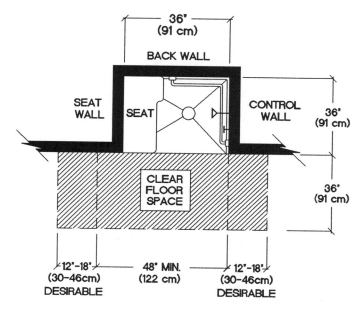

TRANSFER SHOWER

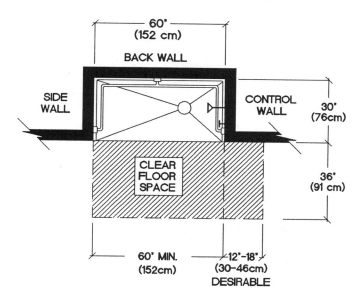

ROLL-IN SHOWER

Guideline 7 Clarification - An additional 12"-18" (30cm-46cm) of clear floor space beyond the control wall is desirable to ease access to controls. The same 12"-18" (30cm-46cm) of clear floor space is desirable beyond the side wall opposite the control wall for maneuvering aids for transfer.

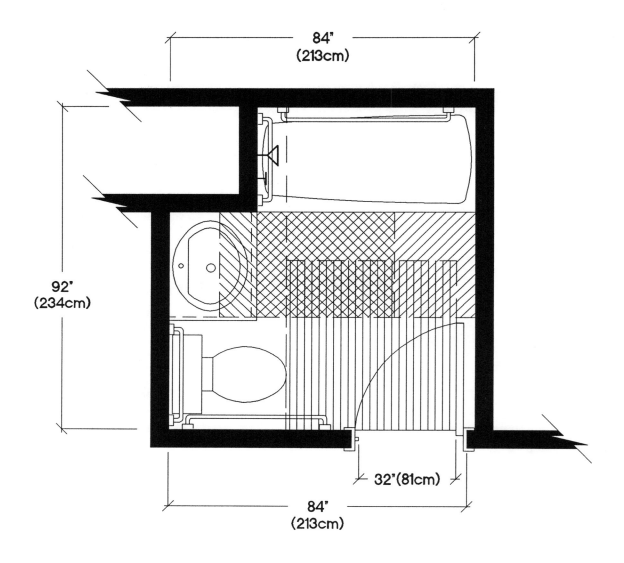

84"
(213cm)

92"
(234cm)

32"(81cm)

84"
(213cm)

Guideline 8 - Clear floor spaces required at each fixture may overlap.

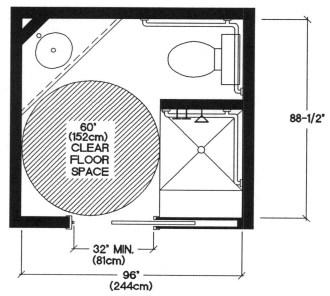

88-1/2"

32" MIN.
(81cm)

96"
(244cm)

MINIMUM 60" (152cm) DIAMETER FOR 360° TURNS

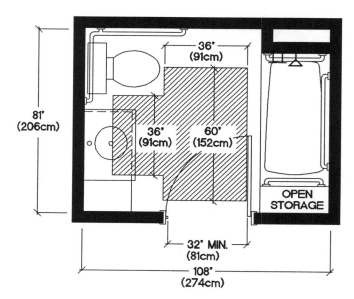

36"
(91cm)

81"
(206cm)

36"
(91cm)

60"
(152cm)

OPEN
STORAGE

32" MIN.
(81cm)

108"
(274cm)

MINIMUM 36" x 36" x 60" (91cm x 91cm x 152cm)
SPACE FOR T-TURNS

Guideline 9 - Space for turning (mobility aids) 180° should be planned in the bathroom.

A minimum diameter of 60" (152cm) for 360° turns and/or a minimum T-turn space of 36" (91cm) x 36" (91cm) x 60" (152cm).

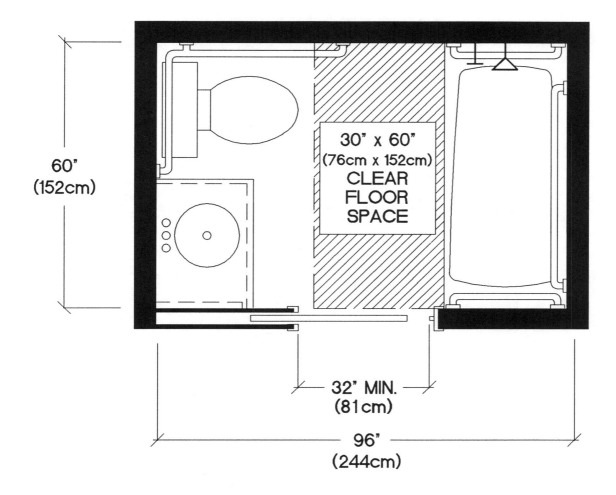

60"
(152cm)

30" x 60"
(76cm x 152cm)
CLEAR
FLOOR
SPACE

32" MIN.
(81cm)

96"
(244cm)

ALTERNATIVE TO TURNING SPACE
30" x 60" (76cm x 152cm) CLEAR FLOOR SPACE

Guideline 9 Clarification - While a designer should always try to meet this goal, physical constraints of a job site may require deviation from the guideline. When space for a 360° diameter or T-turn is unavailable, a 30" x 60" (76cm x 152cm) clear floor space can be substituted, but this compromise will not allow full access by all users.

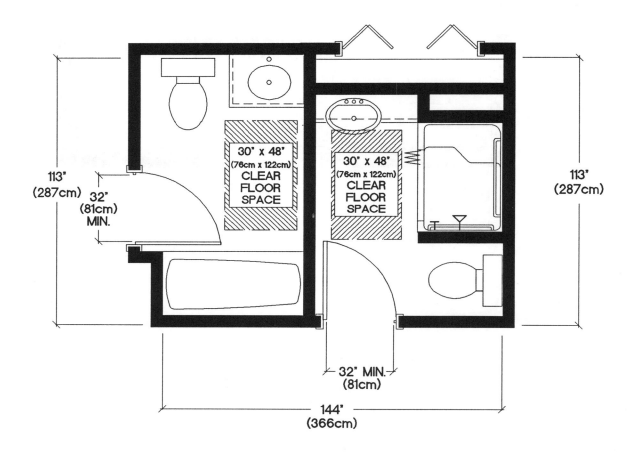

Guideline 10 - A minimum clear floor space of 30" x 48" (76cm-122cm) is **required** beyond the door swing in a bathroom.

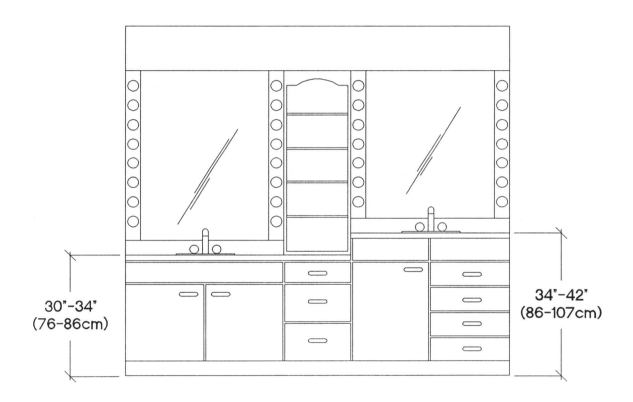

VARIED VANITY COUNTER HEIGHTS ARE DESIRABLE

30"-34"
(76-86cm)

34"-42"
(86-107cm)

Guideline 11 - When more than one vanity is included, one may be 30"-34" (76cm-86cm) high and another at 34"-42" (86cm-107cm) high. Vanity height should fit the user(s).

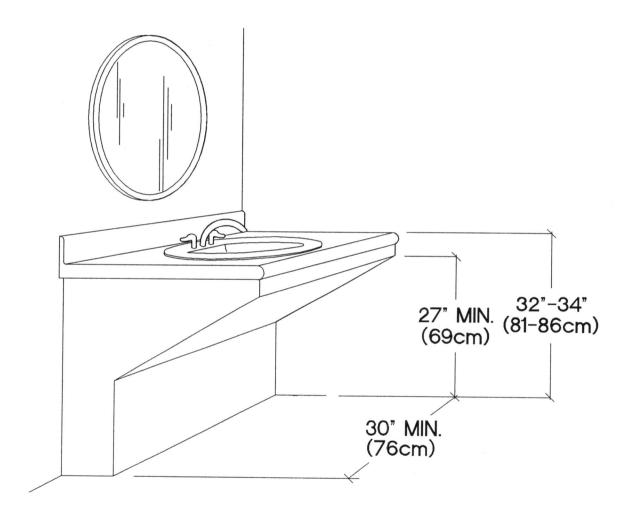

27" MIN.
(69cm)

32"-34"
(81-86cm)

30" MIN.
(76cm)

Guideline 12 - Kneespace (which may be open or adaptable) should be provided at a lavatory. The kneespace should be a minimum of 27" (69cm) above the floor at the front edge, decreasing progressively as the depth increases, and the recommended width is a minimum of 30" (76cm) wide.

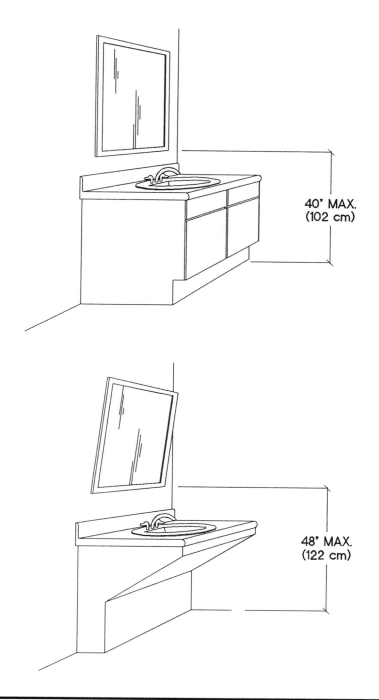

Guideline 13 - The bottom edge of the mirror over the lavatory should be a maximum of 40" (102cm) above the floor or a maximum of 48" (122cm) above the floor if it is tilted.

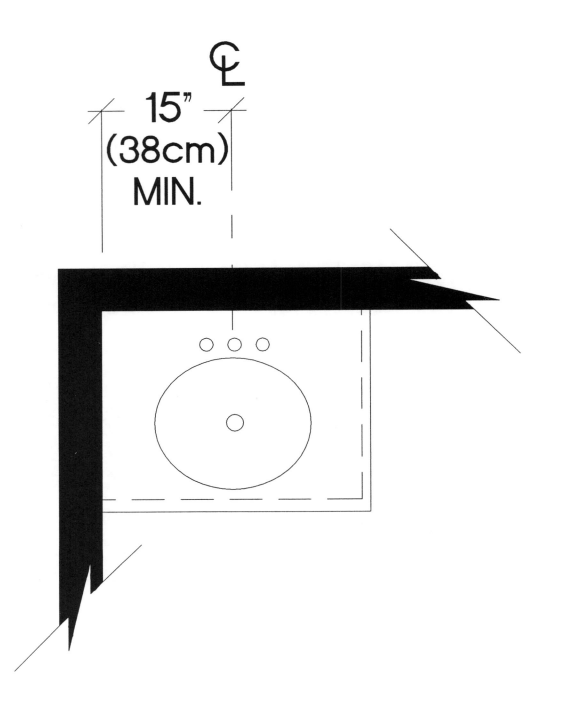

15"
(38cm)
MIN.

C̷L

Guideline 14 - The minimum clearance from the centerline of the lavatory to any side wall is 15" (38cm).

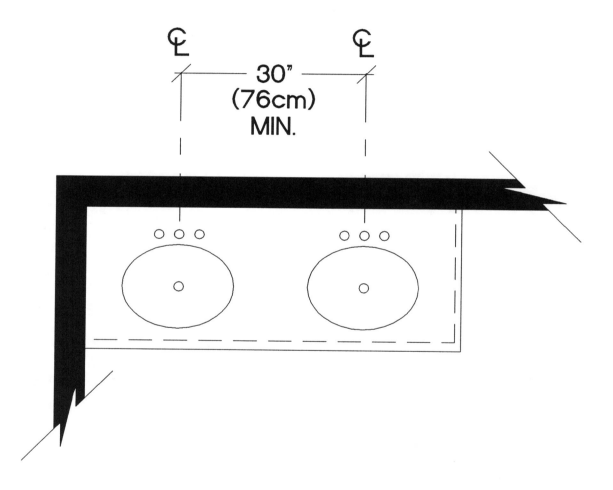

Guideline 15 - The minimum clearance between two bowls in the lavatory center is 30" (76cm), centerline to centerline.

SPACE AS NEEDED FOR PROPER INSTALLATION

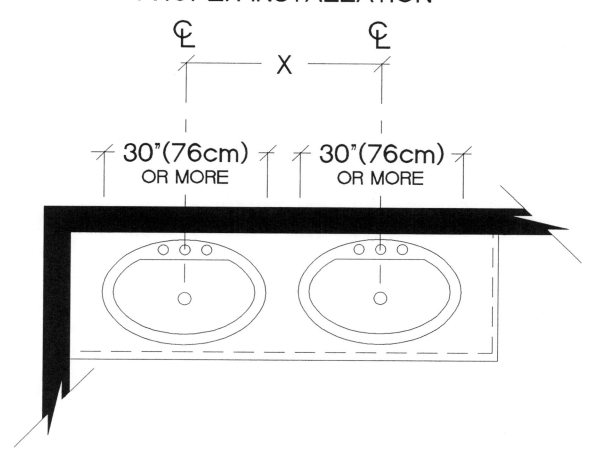

Guideline 15 Clarification - When using lavatories that are 30" (76cm) wide or greater, the minimum distance of 30" (76cm) between centerlines of the two bowls must be increased to allow proper installation of each lavatory.

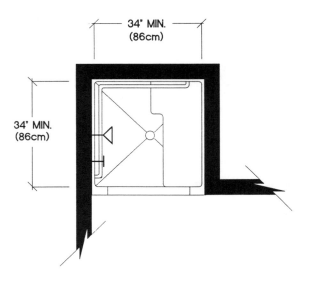

Guideline 16 - In an enclosed shower, the minimum usable interior dimensions are 34" (86cm) x 34" (86cm). These dimensions are measured from wall to wall. Grab bars, controls, movable and folding seats do not diminish the measurement.

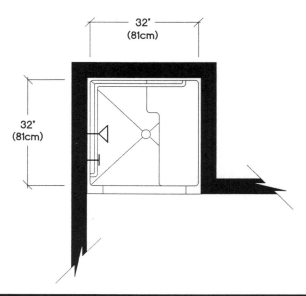

Guideline 16 Clarification - While a designer should always try to meet this goal, physical constraints of a job site may require deviation from the guideline. If a 34" x 34" (86cm x 86cm) interior dimension is unavailable, these dimensions may be reduced to 32" x 32"(81cm x 81cm). Be aware that this compromise may not allow for full use by all people.

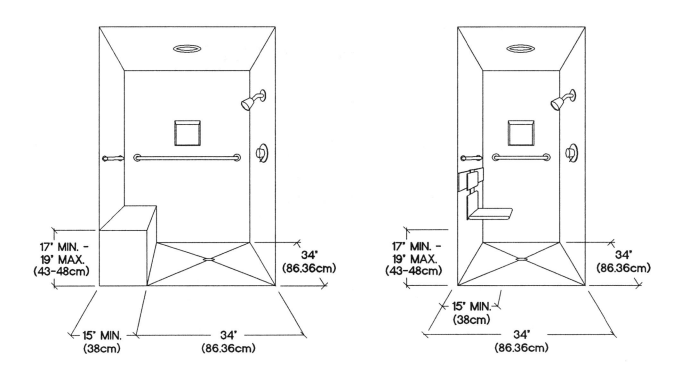

Guideline 17 - Showers should include a bench or seat that is 17-19" (43cm-48cm) above the floor and a minimum of 15" (38cm) deep.

Guideline 17 Clarification 1 - Built-in permanent seats should not encroach upon the minimum 34" x 34" (86cm x 86cm) interior clear floor space of the shower.

Guideline 17 Clarification 2 - Reinforced wall supports for future placement of hanging and folding seat hardware should be planned at the time of shower installation.

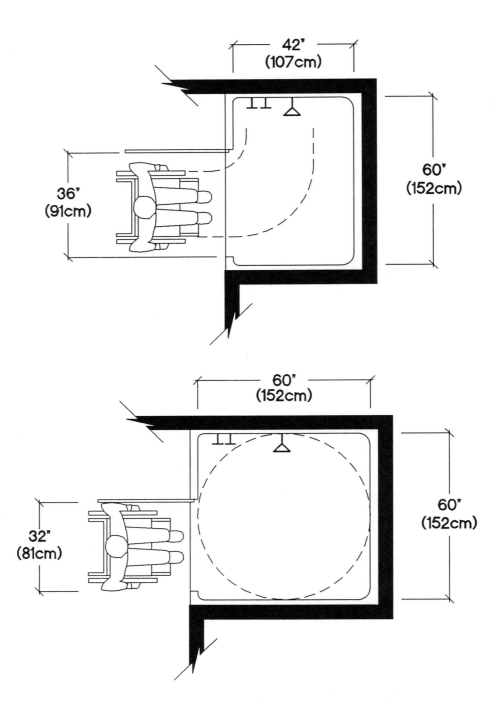

Guideline 18 - The width of the door opening must take into consideration the interior space in the shower for entry and maneuvering. When the shower is 60" (152cm) deep, a person can enter straight into the shower and turn after entry, therefore 32" (81cm) is adequate. If the shower is 42" (107cm) deep, the entry must be increased to 36" (91cm) in order to allow for turning space.

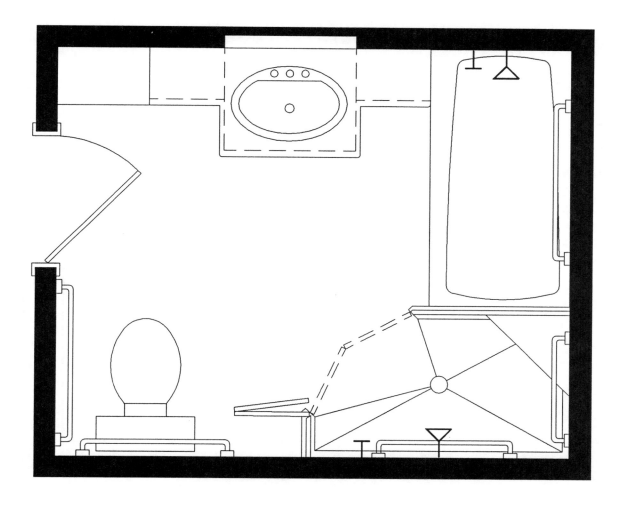

Guideline 19 - Shower doors must open <u>into</u> the bathroom.

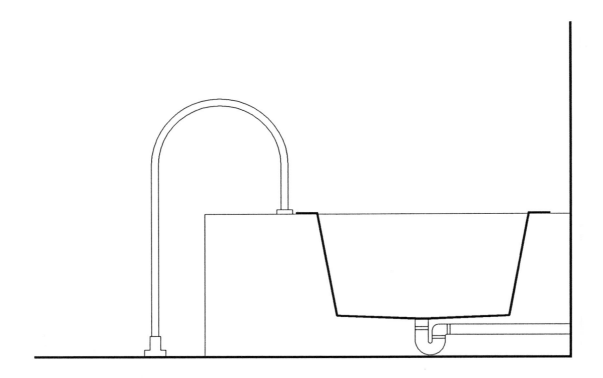

Guideline 20 - Steps should not be planned at the bathtub or shower area. Safety rails should be installed to facilitate transfer to and from the fixture.

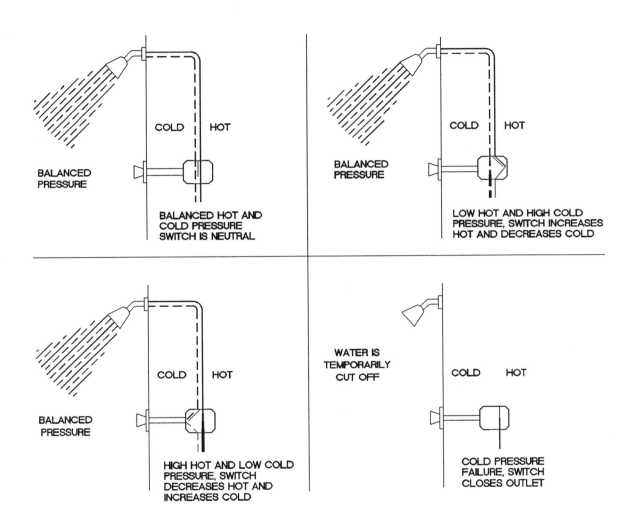

COLD | HOT

BALANCED PRESSURE

BALANCED HOT AND COLD PRESSURE SWITCH IS NEUTRAL

COLD | HOT

BALANCED PRESSURE

LOW HOT AND HIGH COLD PRESSURE, SWITCH INCREASES HOT AND DECREASES COLD

COLD | HOT

BALANCED PRESSURE

HIGH HOT AND LOW COLD PRESSURE, SWITCH DECREASES HOT AND INCREASES COLD

WATER IS TEMPORARILY CUT OFF

COLD | HOT

COLD PRESSURE FAILURE, SWITCH CLOSES OUTLET

Guideline 21 - All showerheads should be equipped with pressure balance/temperature regulator or temperature limiting device.

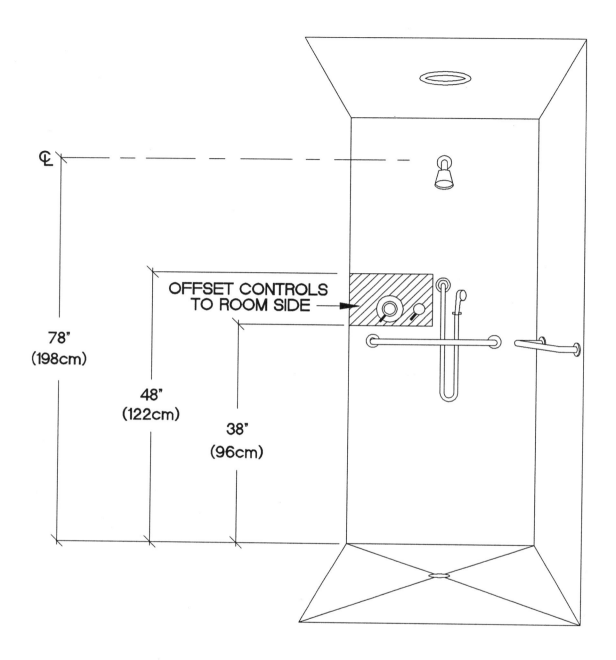

OFFSET CONTROLS
TO ROOM SIDE →

ℂ

78"
(198cm)

48"
(122cm)

38"
(96cm)

Guideline 22a - Shower controls should be accessible from inside and outside the fix-ture. Shower controls should be located between 38"-48" (96cm - 122cm) above the floor (placed above the grab bar) and offset toward the room.

Guideline 22a Clarification - A handheld showerhead may be used in place of or in ad-dition to a fixed showerhead. When mounted, a handheld showerhead should be no higher than 48" (122cm) in its lowest position.

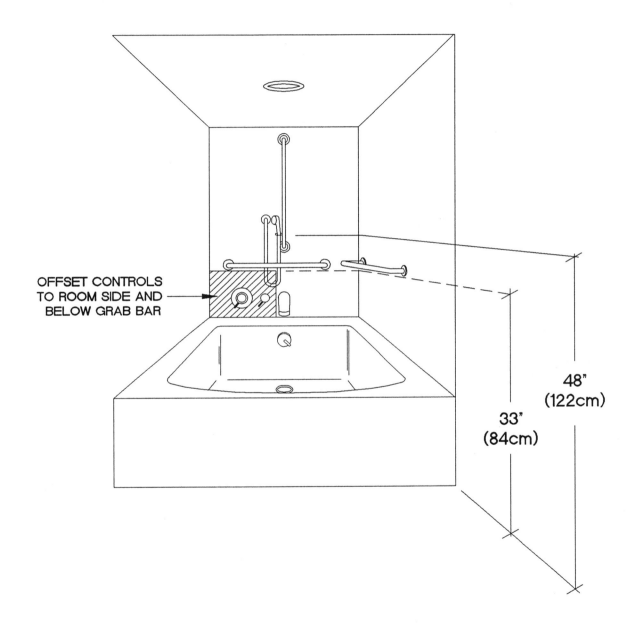

OFFSET CONTROLS
TO ROOM SIDE AND
BELOW GRAB BAR

48"
(122cm)

33"
(84cm)

Guideline 22b - Tub controls should be accessible from inside and outside the fixture. Tub controls should be located between the rim of the bathtub and 33" (84cm) above the floor, placed below the grab bar and offset toward the room.

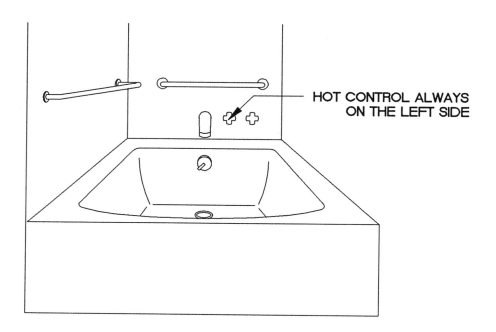

HOT CONTROL ALWAYS
ON THE LEFT SIDE

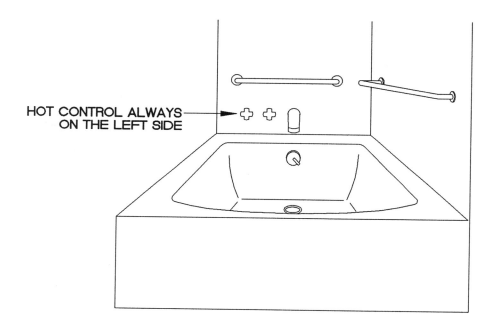

HOT CONTROL ALWAYS
ON THE LEFT SIDE

Guideline 22b Clarification - If separate hot and cold controls are used in a bathtub (not permissible in a shower), for safe use the hot control is always on the left as viewed from inside the fixture.

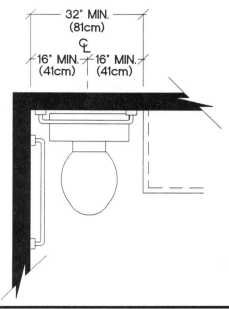

Guideline 23a - A minimum 16" (41cm) clearance should be allowed from the center-line of the toilet or bidet to any obstruction, fixture or equipment (except grab bars) on either side.

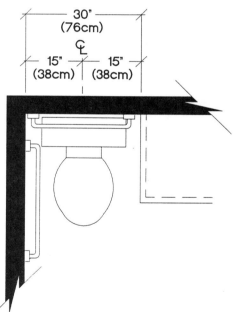

Guideline 23a Clarification - While a designer should always try to meet this goal, physical constraints of a job site may require deviation from the guideline. If a 32" (81cm) clearance is unavailable, this space may be reduced to 30" (76cm). Be aware that this compromise may not allow for full use by all people.

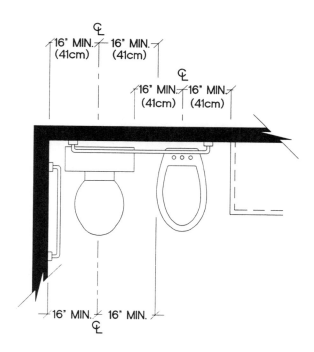

Guideline 23b - When the toilet and bidet are planned adjacent to one another, the 16" minimum (41cm) centerline clearance to all obstructions should be maintained.

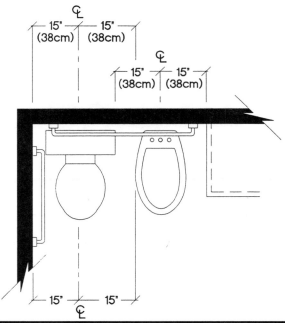

Guideline 23b Clarification - While a designer should always try to meet this goal, physical constraints of a job site may require deviation from the guideline. If a 16" (41cm) centerline clearance to an obstruction is unavailable, this centerline clearance may be reduced to 15" (38cm). Be aware that this compromise may not allow for full use by all people.

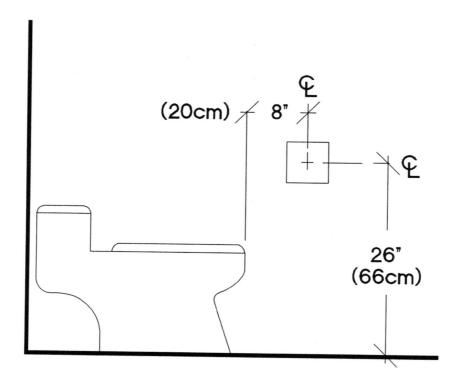

RECOMMENDED TOILET PAPER
HOLDER LOCATION

Guideline 24 - The toilet paper holder should be installed within reach of a person seated on the toilet. Ideal location is slightly in front of the edge of the toilet bowl, centered at 26" (66cm) above the floor.

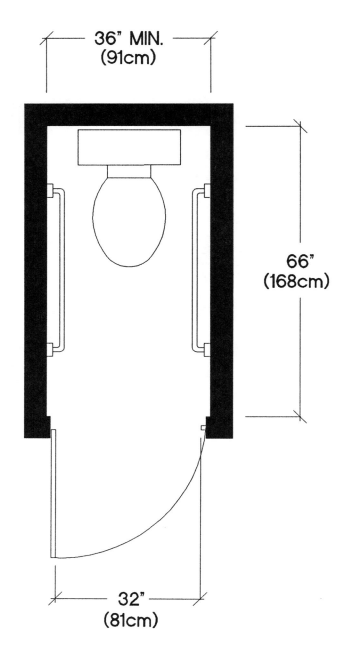

36" MIN.
(91cm)

66"
(168cm)

32"
(81cm)

Guideline 25 - Compartmental toilet areas should be a minimum 36" (91cm) x 66" (168cm) with a swing-out door or a pocket door.

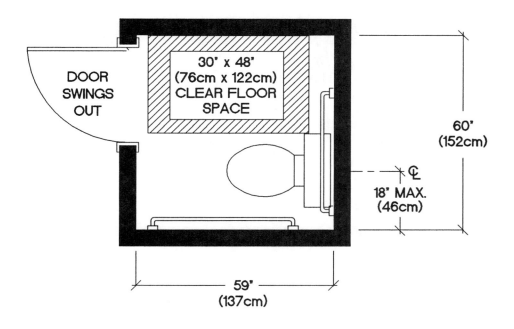

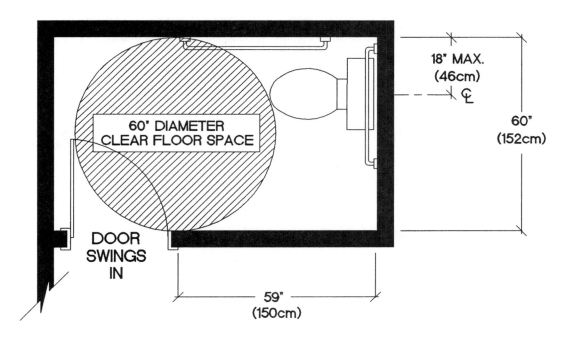

Guideline 25 Clarification - The amount of space needed for a private toilet area will be affected by the mobility of the person using it.

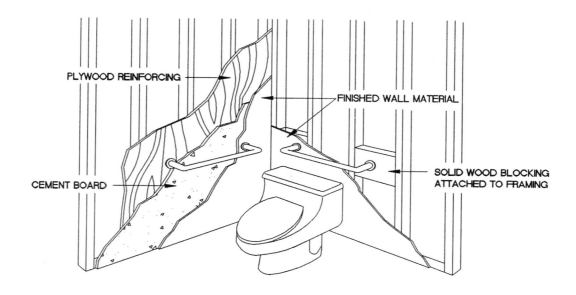

PLYWOOD REINFORCING

FINISHED WALL MATERIAL

CEMENT BOARD

SOLID WOOD BLOCKING ATTACHED TO FRAMING

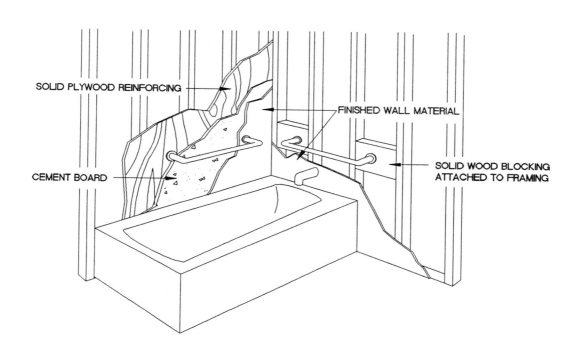

SOLID PLYWOOD REINFORCING

FINISHED WALL MATERIAL

CEMENT BOARD

SOLID WOOD BLOCKING ATTACHED TO FRAMING

Guideline 26 - Walls should be prepared (reinforced) at the time of construction to allow for installation of grab bars. Grab bars should also be installed in the bathtub, shower and toilet areas at the time of construction.

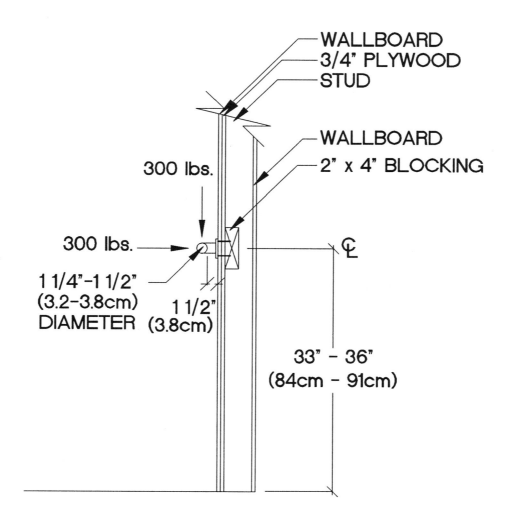

WALLBOARD
3/4" PLYWOOD
STUD

WALLBOARD
2" x 4" BLOCKING

300 lbs.

300 lbs.

1 1/4"-1 1/2"
(3.2-3.8cm)
DIAMETER

1 1/2"
(3.8cm)

₵

33" - 36"
(84cm - 91cm)

GRAB BAR SPECIFICATIONS

Guideline 26 Clarification 1 - Reinforced areas must bear a static load of 300 lbs. (136kg). The use of cement board does not negate the need for blocking or plywood reinforcing.

Guideline 26 Clarification 2 - Grab bars should be installed 33" - 36" (84cm - 91cm) above the floor, should be 1 1/4"-1 1/2" (3.2cm-3.8cm) diameter, extend 1 1/2 (3.8cm) from the wall, support a 300 lbs. (136 kg) load, and they should have a slip-resistant surface. When shapes other than round are used for grab bars, the width of the largest point should not exceed 2" (5.1cm). Towel bars must not be substituted as grab bars.

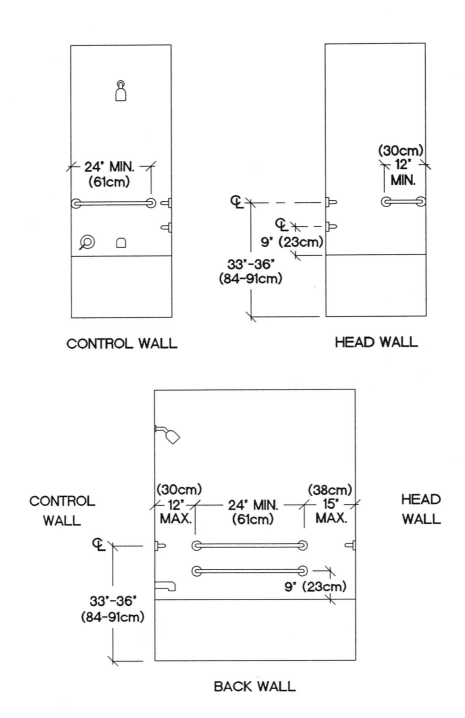

CONTROL WALL

HEAD WALL

CONTROL WALL

HEAD WALL

BACK WALL

Guideline 26 Clarification 3 - Grab bars in bathtub/shower areas should be at least 24" (61cm) wide on the control wall, at least 12" (30cm) wide on the head wall and at least 24" (61cm) wide on the back wall, beginning no more than 12" (30cm) from the control wall and no more than 15" (38cm) from the head wall. If a second grab bar is desired on the back wall, it should be located 9" (23cm) above the bathtub deck, the same width as the grab bar above it.

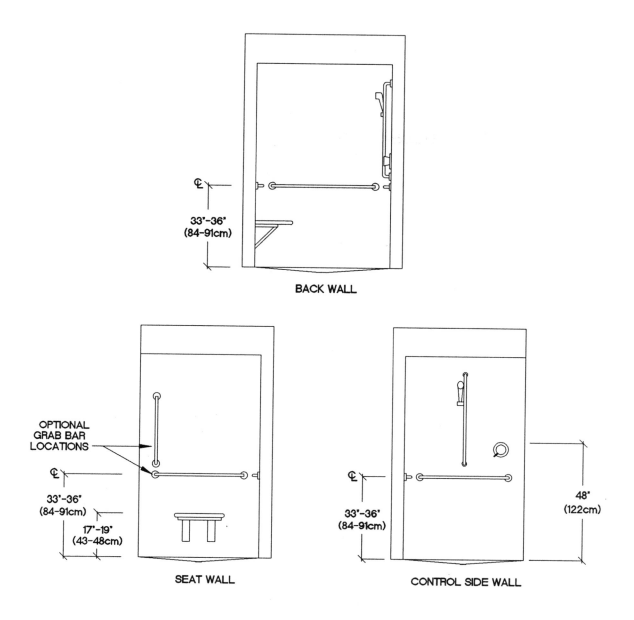

BACK WALL

OPTIONAL
GRAB BAR
LOCATIONS

33"-36"
(84-91cm)

17"-19"
(43-48cm)

SEAT WALL

33"-36"
(84-91cm)

48"
(122cm)

CONTROL SIDE WALL

Guideline 26 Clarification 4 - Grab bars in shower stalls should be included on each surrounding wall (optional on wall where bench is located) and should be no more than 9"
(23cm) shorter than the width of the wall to which they are attached.

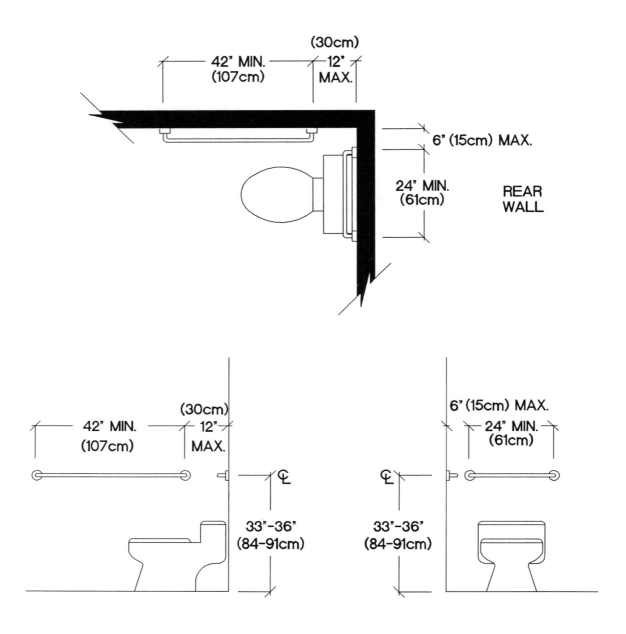

SIDE WALL

42" MIN.
(107cm)

(30cm)
12"
MAX.

6" (15cm) MAX.

24" MIN.
(61cm)

REAR
WALL

42" MIN.
(107cm)

(30cm)
12"
MAX.

33"-36"
(84-91cm)

6" (15cm) MAX.

24" MIN.
(61cm)

33"-36"
(84-91cm)

Guideline 26 Clarification 5a - The first grab bar in the toilet area should be located on the side wall closest to the toilet, a maximum 12" (30cm) from the rear wall. It should be at least 42" (107cm) wide. An optional secondary grab bar in the toilet area may be located on the rear wall, a maximum 6" (15cm) from the side wall. It should be at least 24" (61cm) wide.

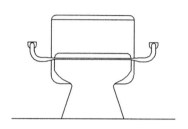

SIDE GRAB BARS ATTACHED BELOW TOILET SEAT

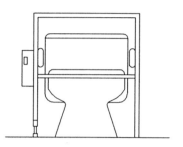

ELECTRONIC SEAT ELEVATOR

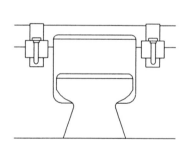

RAIL SYSTEM WITH SUPPORT ARMS

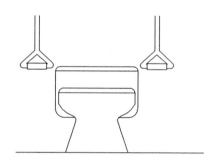

HAND RAILS SUSPENDED FROM CEILING

Guideline 26 Clarification 5b - Alternatives for grab bars in the toilet area include, but are not limited to, side grab bars attached below the toilet seat, a rail system mounted to the back wall with perpendicular support arms at sides of the toilet seat, an electronic seat elevator or hand rails suspended from the ceiling.

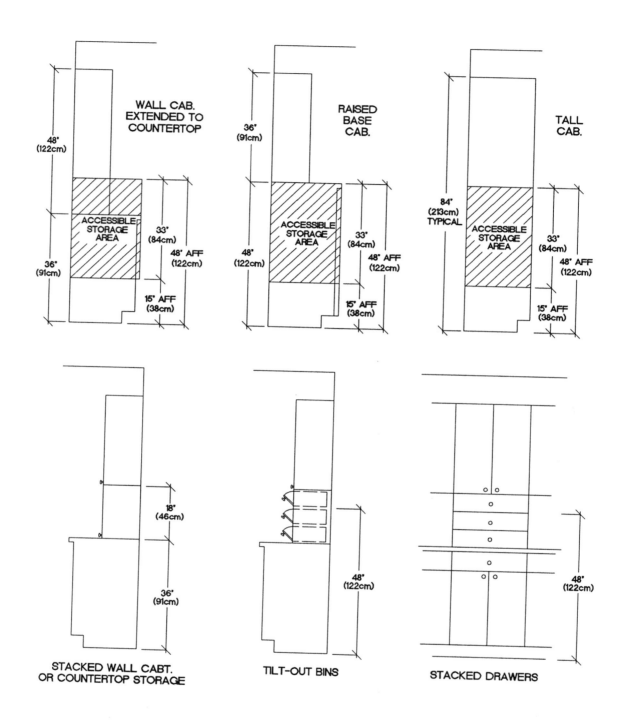

WALL CAB. EXTENDED TO COUNTERTOP

48" (122cm)
36" (91cm)
ACCESSIBLE STORAGE AREA
33" (84cm)
48" AFF (122cm)
15" AFF (38cm)

RAISED BASE CAB.

36" (91cm)
48" (122cm)
ACCESSIBLE STORAGE AREA
33" (84cm)
48" AFF (122cm)
15" AFF (38cm)

TALL CAB.

84" (213cm) TYPICAL
ACCESSIBLE STORAGE AREA
33" (84cm)
48" AFF (122cm)
15" AFF (38cm)

STACKED WALL CABT. OR COUNTERTOP STORAGE

18" (46cm)
36" (91cm)

TILT-OUT BINS

48" (122cm)

STACKED DRAWERS

48" (122cm)

Guideline 27 - Storage for toiletries, linens, grooming and general bathroom supplies should be provided within 15"-48" (38cm-122cm) above the floor.

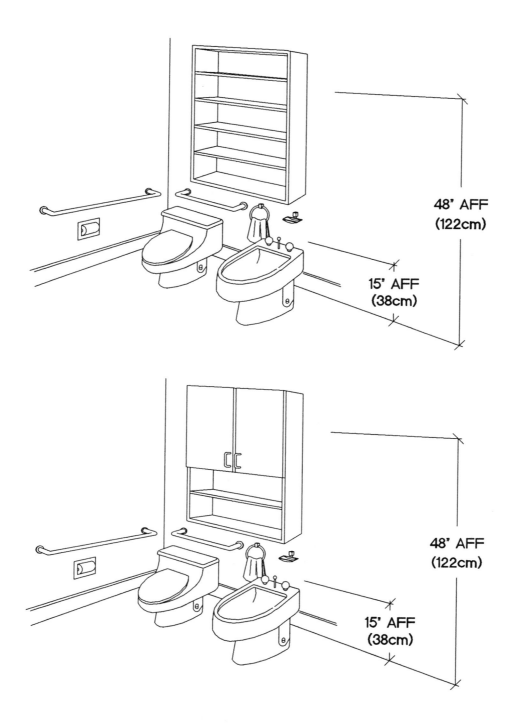

48" AFF
(122cm)

15' AFF
(38cm)

48" AFF
(122cm)

15' AFF
(38cm)

Guideline 28 - Storage for soap, towels and other personal hygiene items should be installed within reach of a person seated on the bidet or toilet and within 15" - 48" (38cm - 122cm) above the floor. Storage areas should not interfere with the use of the fixture.

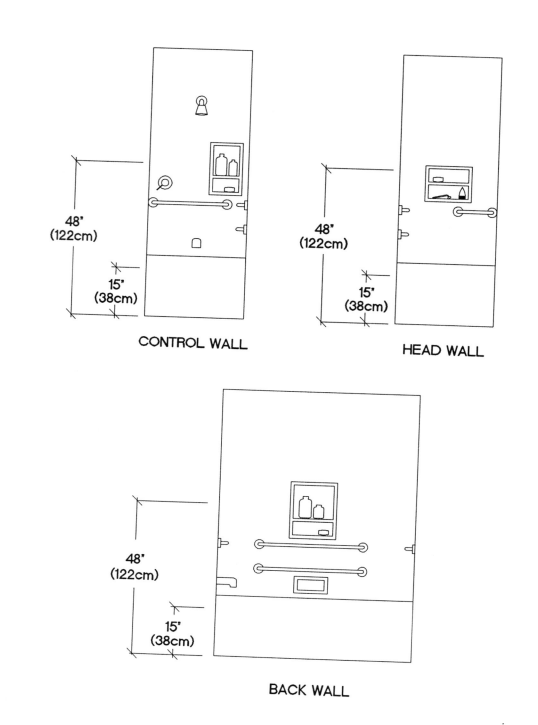

CONTROL WALL

48"
(122cm)

15"
(38cm)

HEAD WALL

48"
(122cm)

15"
(38cm)

BACK WALL

48"
(122cm)

15"
(38cm)

Guideline 29 - In the bathtub/shower area, storage for soap, and other personal hygiene items should be provided within the 15" - 48" (38cm - 122cm) above the floor within the universal reach range.

Guideline 30 - All flooring should be slip resistant.

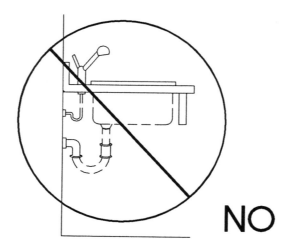

NO

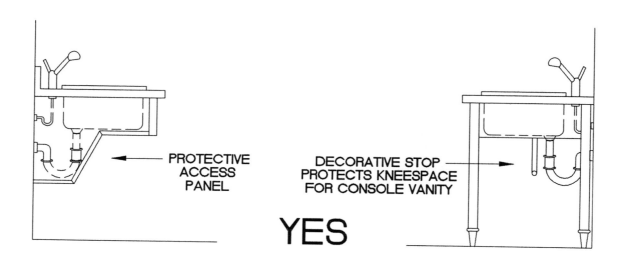

PROTECTIVE
ACCESS
PANEL

DECORATIVE STOP
PROTECTS KNEESPACE
FOR CONSOLE VANITY

YES

Guideline 31 - Exposed pipes and mechanicals should be covered by a protective panel or shroud. When using a console table, care must be given to keep plumbing attractive and out of contact with a seated user.

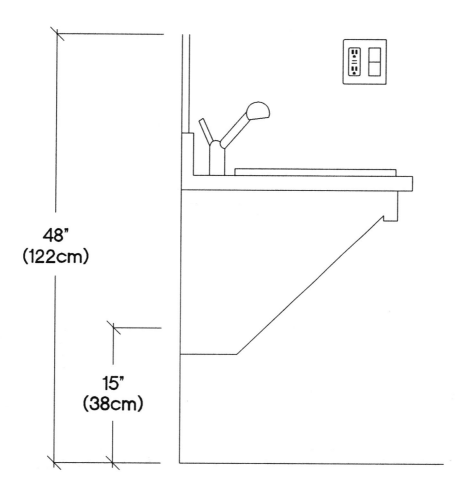

48"
(122cm)

15"
(38cm)

Guideline 32 - Controls, dispensers, outlets and operating mechanisms should be 15"-48" (38cm-122cm) above the floor and should be operable with a closed fist.

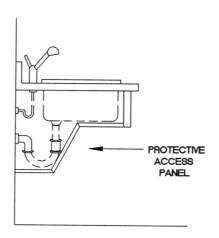

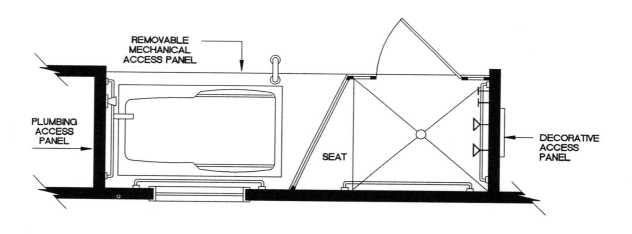

Guideline 33 - All mechanical, electrical and plumbing systems should have access panels.

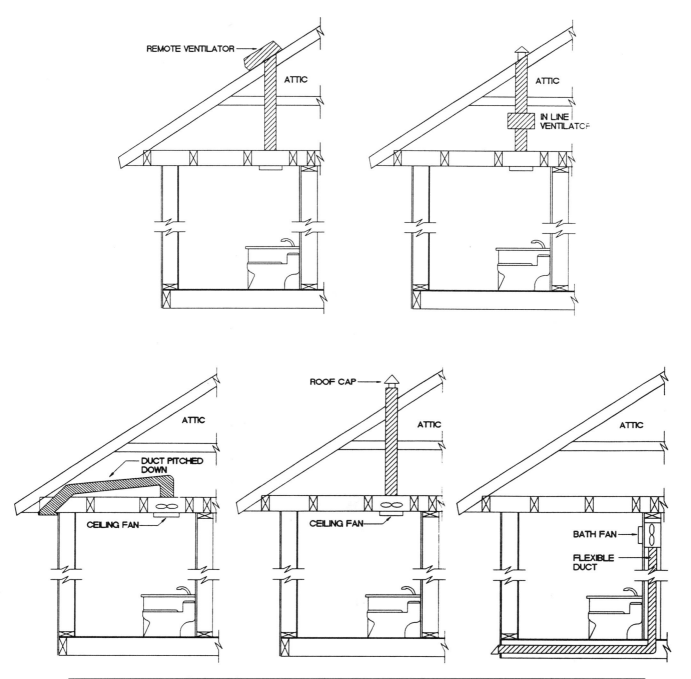

Guideline 34 - Mechanical ventilation systems to the outside should be included in the plan to vent the entire room. The minimum size of the system can be calculated as follows:

$$\frac{\text{Cubic Space (LxWxH) x 8 (changes of air per hour)}}{60 \text{ minutes}} = \text{minimum cubic feet per minute (CFM)}$$

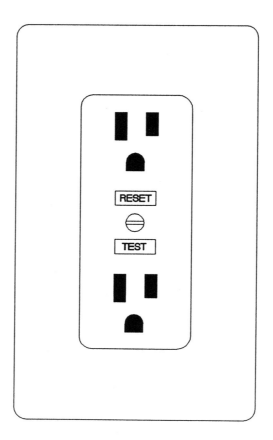

Guideline 35 - Ground fault circuit interrupters must be specified on all receptacles, lights and switches in the bathroom. All light fixtures above the bathtub/shower units must be moisture-proof special-purpose fixtures.

HEAT LAMP

HEAT/FAN/LIGHT

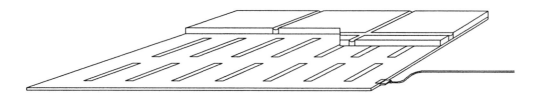

RADIANT FLOOR SYSTEM

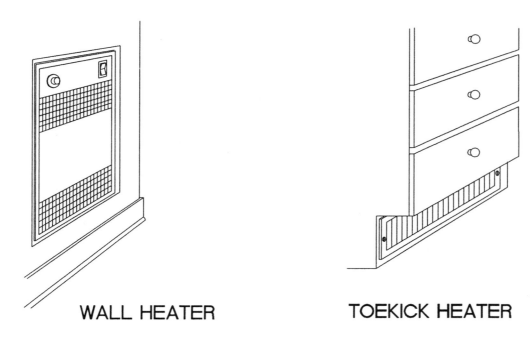

WALL HEATER

TOEKICK HEATER

Guideline 36 - In addition to a primary heat source, auxiliary heating may be planned in the bathroom.

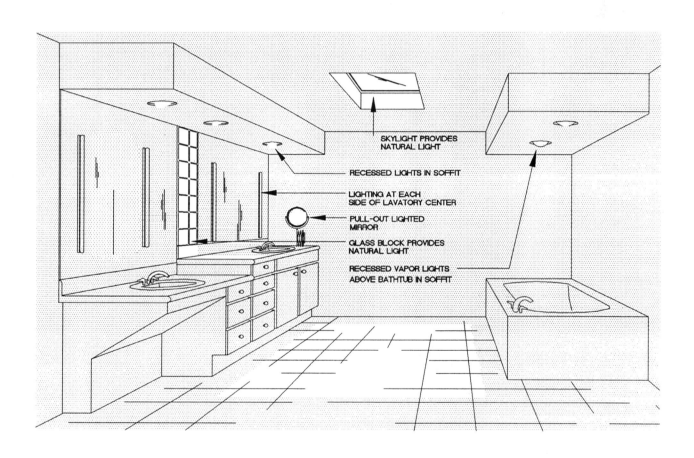

SKYLIGHT PROVIDES
NATURAL LIGHT

RECESSED LIGHTS IN SOFFIT

LIGHTING AT EACH
SIDE OF LAVATORY CENTER

PULL-OUT LIGHTED
MIRROR

GLASS BLOCK PROVIDES
NATURAL LIGHT

RECESSED VAPOR LIGHTS
ABOVE BATHTUB IN SOFFIT

Guideline 37 - Every functional area in the bathroom should be well illuminated by appropriate task lighting, night lights and/or general lighting. No lighting fixture, including hanging fixtures, should be within reach of a person seated or standing in the bathtub/shower area.

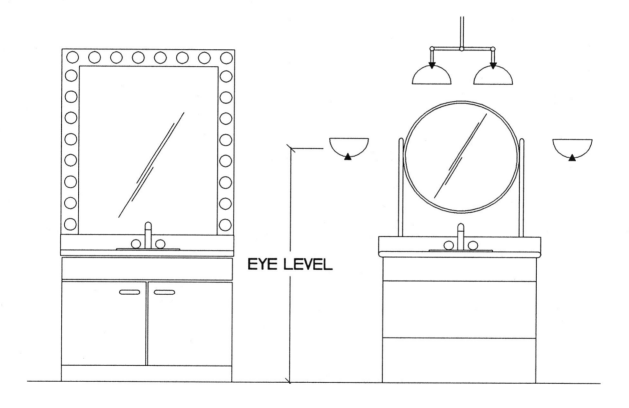

EYE LEVEL

Guideline 37 Clarification - The vanity area should include both overhead and side lighting locations. Side lighting may be planned at eye level which will be approximately 3" (8cm) below a users overall height.

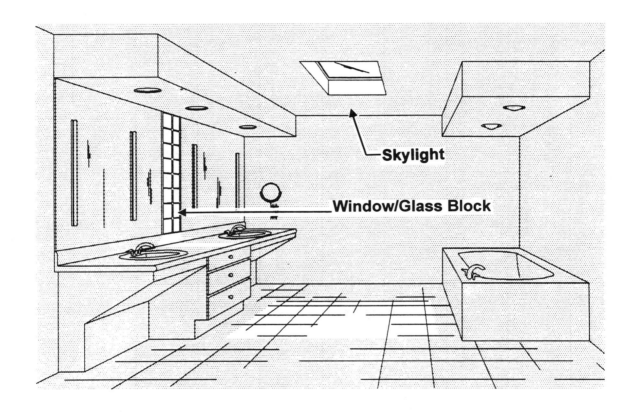

Skylight

Window/Glass Block

Guideline 38 - When possible, bathroom lighting should include a window/skylight area equal to a minimum of 10% of the square footage of the bathroom.

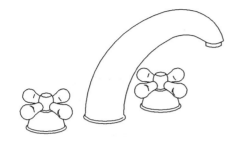

**EASY GRIP
TWO HANDLE
TUB FILLER/CONTROLS**

**SINGLE LEVER
SHOWER CONTROL**

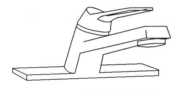

**SINGLE LEVER
LAVATORY FAUCET**

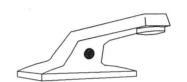

**INFRARED/MOTION SENSOR
LAVATORY FAUCET**

**TOUCH
SENSITIVE**

TOGGLE

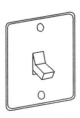

ROCKER

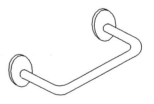

DEEP PULL

Guideline 39 - Controls, handles and door/drawer pulls should be operable with one hand, require only a minimal amount of strength for operation, and should not require tight grasping, pinching or twisting of the wrist. (Includes handles knobs/pulls on entry and exit doors, cabinets, drawers and plumbing fixtures, as well as light and thermostat controls/switches, intercoms, and other room controls.)

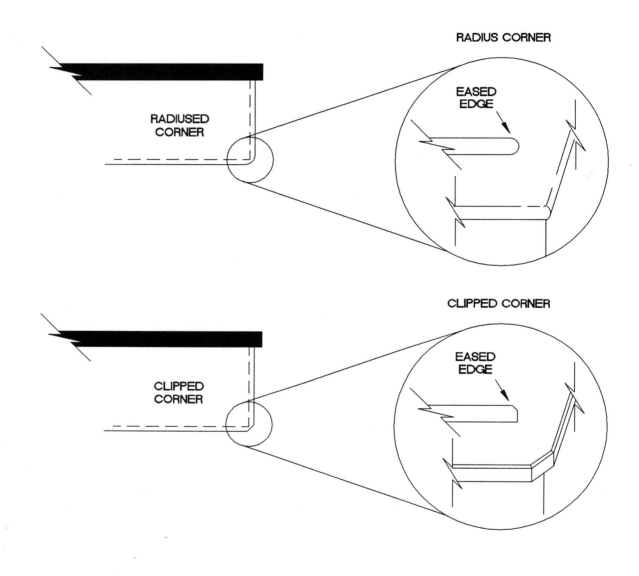

RADIUS CORNER

RADIUSED CORNER

EASED EDGE

CLIPPED CORNER

CLIPPED CORNER

EASED EDGE

Guideline 40 - Use clipped or radius corners for open countertops; countertop edges should be eased to eliminate sharp edges.

Guideline 41 - Any glass used as a bathtub/shower enclosure, partition, or other glass application within 18" (46cm) of the floor should be one of three kinds of safety glazing; laminated glass with a plastic interlayer, tempered glass or approved plastics such as those found in the model safety glazing code.

chapter 3

SPACE

PLANNING

A

CLOSER

LOOK

In some cases, universal design guidelines will be impacted by specific client needs. While the goal of universal design is to meet the needs of the greatest number of people, particular clients may have impairments that require *specific* design considerations. Your purpose may be to design a functional bathroom for a client with a particular disability, or it may be simply to understand the minimum requirements of a person with a specific disability so as to better meet the goal of universal design. Either way, the following design criteria will help.

The Universal Design Approach

A common misconception regarding universal design is that it is nothing more than design for people using wheelchairs. The opposite is true. To be considered universal, a design will be accessible not only to people in wheelchairs, but also to people of most sizes, shapes and abilities. Reference is frequently made to clearances required for wheelchairs because these clearances are generally fine for most other users as well. *For example*, the clear floor space required at a lavatory for a person in a wheelchair is a minimum 30" x 48" (76cm x 122cm), enough for almost anyone. However, 30" (76cm) high countertops for the person in a wheelchair may also work well for a seated person, a shorter person or a child, but they will not work for a tall person or someone who cannot bend.

In this case, to be universal the space must go beyond requirements for the person in a wheelchair, possibly by using adjustable-height counter surfaces or providing a variety of counter surface heights.

This chapter will look mainly at space-planning issues for maneuvering and function in the bathroom for people with mobility impairments. Design considerations for people with visual impairments, hearing impairments, memory loss or confusion, and grip or dexterity impairments will be mentioned here and more clearly addressed in later chapters on products and finishing the space.

Fixtures and Clear Floor Space

Although there are general universal standards for planning spaces, the exact fixture selected and the intended approach and use of the fixture will impact these standards. *For example*, the required clear floor space for a person using a wheelchair is 30" x 48" (76cm x 122cm), but when that person is approaching a bathtub, that dimension needs to be increased to allow for access to controls and safe transfer into the bathtub.

The three main areas to be addressed are:

* lavatory,

* bathtub/shower

* toilet/bidet.

Also important is the approach to and swing of the door into the bathroom. This chapter will look at general universal bathroom space planning. A separate chapter will examine each of the functional areas, including space considerations for those areas.

Space Planning

When planning space for a wheelchair user, you must measure the wheelchair(s) to be used (*see Survey, Chapter 13*). There is no standard wheelchair, but the following dimensions can be a guide when you have no wheelchair available, and want to plan for one.

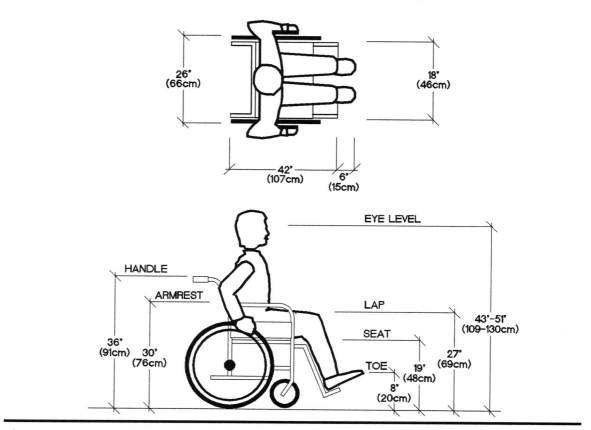

Figure 1 - Dimensions of Adult-Sized Wheelchairs.

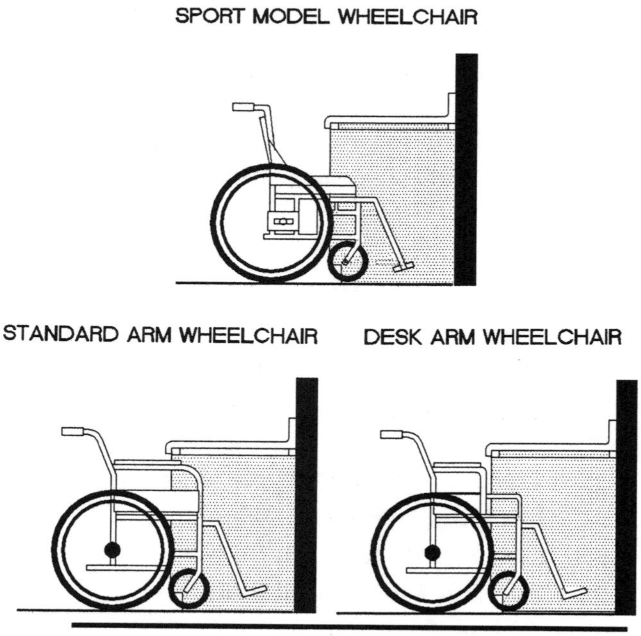

SPORT MODEL WHEELCHAIR

STANDARD ARM WHEELCHAIR DESK ARM WHEELCHAIR

Figure 2 - Common wheelchair styles.

Clear Floor Space

The following clearances are minimums for people who use walkers, crutches or wheelchairs, or stationary seats while working. People who use scooters or bathrooms where one of the users may use a mobility aid will benefit from more space. On the other hand people with vision impairments or low energy or balance will benefit from the minimum amount of space. Layouts that require more turning will require more space.

As noted before, the minimum clear floor space required for a wheelchair user is 30" x 48" (76cm x 122cm). This can be planned for parallel approach or perpendicular (forward) approach. Whenever possible the space for both should be allocated, but this is not always possible or practical in a bathroom. Attention must be given to the client's preference in bathing fixture and in approach or transfer. This should include consideration of a person's handedness, which is the hand or side that is stronger and most able.

Up to 19" (48cm) of this clear floor space may extend under a counter or into a knee space, as at a lavatory.

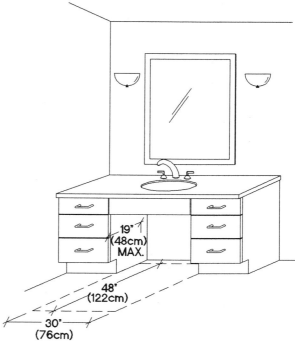

Figure 4 - Perpendicular approach.

KNEE SPACE

Knee spaces are for people who need or wish to sit while using the lavatory or work space. The minimum dimensions for this knee space are 30" wide by 27" high by 48" deep (76cm x 69cm x 122cm) (maximum 19" (48cm) under the counter).

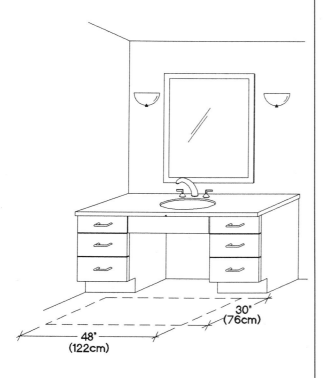

Figure 3 - Parallel approach.

Measuring the Dimensions

When measuring the dimension of the knee space, there are several points to measure.

- At the front edge or apron, the height must be the greatest (27" (69cm) minimum) to allow wheelchair arm clearance. If there is a fixture (sink or countertop) that obstructs this kneespace, it may be beneficial to set the fixture back in the counter to allow maximum wheelchair armrest clearance (provided you do not move it out of functional reach).

- The second height, under the obstruction, must clear knees and should be the maximum possible.

- The third dimension is the depth, which should be clear all the way to the wall, but when there is an obstruction, a minimum of 19" (48cm) allows clearance for wheelchair footrests. If possible a 9" - 12" (23cm - 30 cm) height space off the floor at the back wall will allow greater clearance of the wheelchair footrests.

Depth: Generally a vanity counter is 21" - 24" (53cm - 61cm) deep. However, only 19" (48cm) of this can be counted in the total of 48" (122cm) clear floor space at the knee space.

Width: Although 30" (76cm) is given as a minimum, 36" (91cm) works much better as it allows for the possibility of a 3-point turn for a wheelchair user.

Height: A minimum knee space height of 27" (69cm) is recommended, and the exact minimum for a specific client will be determined by the height of the arm of his/her wheelchair. While each wheelchair is custom, several styles with variations in the armrests allow flexibility in the required knee space height.

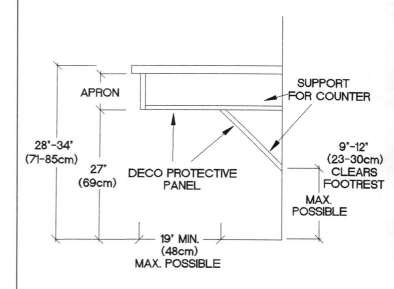

Figure 5 - Kneespace considerations.

The knee space under a lavatory has special considerations. The dimensions of the clear knee space are affected by the height of the counter and the depth of the sink as well as the drain and plumbing location.

Any exposed electrical or plumbing systems (drain pipes, shut off valves, wires) should be insulated or padded and concealed to improve the look and protect users from contact with hot or sharp surfaces.

Turning Space

A space that requires as few turns as necessary provides easier maneu-vering for a person in a wheelchair in the bathroom. It is desirable that space be provided in the bathroom for a person using a wheelchair to turn 180°. Two types of clear floor spaces for two types of turns make this possible.

The first is the easily recognized 60" (152cm) diameter circle and the second is a 36" x 36" x 60" (91cm x 91cm x 152cm) T-turn. The full 60" (152cm) circle is usually the preferred, but if space or energy levels make this difficult or if visual impairments exist, a T-turn that takes less space and allows for easier *way-finding* may be the choice.

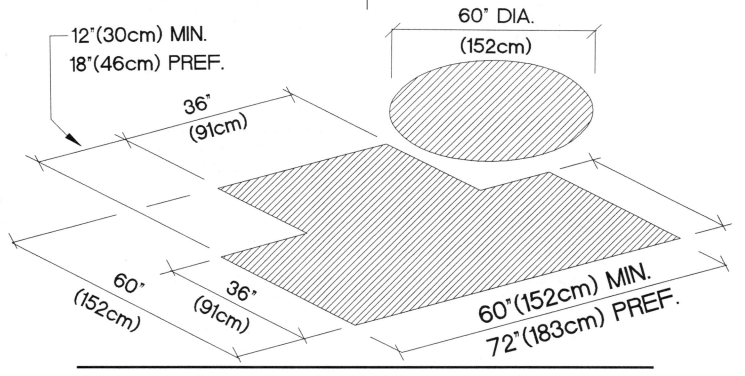

Figure 6 - Clear floor space for turning wheelchairs.

The actual space required for a 360° pivoting turn is 60" (152cm) at the floor and less as you rise above the floor. At approximately 12" (30cm) off the floor, the required space gets smaller because it is above the wheelchair footrests. At 30" (72cm) off the floor the required space again becomes smaller because it has cleared the wheelchair armrest.

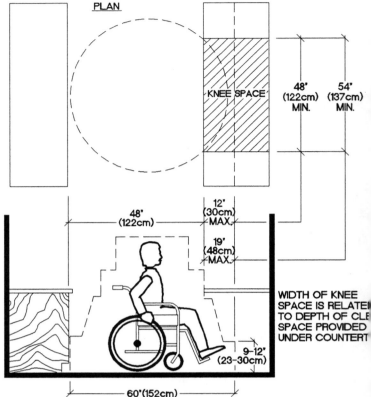

PLAN

KNEE SPACE

48" (122cm) MIN.

54" (137cm) MIN.

48" (122cm)

12" (30cm) MAX.

19" (48cm) MAX.

WIDTH OF KNEE SPACE IS RELATE[] TO DEPTH OF CLE[] SPACE PROVIDED UNDER COUNTERT[]

9-12" (23-30cm)

60"(152cm)

Figure 8 - Clear floor space with enlarged toe space.

This information can be useful when working with limited space. Up to 6" (15cm) of the required 60" (152cm) can be provided by a toekick that is a minimum 6" (15cm) deep and 9" - 12" (23cm - 30cm) high. Up to 19" (48cm) of the required 60" (152cm) can be provided by the clear floor of a knee space if the knee space is a minimum of 48" - 54" (122cm - 137cm) wide. Considering that smaller spaces will sometimes work better for a person with visual impairments or reduced stamina, this can provide a better option.

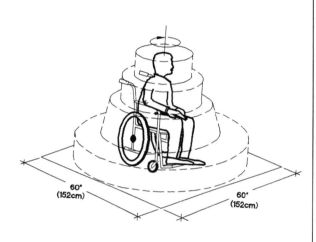

60" (152cm)

60" (152cm)

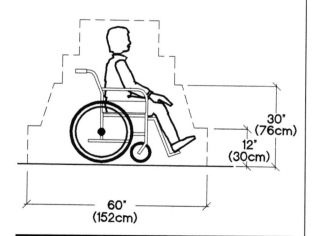

30" (76cm)

12" (30cm)

60" (152cm)

Figure 7 - Clear floor space for a circular turn.

UNIVERSAL BATHROOM PLANNING

The other type of turn, the T-turn, requires minimum clear floor space of 36" x 36" x 60" - 72" (91cm x 91cm x 183cm). The turn is made by pulling into the side arm of the T and backing out going in the opposite direction.

By making a knee space a minimum 36" (91cm) wide, it can be one leg of the T. This is useful information as it allows for flexibility, and wheelchair accessibility without greatly enlarging spaces.

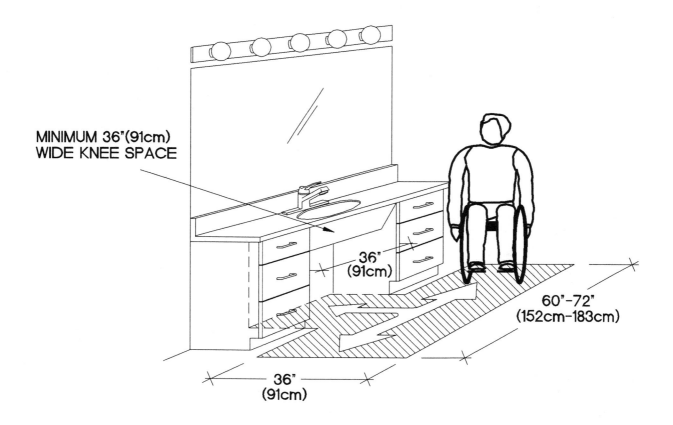

MINIMUM 36"(91cm) WIDE KNEE SPACE

36" (91cm)

60"-72" (152cm-183cm)

36" (91cm)

Figure 9 - Optional turning space - T-Turn.

Heights and Reach Ranges

The average person who remains seated to maneuver in the bathroom has a forward reach range of 15" - 48" (38cm - 122cm) off the floor. If there is an obstruction greater than 20" (51cm) deep, like a counter, the upper limit drops to 44" (112cm). From a seated position reaching to the side, the range is 15" - 54" (38cm - 137cm). If the obstruction is greater than 10" (25cm) deep, the upper limit drops to 46" (117cm).

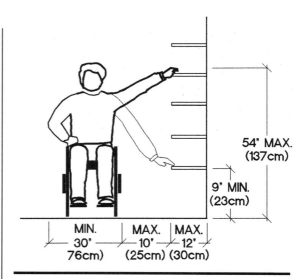

Figure 11 - Reach Range Guidelines - Seated Person.

The person who uses crutches, a walker or in some way needs to use his arms or hands to maintain balance has a slightly different reach range. This person will have trouble reaching very low or very high.

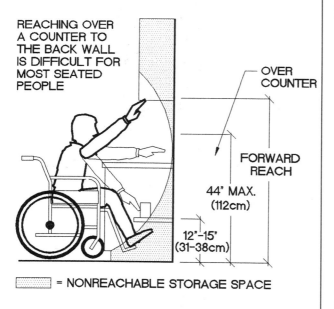

REACHING OVER A COUNTER TO THE BACK WALL IS DIFFICULT FOR MOST SEATED PEOPLE

OVER COUNTER

FORWARD REACH

44" MAX. (112cm)

12"-15" (31-38cm)

☐ = NONREACHABLE STORAGE SPACE

Figure 10 - Reach Range Guidelines - Seated Person.

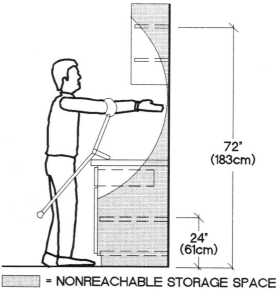

72" (183cm)

24" (61cm)

☐ = NONREACHABLE STORAGE SPACE

Figure 12 - Reach Range Guidelines - Standing, Mobility-Impaired Person.

The lower end of this forward reach range is 15" - 24" (38cm - 61cm) off the floor, depending on a person's ability to bend (back or knee). The upper limit is 69" - 72" (175cm -183cm), depending on the depth of any obstruction.

Combining these reach ranges with the functional limits previously established for individuals 5' 3" - 5' 7" (160cm - 170cm) (24" (61cm) without bending - 69" (175cm) over

a 25" (64cm) deep counter, a universal reach range of 15" - 48" (38cm - 122cm) is suggested as a guide.

Information on reach range will impact how you design storage spaces and counter heights. Configuration of cabinetry and accessorization for storage will have an impact on how well the area within the universal reach range is utilized *(see Chapter 7)*.

	Seated User	Standing, Mobility Impaired Person	Standing Person 5'3" - 5'7" (160cm-170cm)	Universal
Lower Limit - bending	15" (38cm)	15" (38cm)	15" (38cm)	15" (38cm)
Lower Limit - no bending	_____	24" (61cm)	24" (61cm)	24" (61cm)
Upper Limit	48" (122cm)	72" (183cm)	79 1/2" (202cm)	48" (122cm)
Upper Limit - Obstructed up to 25" (64cm)	44" (112cm)	69" (175cmn)	69" (175cm)	44" (112cm)

Space Planning Considerations Involving Doors

Because the bathroom is a private area, a door is an important consideration. In a private or master bathroom suite, one option might be to eliminate unnecessary doors. In a powder room or a shared bathroom, a door is usually a necessity and its impact on maneuvering space must be addressed. To maintain universal access to and use of a bathroom, a designer must look at the door swing, the clear space on either side of the door, and the approach to the door.

The first consideration is the clear opening at the door, a minimum 32" (81cm), which is the opening minus the thickness of the door stop, the thickness of the door and the space between the door and frame at the hinge side. This requires a 36" (91cm) standard door. It is possible to increase the clear opening at a door by changing to a hinge that allows the door to move out of the door opening.

Clear Floor Space at Doors

The clear floor space required at a door varies with approach and swing or style of door. Basically, a larger clear floor space must be allowed on the pull side of the door beyond the latch to allow space to operate the door and move out of the door swing. A narrower clear floor space will be needed on the push side of the door, depending on approach.

The goal of the clearance requirements set down in the codes (**ANSI, UFAS, ADA**) is to allow a person using a mobility aid to approach the door, operate the latch and maneuver through the door. Based on the direction of approach, the maneuvering space will vary. These requirements are called out for commercial buildings, but they will also be of assistance in planning a residential space.

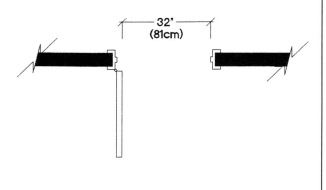

Figure 13 - Clear opening at the door.

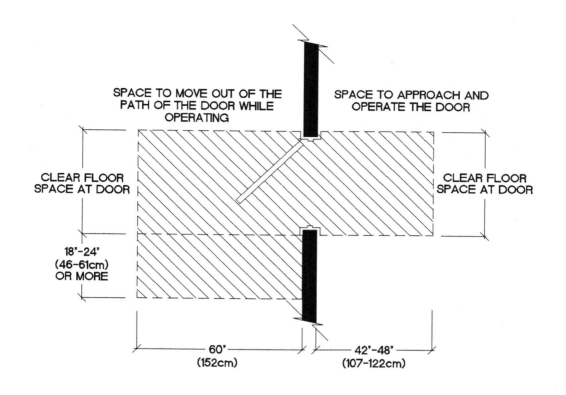

SPACE TO MOVE OUT OF THE
PATH OF THE DOOR WHILE
OPERATING

SPACE TO APPROACH AND
OPERATE THE DOOR

CLEAR FLOOR
SPACE AT DOOR

CLEAR FLOOR
SPACE AT DOOR

18"-24"
(46-61cm)
OR MORE

60"
(152cm)

42"-48"
(107-122cm)

Figure 14 - General minimum clear floor space at doors (varies based on approach.

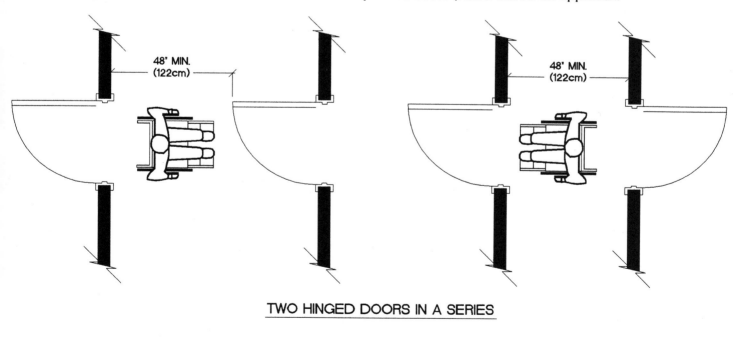

48" MIN.
(122cm)

48" MIN.
(122cm)

TWO HINGED DOORS IN A SERIES

Figure 15 - Clear floor spaces at doors in commercial buildings.

Because requirements for clear floor spaces at doors will impact hallway widths and space within the bathroom, they must be examined together. The actual passage width needed for a person in a wheelchair to make a 90° turn into an opening 32" (81cm) wide is 42" (107cm). Given that often the hall width is less flexible, solutions might involve widening the door or recessing the bathroom entry.

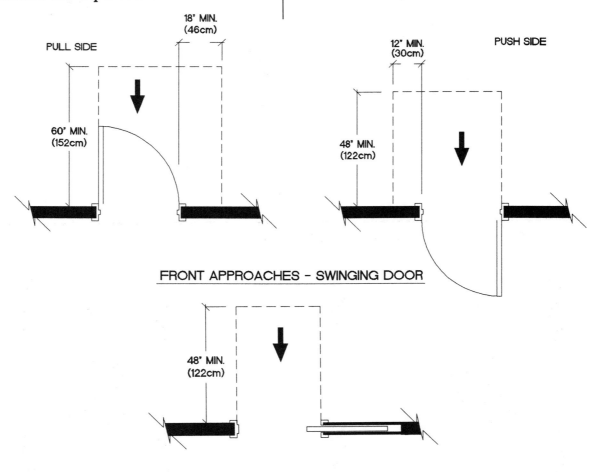

FRONT APPROACHES - SWINGING DOOR

FRONT APPROACHES - SLIDING DOOR

Figure 16 - Clear floor spaces at doors.

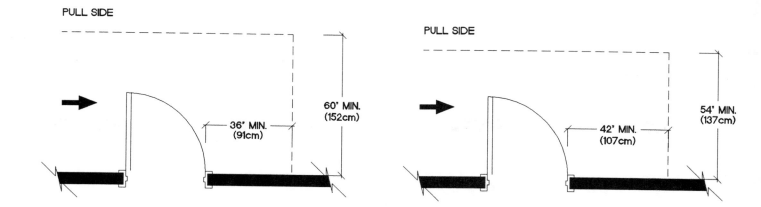

PULL SIDE

36" MIN.
(91cm)

60" MIN.
(152cm)

PULL SIDE

42" MIN.
(107cm)

54" MIN.
(137cm)

HINGE-SIDE APPROACHES - SWINGING DOOR

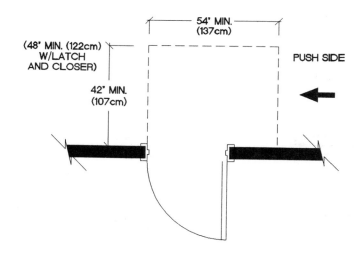

54" MIN.
(137cm)

(48" MIN. (122cm)
W/LATCH
AND CLOSER)

42" MIN.
(107cm)

PUSH SIDE

Figure 17 - Clear floor spaces at doors.

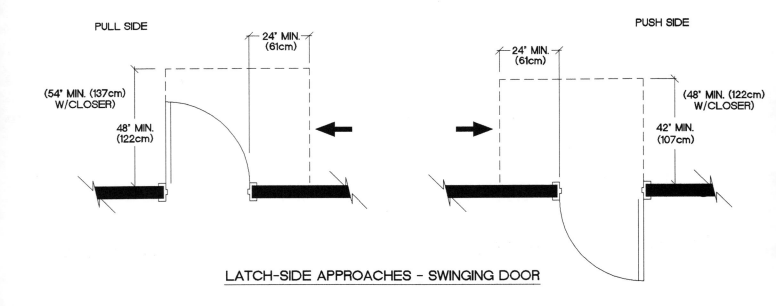

PULL SIDE

PUSH SIDE

24" MIN.
(61cm)

(54" MIN. (137cm)
W/CLOSER)

48" MIN.
(122cm)

24" MIN.
(61cm)

(48" MIN. (122cm)
W/CLOSER)

42" MIN.
(107cm)

LATCH-SIDE APPROACHES - SWINGING DOOR

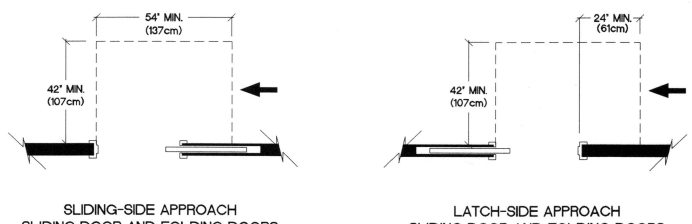

54" MIN.
(137cm)

42" MIN.
(107cm)

24" MIN.
(61cm)

42" MIN.
(107cm)

SLIDING-SIDE APPROACH
SLIDING DOOR AND FOLDING DOORS

LATCH-SIDE APPROACH
SLIDING DOOR AND FOLDING DOORS

Figure 18 - Clear floor spaces at doors.

As in other aspects of universal design, the threshold should not be higher than 1/2" (1.27cm) (beveled) or 1/4" (.64cm) (square), and the door handle should be a lever or a type that will allow use without firm grasp. Automatic door controls or door closers may be a solution.

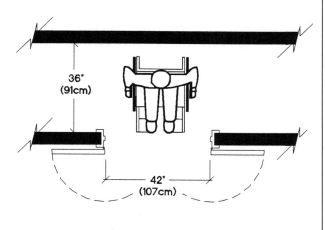

Figure 19 - Minimum Door and Passage Width.

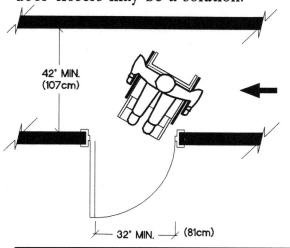

Figure 20 - Alternative use of space at doors.

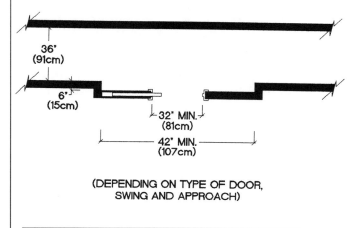

(DEPENDING ON TYPE OF DOOR, SWING AND APPROACH)

Figure 21 - Alternative use of space at doors.

A WORD OF CAUTION

We are moving from a *"Peter Pan"* world, where everyone was to have been the same-size, lifestyle, ability and age, to a world that encourages diversity. Our changing bathroom design guidelines reflect this shift in attitudes.

Do not mistake universal design as a new form of *"one size fits all"*, and do not mistake the guidelines explained in this chapter as optimum for everyone. These guidelines, based mainly on **ANSI, UFAS** (*see Chapter 12*), and the **Accessible Housing Design Files** are minimums. Each client and each space must be considered separately as always. Again, use these guidelines as minimums and as a basis from which to expand creatively.

The planning of clear floor spaces for maneuvering and use of the basic stations of the bathroom is complex. It is impacted by space requirements for mobility aids and strengths and abilities of the people using the bathroom. *Appendix 5, Transfer Techniques*, will assist the designer in understanding the exact goals of these space allotments, enabling the designer to choose optimally within the constraints of each job.

A complete understanding of the required clear floor spaces and the reasons behind the requirements gives you the opportunity to make optimum choices when balancing these considerations with the other parameters of the job. Several points are worth reiterating here.

- First, remember these allowances are minimums. Understanding the reason for these allowances and your clients needs in terms of maneuvering will help you to determine where you might be more generous and where your client's interests will be best met by sticking to the minimum. In particular, people using scooters and bathrooms where there will be multiple users will benefit from more generous spaces.

- Second, whenever possible, measure your client's space requirements, as mobility aids are unique.

- Finally, keep in mind that these spaces will overlap in a bathroom and do not greatly increase the overall size of the space.

chapter 4

THE LAVATORY AREA

The first of the three main functional areas of the bathroom, the lavatory area, requires careful consideration in terms of universal design. The space allowances, the style and installation, and to a lesser degree the material, of the lavatory will have tremendous impact on safe and universal access to the area. This chapter will examine the lavatory and the spaces surrounding it, in terms of universal design.

SPACE CONSIDERATIONS FOR THE LAVATORY AREA

Universal space planning in the lavatory area involves several key considerations, all of which impact one another. They are:

- counter height
- sink depth
- plumbing location
- knee space height and width
- clear floor space for approach and use
- the impact on adjacent clear floor space
- storage.

Counter Height, Sink Depth, Plumbing Location, Knee Space Height

The maximum height lavatory for a seated user should be 34" (86cm), with 30" (72cm) being a more comfortable choice. Sink depth, and needed knee space height (based on height of wheelchair armrest) will impact this. NKBA suggests that a sink be no deeper than 6 1/2" (17cm). To function properly, 4" (10cm) is adequate. Given that the recommended knee space clearance is 27" (69cm) high minimum, and 29" (74cm) preferred to the bottom of the front edge or apron, the designer must work within these constraints to arrive at an optimum solution.

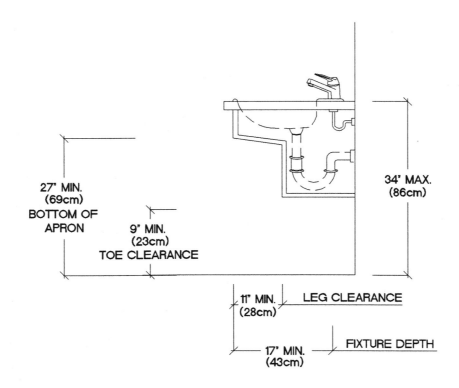

Figure 22 - Kneespace at lavatory.

A comfortable height for a lavatory for a standing user is typically 36" - 38" (91cm - 97cm). Both the standing and seated user can be accommodated if there is room for two sinks or if an adjustable height sink can be used.

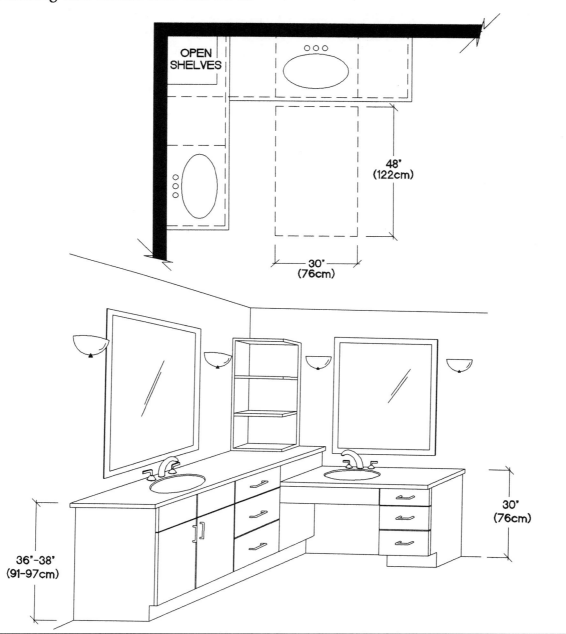

Figure 23 - Example of two lavatories at different heights.

Knee Space Width, Clear Floor-Space, and Storage

The minimum width for a knee space is 30" (72cm) with 36" (91cm) preferred. Remember that 36" (91cm) width will allow for a T-turn and 48" - 54" (122cm - 137cm) width will allow for enough clear space to include up to 19" (48cm) under the knee space to be used in a 60" (152cm) turning radius. When appropriate, planning the open knee space of the lavatory adjacent to the clear space at another fixture will be beneficial for maneuvering.

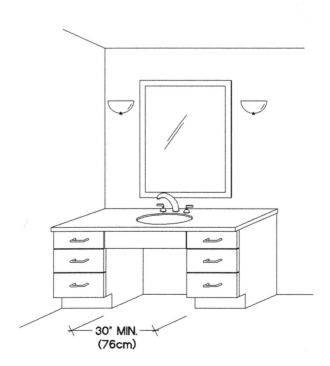

Figure 24 - Minimum width kneespace.

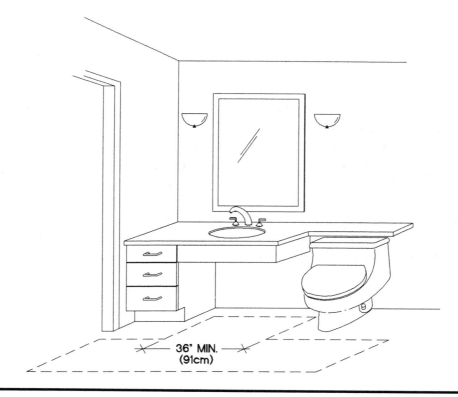

Figure 25 - 36" (91cm) knee space allows for use in T-turn.

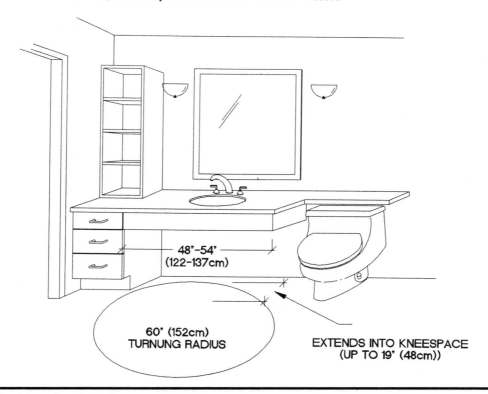

Figure 26 - 48" - 54" (122cm - 137cm) wide kneespace, using up to 19" (48cm) to complete 60" (152cm) turning space.

Storage in the lavatory area for towels, equipment, and supplies must be within the universal reach range of 15" - 48" (38cm - 122cm) and should be within reach of a person using the lavatory. Drawers adjacent to a knee space, open shelves on adjacent counter areas, or rolling storage help to achieve this convenience.

THE FIXTURE

The lavatory or sink must be chosen carefully to provide functional counter and storage space while allowing for needed clear floor space. The main types of lavatories to be considered are Wall Hung, Pedestal, Drop-In, Undermount, Integral, and Console.

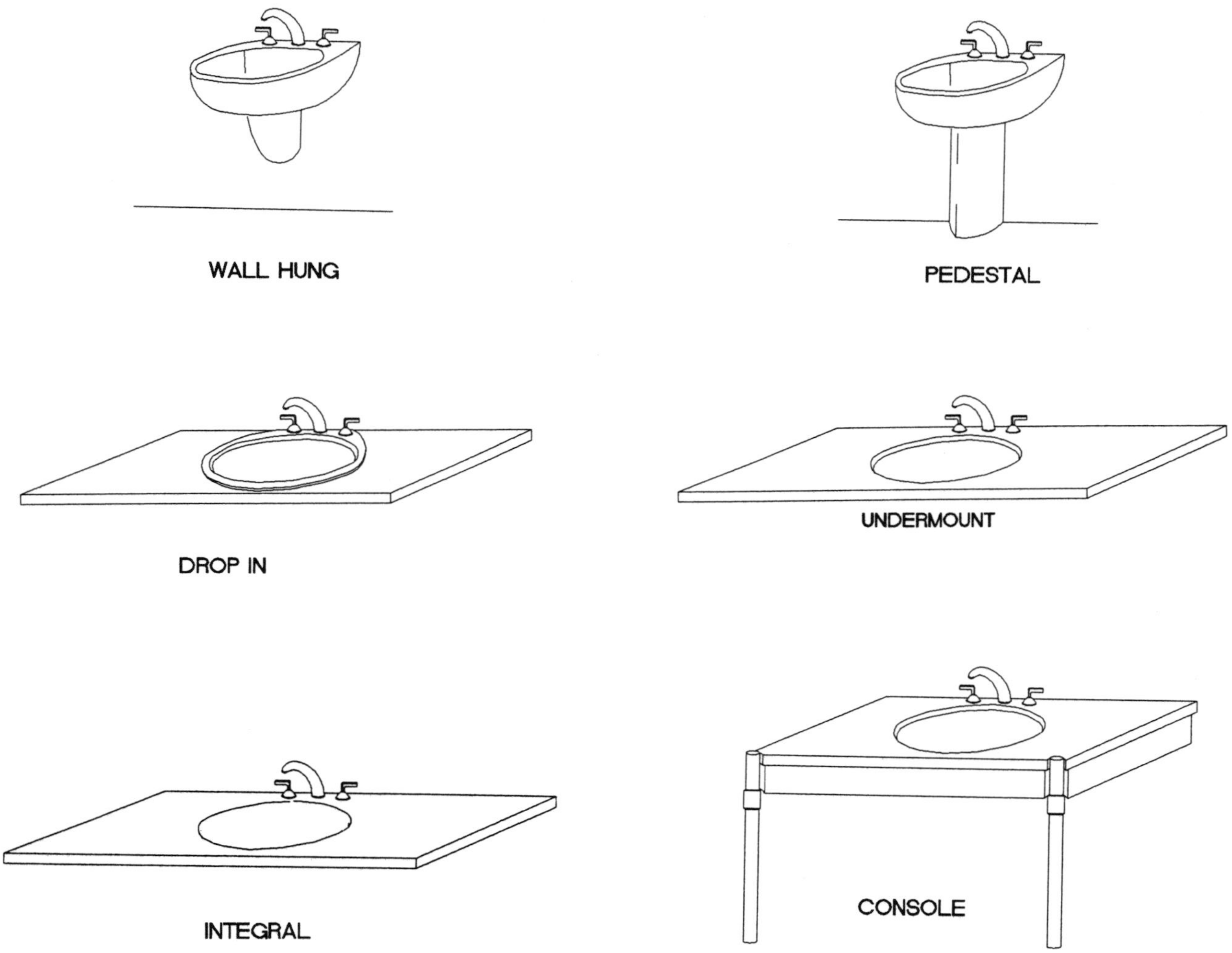

WALL HUNG

PEDESTAL

DROP IN

UNDERMOUNT

INTEGRAL

CONSOLE

Figure 27 - Main types of lavatories.

Lavatory Designs

Certain characteristics will improve the universal design application for any of these lavatories. The maximum depth recommended for an accessible sink is 6 1/2" (17cm). A sink depth of 4" (10cm) is sufficient, and a design that is shallower in the front, leading back to the deepest part of the bowl with a drain at the rear, is the preferred configuration.

If the space under the lavatory is to be open, it must include some type of protective covering for the drain and water pipes. This covering should extend to the bottom side of the sink if needed to protect against heat, insulated for sound, and to cover any rough surfaces. A variety of options exist to do this attractively.

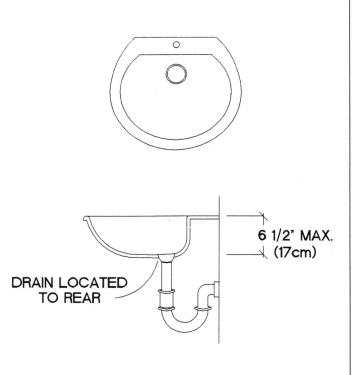

Figure 28 - Ideal lavatory configuration.

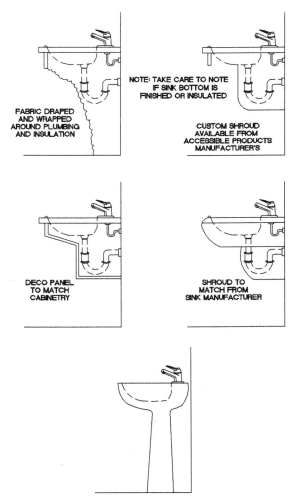

Figure 29 - Options for covering pipes and sink underside.

Accessing the Knee Space

Several adaptable solutions would allow for the space under the sink to be used in a variety of ways. The face frame and doors of the cabinet might be made removable with the plumbing protected inside. This would allow the undersink area to be used for storage and when desired, removal of the face frame and doors would create a knee space for seated use. Another option would be to use retractable doors, taking care to allow for a 30" (72cm) minimum width interior space when the doors are in the retracted position. A third option would be to create bi-fold doors that fold 180° to lie flat on the adjacent cabinets. A hinge is available to facilitate this.

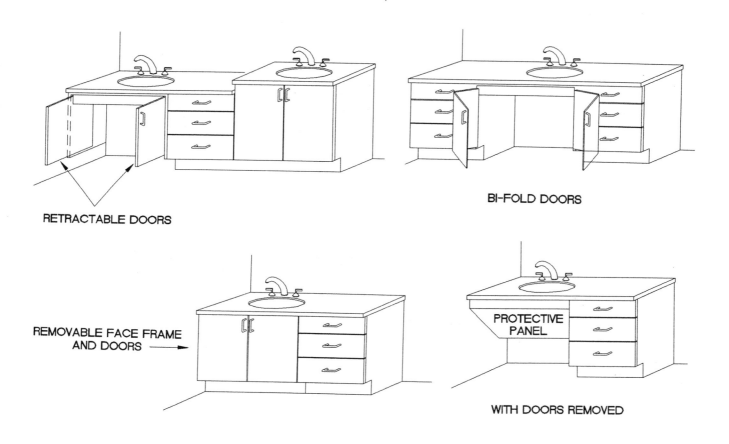

RETRACTABLE DOORS

BI-FOLD DOORS

REMOVABLE FACE FRAME AND DOORS →

PROTECTIVE PANEL

WITH DOORS REMOVED

Figure 30 - Adaptable lavatory options.

Wall Hung Lavatories

The wall hung lavatory provides great flexibility in the height of the area, with full clear floor space. However, it does not provide storage or counter options. Several solutions involve wall hung cabinets and the possible use of a counter or shelf above the sink, with care being taken to keep the counter surface within reach of users of various stature.

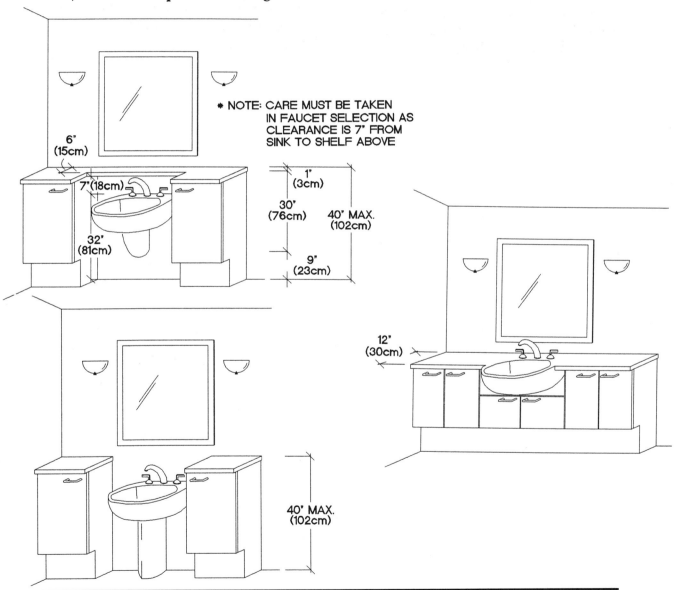

* NOTE: CARE MUST BE TAKEN IN FAUCET SELECTION AS CLEARANCE IS 7" FROM SINK TO SHELF ABOVE

Figure 31 - Examples - Wall hung or pedestal lavatory areas.

Pedestal Lavatories

These same options apply to pedestal sinks.

The pedestal sink allows for clear floor space, with some interruption from the pedestal. Styles are available with the sink itself having an integral work surface.

In other designs, adjacent work surfaces can be created as illustrated for the wall-hung lavatory. The typical height of a pedestal sink is 30" (72cm), which will usually be too low to allow for a knee space, depending on the sink depth. The sink can be elevated by building a base for the pedestal.

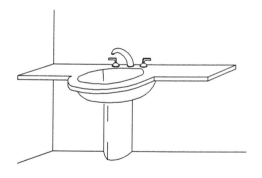

Figure 32 - Pedestal sink with integral work surface.

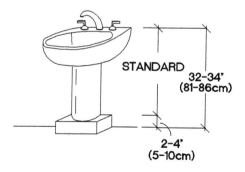

Figure 33 - Pedestal Sink with Built-up Base.

While the pedestal sink does provide some clear floor space, it may be desirable to opt for the same sink bowl with a matching wall shroud to make the knee space totally clear. Many pedestal sinks are available either way.

* NOTE: ONLY WHEN SO INTENDED BY MANUFACTURER

Figure 34 - Pedestal sink converted to wall hung sink with shroud

Drop-In and Undermount Lavatories

When using either a drop-in or an undermount sink, the lavatory area can be universally designed if the depth of the sink does not exceed 6 1/2" (17cm) and the drain is located to the rear. This would be done following the steps for creating a knee space. Unfortunately, the depth limitation makes most current sinks too deep when undermounted, but there are a few models available that will allow for this. The undermount sink eliminates any lip or rise in the surface around the sink rim, so it is desirable for a person with limited grip to access its interior.

Integral Lavatories

The integral sink fitted without apparent seams into the counter offers unique universal design solutions, particularly when formed from solid surface materials that can be formed and shaped. The sink depth can sometimes be adjusted by trimming the bowl before it is bonded to the counter surface. The area immediately surrounding the sink can be trimmed and shaped to suit user and space needs. The front edge of the counter can be extended to create an apron to conceal support for the sink. Handholds and towel bars can be cut into the counter surface.

Console Lavatories

The console sink is an attractive way to provide a sink with a kneespace, provided there are sufficient clearances and maneuvering spaces. Carefully check the height of the console, the height of the kneespace below, and the adjacent clear floor space. The console sink will also require special attention to protecting the user from exposed pipes and potentially sharp edges.

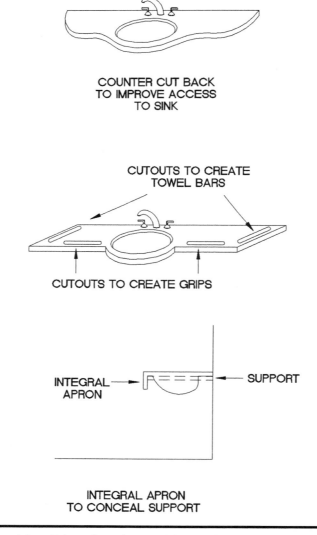

COUNTER CUT BACK
TO IMPROVE ACCESS
TO SINK

CUTOUTS TO CREATE
TOWEL BARS

CUTOUTS TO CREATE GRIPS

INTEGRAL APRON ← → SUPPORT

INTEGRAL APRON
TO CONCEAL SUPPORT

Figure 35 - Options with solid surface/integral lavatories.

Adjustable Height Sinks

Several products exist that allow for height adjustment of the lavatory and/or adjacent counter area on a moment-to-moment basis. To use a motorized system, flexible plumbing lines must be installed which will require approval from local plumbing inspectors. While this is non-traditional, a careful examination of the system and its goals will usually result in approval. The system works via a motor installed against the wall that will raise and lower the counter, sink included.

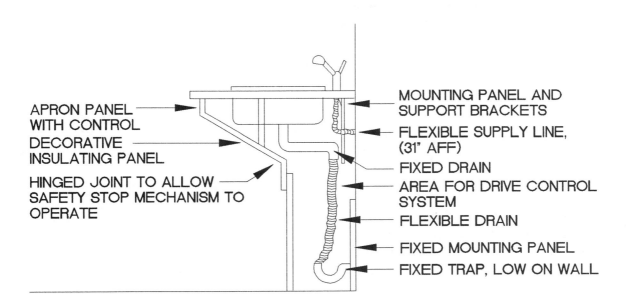

APRON PANEL WITH CONTROL

DECORATIVE INSULATING PANEL

HINGED JOINT TO ALLOW SAFETY STOP MECHANISM TO OPERATE

MOUNTING PANEL AND SUPPORT BRACKETS

FLEXIBLE SUPPLY LINE, (31" AFF)

FIXED DRAIN

AREA FOR DRIVE CONTROL SYSTEM

FLEXIBLE DRAIN

FIXED MOUNTING PANEL

FIXED TRAP, LOW ON WALL

Figure 36 - Flexible plumbing lines.

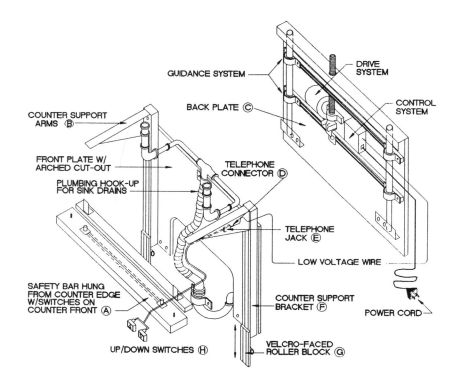

Figure 37 - Drive assembly for motorized sink and counter support.

The result is a totally flexible, easy-to-operate system that truly works for everyone.

Another product available includes the lavatory, flexible plumbing lines and a wall bracketing system that allows a person to adjust the position of the lav to the right or left or up and down by pressing a release lever.

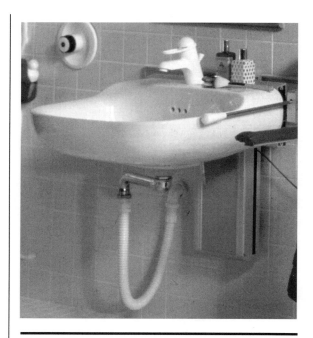

Figure 38 - Adjustable lavatory. (pressalit by American Standard)

These types of adjustability may be costly, but the total flexibility they provide will be worth the added benefits. A more moderately priced option would be a hand crank lift mechanism.

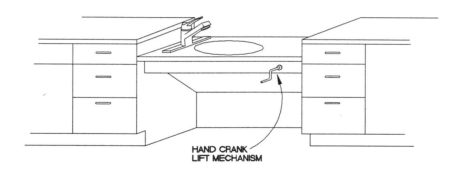

HAND CRANK
LIFT MECHANISM

Figure 39 - Hand crank lift mechanism.

Yet another option is to create adaptable-height lavatory and vanity areas. This will again require the use of flexible plumbing lines which must be approved. The counter, including the sink, is hung on support brackets. The brackets may be mounted at several heights without needing major construction changes. This type of adjustability is not meant for day-to-day changes, but for changes when users' needs change.

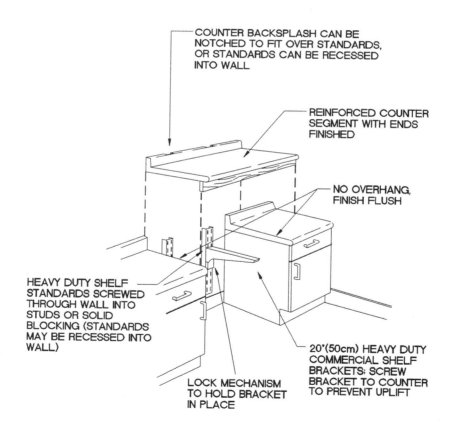

COUNTER BACKSPLASH CAN BE NOTCHED TO FIT OVER STANDARDS, OR STANDARDS CAN BE RECESSED INTO WALL

REINFORCED COUNTER SEGMENT WITH ENDS FINISHED

NO OVERHANG, FINISH FLUSH

HEAVY DUTY SHELF STANDARDS SCREWED THROUGH WALL INTO STUDS OR SOLID BLOCKING (STANDARDS MAY BE RECESSED INTO WALL)

LOCK MECHANISM TO HOLD BRACKET IN PLACE

20"(50cm) HEAVY DUTY COMMERCIAL SHELF BRACKETS: SCREW BRACKET TO COUNTER TO PREVENT UPLIFT

Figure 40 - Manually adjustable height lavatory/counters.

UNIVERSAL BATHROOM PLANNING

LAVATORY MATERIALS

Finally, the materials used to fabricate lavatories have some impact on universal design. Materials chosen should be slow to transfer heat and/or sound. The underside of the lavatory should be smooth and insulated to protect the legs of a seated user.

Stainless steel and other decorative metals are usually easy to maintain and several manufacturers are now insulating them against sound and heat transfer. There are several stainless steel sinks that can be ordered with the depth and drain location called out by the designer.

Sinks of solid surface material are more costly, but they transfer less heat and sound. Also, they offer tremendous flexibility in fabrication. Cast polymer or cultured marble are less flexible in terms of fabrication, but manufacturers of these products have paid particular attention to universal design considerations, so there is a wide variety of standard shapes to choose from.

Vitreous china or cast iron lavatories are often deeper than the maximum 6 1/2" (17cm). There are growing numbers of china lavatories designed specifically to meet this need, so the selection is expanding.

For a more extensive discussion of materials, refer to **Volume 3** of **NKBAs Bathroom Industry Technical Manual's, Bathroom Equipment and Materials**.

chapter 5

THE BATHTUB/ SHOWER AREA

Universal considerations for the bathtub or shower area include space planning, style and universal installation, material selection and controls. The main focus for the bathtub or shower area is on safe transfer into and out of the fixture and on ease of use.

SPACE CONSIDERATIONS FOR THE BATHTUB/SHOWER AREA

In planning the space for the bathtub and/or shower area, how the user will approach and transfer, into and out of the fixture will influence the use of space. A truly universal space would allow for a variety of approaches. In addition, the type of fixture and its intended use will affect the space plan. The three main fixtures are; a bathtub, a roll-in shower (large enough for a person using a wheelchair to roll into), and a transfer shower (a shower that a person using a wheelchair would transfer into).

The Bathtub

The bathtub space can be handled several ways. The first is to provide a seat or transfer surface in the bathtub space. One advantage to this option is that it requires the minimum amount of space, fitting within the bathtub. This is often a portable item, requiring no structural changes for its use. The disadvantages are that the seat will take up space wihin the bathtub, eliminating the option of soaking in the bathtub. Storage space must be provided when it is to be removed, and care must be given to ensure its stability. To create a better transfer surface, the bathtub seat should extend slightly beyond the edge of the bathtub.

Clear Floor Space at Bathtub

The clear floor space required at this type of bathtub is the length of the bathtub x 30" (72cm) with a preferred width of 36" (91cm).

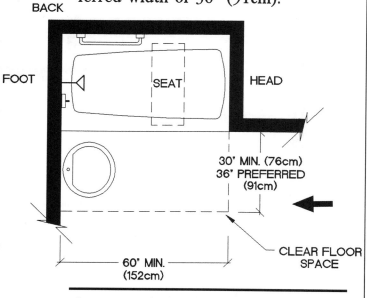

Figure 41 - Clear floor space - parallel approach.

For a perpendicular approach, the clear floor space required increases to a 48" (122cm) depth.

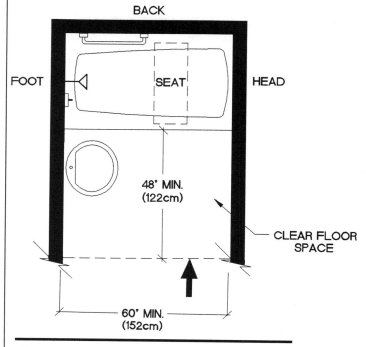

Figure 42 - Clear floor space - - forward or perpendicular approach.

The preferred clear floor space would include 12" - 18" (30cm - 46cm) at both ends of the bathtub to allow for better access to controls and better maneuvering for a parallel transfer for a person using a mobility aid.

The added clearance at the foot of the bathtub allows for an added wheelchair footrest to extend beyond the control wall. The added clear floor space at the head of the bathtub allows for better positioning of the back portion of a wheelchair.

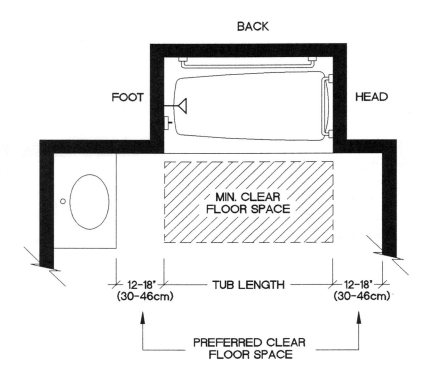

BACK

FOOT   HEAD

MIN. CLEAR
FLOOR SPACE

12-18"   TUB LENGTH   12-18"
(30-46cm)   (30-46cm)

PREFERRED CLEAR
FLOOR SPACE

Figure 43 - Preferred clear floor space.

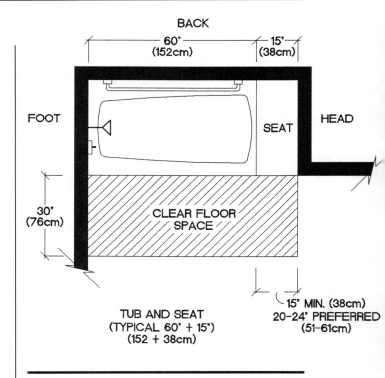

BACK

60"   15"
(152cm)   (38cm)

FOOT   SEAT   HEAD

30"   CLEAR FLOOR
(76cm)   SPACE

TUB AND SEAT   15" MIN. (38cm)
(TYPICAL 60" + 15")   20-24" PREFERRED
(152 + 38cm)   (51-61cm)

Another option for the bathtub area is to create a built-in transfer surface at the head of the bathtub. The depth of this built-in surface must be a minimum of 15" (38cm), with 20" - 24" (51cm - 61cm) preferred.

Figure 44 - Built-in seat at head of bathtub.

Remember, the minimum clear floor space required is 30" (72cm) x the length of the bathtub plus the seat. Better access to controls and better positioning of a wheelchair again call for an additional 12" - 18" (30cm - 46cm) clear floor space at the foot and the head of the bathtub.

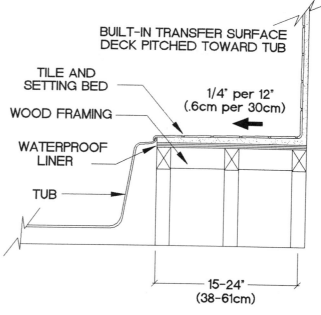

Figure 46 - Construction details - built-in transfer surface.

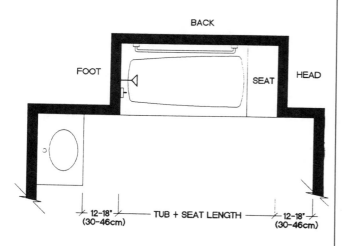

Figure 45 - Preferred clear floor space - bathtub with built-in seat.

Both the built-in or the removable bathtub seat must withstand a minimum of 300 pounds (136kg) of pressure. To construct a built-in seat, framing that will withstand this weight must be provided. In addition, the area must have a waterproof liner and should be sloped slightly toward the bathtub (1/4" per 12") (.64cm per 30cm) to avoid excess water standing on the seat.

BATHTUB CONTROLS, ACCESSORIES AND GRAB BARS

Controls

Controls should be located at the foot of the bathtub below the grab bar and offset toward the outside of the bathtub. Sometimes, a second control and a handheld spray will be located on the back wall for ease of use by someone in the bathtub.

Showerhead

A fixed showerhead, if used, should be mounted at the standard 78" (198cm) above the floor. A handheld showerhead should be mounted not higher than 48" (122cm) and in a position not to obstruct the use of grab bars. If the hand-held shower head is mounted on a slide-bar, the bar must allow for positioning the shower head with its lowest position not higher than 48" (122cm). *(See Chapter 7 for a greater discussion of controls, fittings and accessories).*

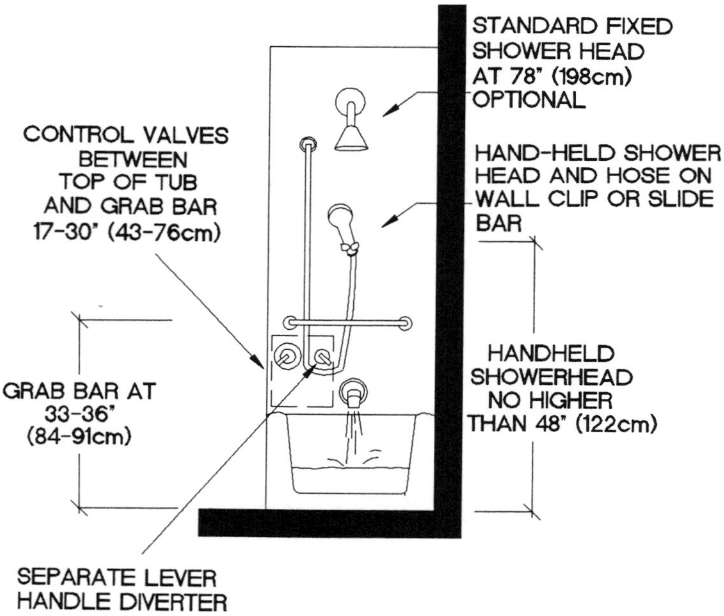

Grab Bars

Grab bars improve safety and stability. While they are integral in certain bathtubs, they are optional with others, and the most universal choice is to build support into the entire bathtub surround so that grab bars may be added when and where needed.

Standards will dictate several locations for grab bars, yet it may not be a current need or desire of a client as you plan. Keep in mind that the point of entry where a person shifts from sitting to standing or from transfer surface down into the bathtub are the areas most likely to need grab bars.

The location of grab bars in the bathtub area will be affected by how a person intends to transfer into and out of the bathtub. A universal approach is to install blocking throughout the bathtub area, as previously mentioned, so that grab bars can be positioned when and where they will be most effective.

At the foot of the bathtub the grab bar should be a minimum of 24" (61cm) long beginning at the front edge of the bathtub. On the

CONTROL VALVES BETWEEN TOP OF TUB AND GRAB BAR 17-30" (43-76cm)

GRAB BAR AT 33-36" (84-91cm)

SEPARATE LEVER HANDLE DIVERTER

STANDARD FIXED SHOWER HEAD AT 78" (198cm) OPTIONAL

HAND-HELD SHOWER HEAD AND HOSE ON WALL CLIP OR SLIDE BAR

HANDHELD SHOWERHEAD NO HIGHER THAN 48" (122cm)

Figure 47 - Bathtub control wall.

back wall, the grab bar should be a minimum 24" (61cm), although a longer bar is preferred. This bar may not be more than 24" (61cm) from the foot-end wall and not more than 12" (30cm) from the head-end wall.

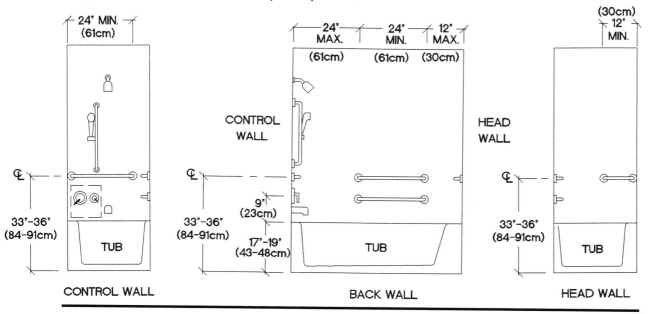

Figure 48 - Grab bars at bathtub without built-in seat

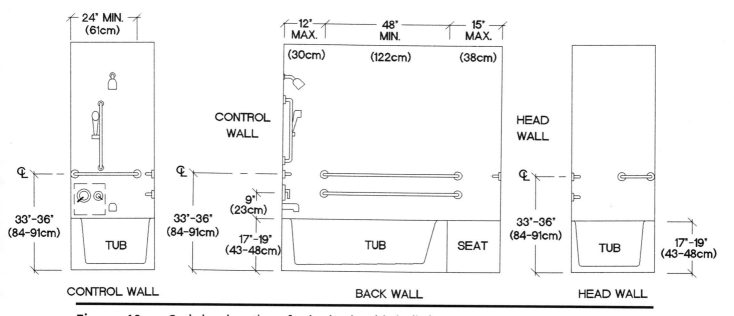

Figure 49 - Grab bar locations for bathtub with built-in seat

A second grab bar, 9" (23cm) above the rim of the bathtub, the same length as the first should be included. The bar at the head of the bathtub is to be a minimum 12" (30cm) long, beginning at the front edge of the bathtub. If a built-in transfer seat is used, the bar at the head of the bathtub may be omitted and the grab bar(s) on the back wall becomes a 48" (122cm) minimum length, not more than 12" (30cm) from the foot of the bathtub and not more than 15" (38cm) from the head of the bathtub. For more information on how a person might transfer into the bathtub, *see Appendix 5, Transfer Techniques*.

THE FIXTURE

There are many varieties of bathtubs on the market today, with growing numbers of styles lending themselves to universal design. The traditional 30" w x 60" l x 14" - 21" d (72cm w x 152cm l x 36cm - 53cm d) bathtub can be challenging to even the most able-bodied user in terms of safe entry, exit and control.

• Any bathtub that does not include a seat in its design can be more safely installed by planning a transfer seat or surface into the decking around the bathtub.

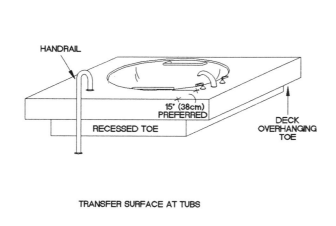

TRANSFER SURFACE AT TUBS

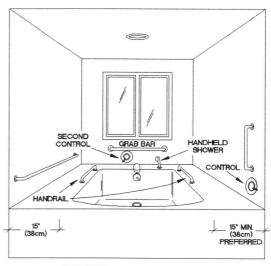

TRANSFER SURFACE AT TUBS

Figure 50 - Transfer surface at bathtubs.

- Changing from hazardous steps around a bathtub to an increased platform or deck will improve safe access for all, particularly if a handrail or grab bar is planned to further aid stability.

- A minimum depth of 15" (38cm) is recommended for a transfer surface, but if this is not possible, plan the deepest available space.

- Finally, a slip-resistant surface on the floor of the bathub will improve safe access.

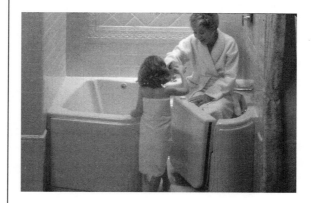

Figure 51 - Courtesy of Kohler - Bathtub with door.

Bathtub Styles

Although the style of the basic bathtub, which has never been user-friendly, has changed very little, there are a number of styles that provide assistance to the bather in entry and exit. Several bathtubs have doors.

In addition, molded bathtubs and surround systems are available with seats as an integral part of the bathtub.

Another option in the molded bathtub products may be fold-down seats or grab bars.

There are bathtubs with built-in lifts or seats that rotate out to allow

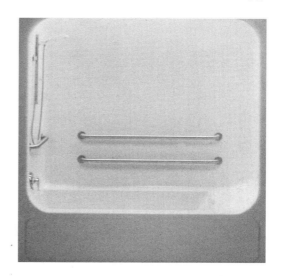

Figure 52 - Bathtub with integral seat.

a bather to transfer onto the seat, then back in and down to allow the bather to soak in the bathtub or whirlpool.

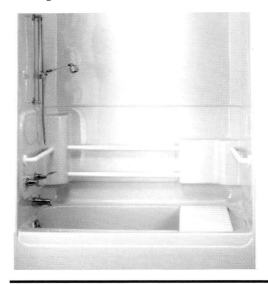

Figure 53 - Bathtub with fold-down seat.

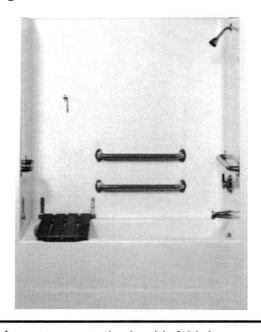

Figure 54 - Bathtub with fold-down seat.

Figure 55 - Bathtub with built-in lift.

Several bathtubs are designed so that the floor of the bathtub is accessible by means of a door or rotating panel, and the bathtub floor is 18" - 20" (46cm - 51cm) high. This results in easy transfer directly onto the bathtub floor. It also means a person can sit while cleaning the bathtub or bathing a child, rather than kneeling on the floor.

designer to create an area where function and aesthetics don't conflict.

Bathtub Materials

For the most part, materials used to fabricate bathtubs do not impact their universal application.

- Fiberglass, acrylic or molded materials typically retain heat better than cast iron, steel or china, but beyond that, there is little universal design advantage in using one over another.

- Custom bathtubs made of stone, tile, concrete, wood or other materials allow for custom shapes that can be universal, but care must be taken to make these surfaces slip-resistant.

- There is a soft bathtub on the market, created by using a fiberglass shell, lining it with foam and then sealing it with a non-porous elastomeric material. The result is a non-slip, soft surface that retains heat and decreases accidents and injuries from falls.

Figure 56 - Bathtub with raised height floor and rotating front panel.

Bathtub Aesthetics

While the growing availability of accessible bathtubs are welcome, the institutional or medical appearance of many of them is unfortunate.

It requires continued effort from the manufacturers to improve the appearance of the bathubs and continued effort from the bathroom

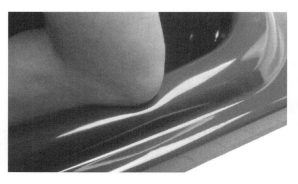

Figure 57 - Soft bathtub.

Universal Design Critera for Bathtubs

Whether a bathtub is a whirlpool or not, standard size and shape or larger, intended for use by one or several, there are basic universal design criteria that should be applied in the selection process.

- First, entry and exit from the bathtub should be made safer by providing transfer surfaces and hand-holds.

- Second, non-slip surfaces should be chosen or added.

- Third, there should be easy access to the controls, whether the bather is inside or outside of the bathtub.

- Fourth, there should be a minimum amount of protruding objects in the bathtub area to avoid the risk of body parts bumping into anything.

Applying these criteria will improve safety and access for anyone using the bathtub.

THE SHOWER AREA

Space Considerations for the Roll-in Shower

A roll-in shower is a water-proofed area large enough for a person in a wheelchair to roll in and remain in the chair while showering. This type of shower lends itself to current trends toward the shower as a place of relaxation and retreat. It's size allows for one or more users and for the addition of multiple sprayheads, body sprays or rain bars.

To be considered a roll-in shower, the area must be a minimum 60" (152cm) wide by 30" (72cm) deep, with no threshold greater than 1/4" (.64cm) high if square, or (1/2" (1.27cm) if beveled). Because this is a standard bathtub size, it allows for the conversion from bathtub to shower within an existing space. However, this size creates some problems in that 30" (72cm) is too shallow to retain water. A better size for the roll-in shower would be 60" x 48" (152cm x 122cm) or greater. Another option in designing the space is to waterproof the adjacent area and slope the floor slightly to the drain.

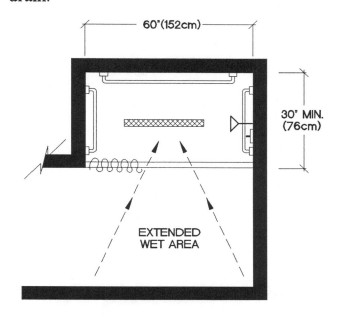

Figure 59 - Minimum size roll-in Shower with extended wet area.

Clear Floor Space - Roll-In Shower

The clear floor space required adjacent to a roll-in shower is 60" x 36" (152cm x 91cm). An additional benefit to this dimension is that the combined space creates the clearance needed for a chair to turn 360°.

A preferred clear floor space would include 12" - 18" (30cm - 46cm) beyond the control wall to allow for better access to the controls.

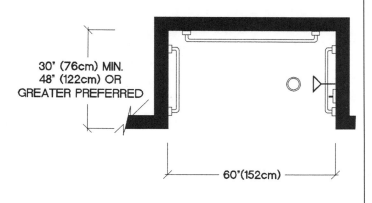

Figure 58 - Roll-in Shower.

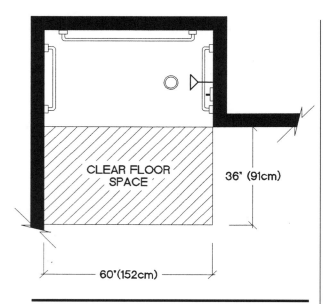

Figure 60 - Clear floor space at roll-in shower.

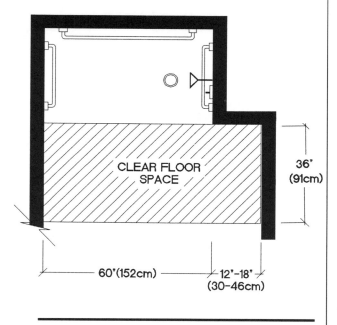

Figure 61 - Preferred Clear Floor Space at Roll-in Shower

ROLL-IN SHOWER CONTROLS, GRAB BARS AND ACCESSORIES

Controls

Controls may be placed on any of the walls, in the area above the grab bars, no higher than 48" (122cm). Placement on either or both of the side walls improves access to controls for a person who is in the shower. This placement is safer and more convenient for adjusting water temperature and flow prior to entering the shower. A control on the back wall will be more accessible to a person seated in the area while showering.

Showerhead/Hand-Held Spray

If a fixed showerhead is used, 78" (198cm) is a good height for most people. A hand-held spray should be used, mounted no higher than 48" (122cm) in its lowest position. The use of an adjustable height hand spray may eliminate the need for a fixed shower head if the mounting bar allows for adjustment from 78" high to not more than 48" (122cm) above the floor.

Grab Bars

Horizontal grab bars should be placed on all three walls of a roll-in shower, 33" - 36" (84cm - 91cm) high. Vertical grab bars may be

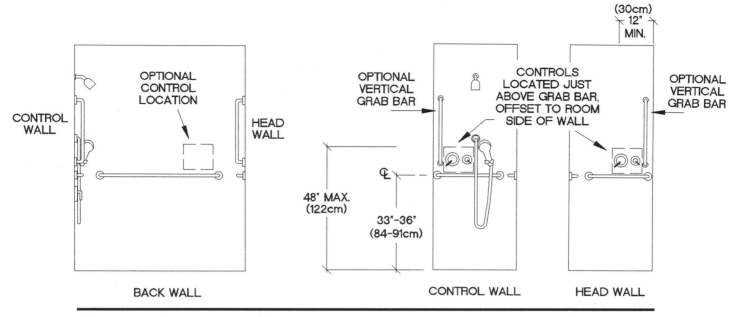

Figure 62 - Control and Other Walls - Roll-in Shower.

placed on the side walls to aid in balance and as a safety measure.

TRANSFER SHOWER

The transfer shower is designated at 36" x 36" (91cm x 91cm). Recent revisions to this standard acknowledge that a shower unit installed in a 36" x 36" (91cm x 91cm) space may result in an interior clear floor space slightly less, closer to 34" x 34" (86cm x 86cm) overall dimensions. Usually dimensions given are minimums, in this case the dimensions are the optimum. This type of shower is designed precisely to provide safe transfer for people with or without mobility impairments and it is one of the most universal of bathing options. It creates a space in which a person has both support and fixture controls within his reach at all times.

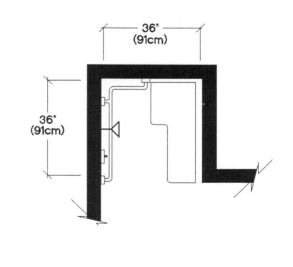

Figure 63 - 36" x 36" (91cm x 91cm) transfer shower.

The minimum clear floor space at a transfer shower is 36" x 48" (91cm x 122cm), measured from the control wall.

The preferred clear floor space would include an additional 12" - 18" (30cm - 46cm) beyond the control wall for better access to controls and to improve maneuvering space.

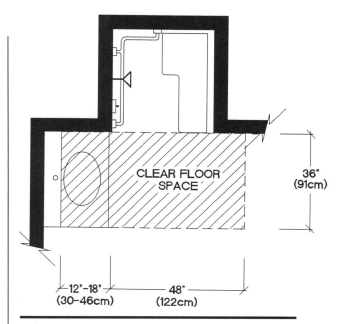

Figure 65 - Preferred clear floor space at transfer shower

TRANSFER SHOWER CONTROLS, GRAB BARS AND ACCESSORIES

To create a true transfer shower, not only its size, but also the exact locations of the controls, the grab bar, and the seat are important.

Controls

The controls are to be located above the grab bar, not higher than 48" (122cm), offset to the room side on the control wall (opposite the seat).

Showerhead/Hand-Held Spray

The showerhead and the hand-held spray are to be centered on the control wall.

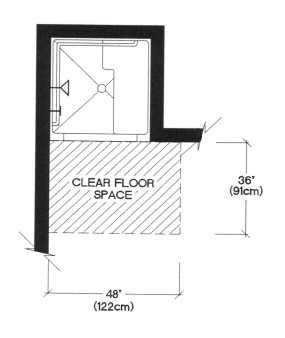

Figure 64 - Minimum clear floor space at transfer shower.

Handedness or strength on one side or another will affect the location of the control wall and the seat.

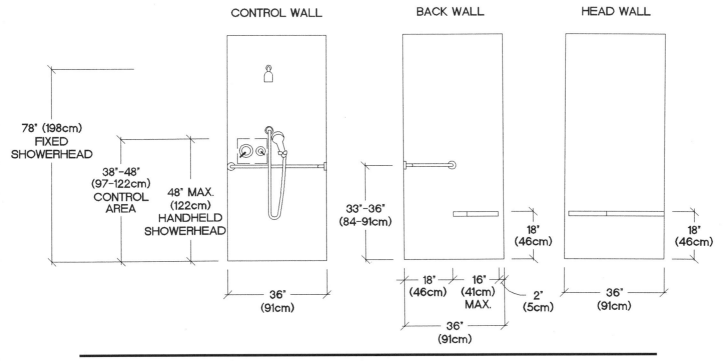

CONTROL WALL   BACK WALL   HEAD WALL

78" (198cm)
FIXED
SHOWERHEAD

38"-48"
(97-122cm)
CONTROL
AREA

48" MAX.
(122cm)
HANDHELD
SHOWERHEAD

33"-36"
(84-91cm)

18"
(46cm)

18"
(46cm)

36"
(91cm)

18"
(46cm)

16"
(41cm)
MAX.

2"
(5cm)

36"
(91cm)

36"
(91cm)

Figure 66 - Transfer shower - controls and other walls.

Grab Bars and Seats

The grab bar is to be L-shaped, the length of the control wall plus 18" (46cm) on the back wall. The seat may be L-shaped or straight. The dimensions of the seat, its location, and its shape are intended to provide maximum safety and support on two walls.

A fold-up seat is more universal in that it allows for use in a standing or seated position.

For more information and examples of how a person might transfer into this shower, see *Appendix 5, Transfer Techniques.*

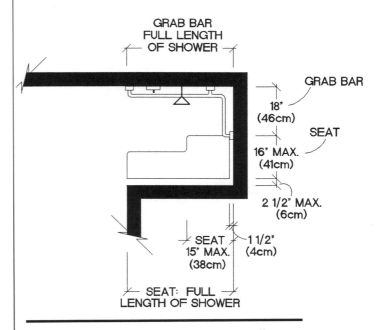

GRAB BAR
FULL LENGTH
OF SHOWER

GRAB BAR

18"
(46cm)

SEAT

16" MAX.
(41cm)

2 1/2" MAX.
(6cm)

SEAT
15" MAX.
(38cm)

1 1/2"
(4cm)

SEAT: FULL
LENGTH OF SHOWER

Figure 67 - Grab bar and seat configuration for transfer shower.

THE SHOWER FIXTURE

Transfer Showers

The transfer shower, created in a 36" x 36" (91cm x 91cm) space with an L-shaped grab bar, an L-shaped seat, and little or no threshold is the most versatile bathing fixture available. This shower allows a standing person support while showering and provides for transfer from a wheelchair with the greatest ease and privacy.

Keep in mind that this bathing system provides total independence for most people using mobility aids who can stand to transfer. While this shower can be a molded unit or one made with separate component parts, its dimensions and specifications are precise to create a space where anyone using the shower will have support and control within their reach at all times. Choosing a folding seat allows a person to stand or sit while showering.

Although not essential for a transfer shower, little or no threshold, 1/2" (1.27cm) maximum is preferred as it makes transfer and entry easier and safer. Because the space is small, and water may escape the shower, care must be given to retain the water. The floor of the shower and adjacent floor space should be waterproofed and sloped towards the shower drain (suggested pitch is 1/4" per 12") (.64cm x 30cm). In some cases, a grate-type drain will ease in the containment of water, but it should not interfere with the floor surface.

Often times a shower curtain is preferred over a door because the curtain in no way interferes with maneuvering. A shower curtain of extra length will assist in retaining water. The exact dimensions of the space must be followed for a transfer shower to work properly. Transfer showers are available in molded units with fold-up or integral seats, and with grab bars and controls.

USE OF THE 36" X 36"(91 x 91cm) TRANSFER SHOWER BY WHEELCHAIR USERS

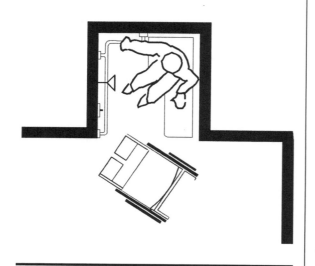

Figure 68 - Transfer shower.

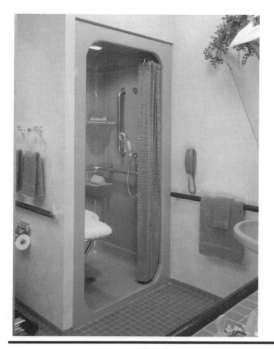

Figure 69 - Transfer shower module.

Figure 70 - Transfer shower module.

Roll-In Showers

The roll-in shower is simply a water-proofed area large enough for a person in a wheelchair to remain in the chair to shower. While this seems at first to be the easiest showering system, in fact usually the person in a wheelchair must transfer into a shower chair, so transfer is still a part of the process.

In addition, shower chairs often do not have front controls and must be pushed from behind, which translates to the need for an assistant to move a person into and out of the shower. For those who can transfer, the 36" x 36" (91cm x 91cm) transfer shower may offer greater independence.

That said, the roll-in shower does have tremendous flexibility and universal design appeal. The aesthetic appeal of a shower area or wet room is wonderful. The size of the space lends itself to a variety of uses - bathing pets, sitting or standing to shower, in or out of a wheelchair, and multiple users at one time. It's size also reduces concerns for water escaping the shower area, and provides useful clear floor space for ease in maneuvering.

The minimum size for a roll-in shower is 30" x 60" (72cm x 152cm), good for replacing a traditional bathtub, but small for water retention. As mentioned previously, planning adjacent wet areas will help to take care of the water concern. A size of 36" - 48" x 60" (91cm - 122cm x 152cm) is better, with a 60" x 60" (122cm x 122cm) roll-in shower having the added advantage of providing a full turning circle.

There are molded units with or without fold-up seats and grab bars in the 30" x 60" (72cm x 152cm) size. These units must be designed with low (maximum) or no thresholds for a true roll-in surface. In some cases, the base of the unit will have a curb and in such cases, the floor of the module must not be recessed greater than 1/4" (.64cm), (1/2" (1.27cm) beveled from the front edge.

Figure 72 - Roll-in shower module.

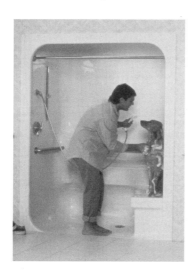

Figure 71 - Roll-in shower module.

Figure 73 - Roll-in shower module.

UNIVERSAL BATHROOM PLANNING

Wet Areas

The concept of a wet area eliminates many of the concerns in other bathing systems. A wet area is created by making the space adjoining the shower waterproof as well, sloping the entire floor towards the shower.

Creating a wet room means that fewer walls and divisions of space are needed. So a person can more easily maneuver using a wheelchair, walker or crutches and has a choice of whether to use a seat to shower. It is important to waterproof the entire area and to locate GFI electrical outlets out of the spray and splash of the water.

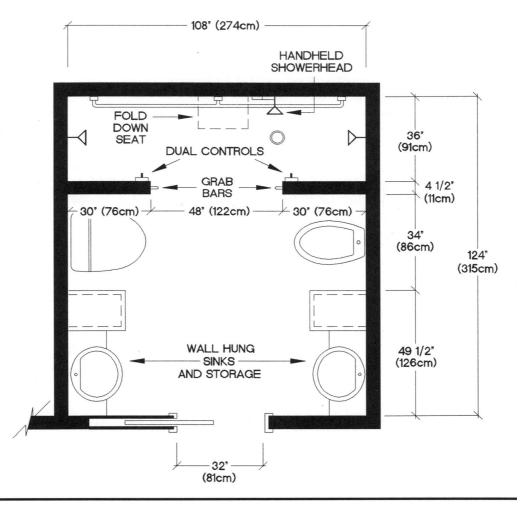

Figure 74 - Wet room.

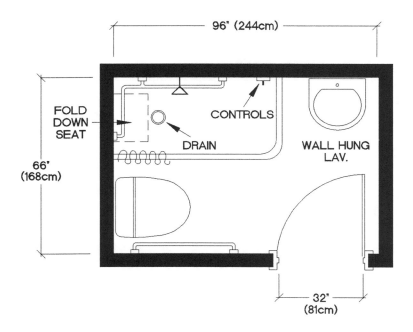

96" (244cm)

FOLD
DOWN
SEAT

CONTROLS

DRAIN

WALL HUNG
LAV.

66"
(168cm)

32"
(81cm)

ENTIRE FLOOR IS WATERPROOF
AND SLOPES TO SHOWER DRAIN

Figure 75 - Wet room.

Materials and Aesthetics

Transfer showers are available in molded units with fold up or integral seats, and with grab bars and controls. They can also be fabricated from tile, solid surface, stone, or concrete, following the specifications. As with any bathing system, when planning for a shower area this size, blocking in the walls will provide for easy addition of the seat and grab bars.

One way to create a custom universal shower is to begin with a shower base designed to have a flush threshold. These are available with slight ramps which eliminate the need for a floor recess, and removable thresholds. Another option is a custom shaped shower base made of solid surface material with an integral curve to help retain water but allow easy access.

The base can also be formed from tile, small tiles being the better choice as they help with slip-resistance and they most easily incorporate the floor sloping to the drain. Once the base is created, wall treatments can be personal preference.

When planning the use of materials, consider contrast at entry, controls and grab bars, and seats for visual cuing. Keep in mind that the floor in and beyond the shower must be waterproof and that reinforcing should be in all the walls for installation of seats and grab bars.

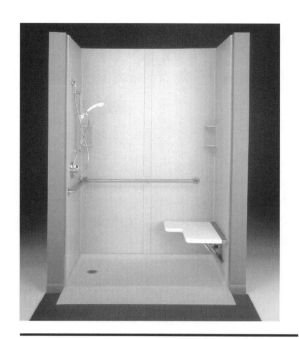

Figure 76 - Shower base with flush threshold.

Universal Design Criteria for Showers

Whatever the style or material used in a shower, the following universal design criteria will apply.

- The floor should be non-slip and the threshold should be low or flush.

- Hand-holds for support and flexible seating should be planned either for present or future installation.

- The clear floor space approaching and in the shower should allow for flexibility.

- Safety and ease of use benefit everyone.

Figure 77 - Solid surface custom base without threshold.

chapter 6

THE TOILET AND THE BIDET

Like the bathtub or shower, the toilet and the bidet require transfer. The same careful consideration must be given to space, materials, fixtures and supports, to ensure safe transfer and ease of use.

SPACE CONSIDERATION FOR THE TOILET/BIDET AREA

In planning the space for the toilet and bidet area, mobility, balance, handedness, and transfer will again be important. Planning appropriate storage space in this area is also important and should not be overlooked.

The addition of a bidet or an integral personal hygiene system in the toilet is particularly beneficial to a client who is unable to clean in traditional ways.

Codes and Standards

While the bidet is not mentioned in codes or standards, space considerations similar to those of toilets may be applied.

Most codes and standards detail toilet areas as part of non-residential spaces, but not as clearly for private residences. Both **ANSI** and the **Fair Housing Guidelines** provide some specification for toilets in residential baths.

The following is based on these two sources of information and draws from codes and standards. The configuration of the toilet area includes one side wall to return a minimum 54" (137cm), and a back wall width a minimum of 32" (81cm).

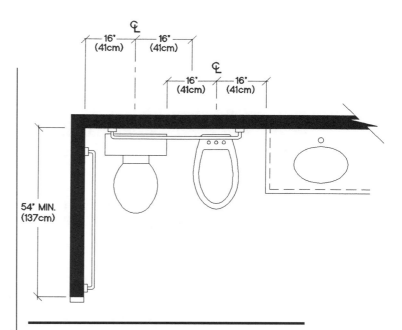

Figure 79 - Toilet and bidet area.

Clear Floor Space

The clear floor space suggested at a toilet is 48" (122cm) in front of the fixture by 48" (122cm) off the side wall.

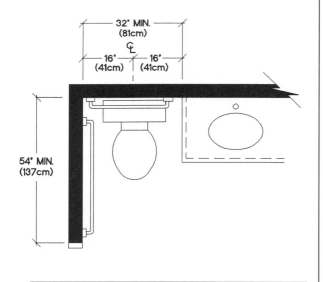

Figure 78 - Toilet area.

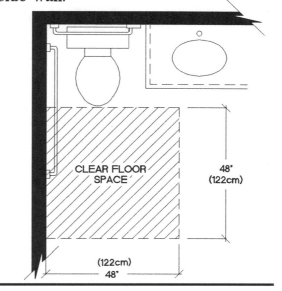

Figure 80 - Clear floor space at toilet.

This would allow a person to transfer from a perpendicular approach or a forward approach (*see Appendix 5 - Transfers*), making it fairly flexible and universal.

Increasing the clear floor space off the side wall to 60" (152cm) with no lavatory directly adjacent to the toilet, increases the transfer options to allow for a parallel transfer. In this case recessing the back wall adjacent to the toilet further improves maneuvering space. Rolling storage of personal hygiene equipment can be a flexible way to use this space.

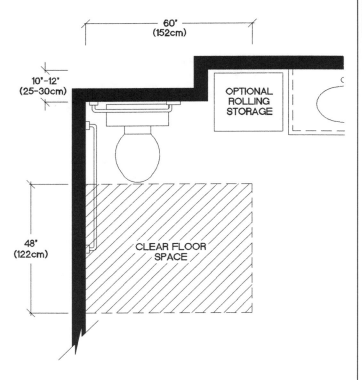

Figure 81 - Optional plan for clear floor space at toilet.

When a toilet and a bidet are located adjacent to each other, the clear floor spaces will overlap, with the clear floor space extending at least 16" (41cm) to either side of the center line of both fixtures.

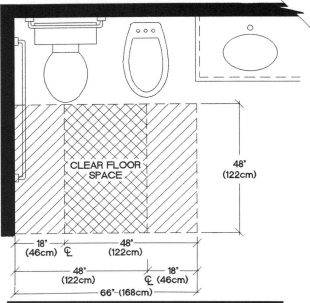

Figure 82 - Overlapping clear floor space at toilet and bidet.

Location of Grab Bars, Controls, and Accessories

If there are space constraints, some alternatives can be found by examining the following minimums for toilets.

The grab bars are to be located 33" - 36" (84cm - 91cm) off the floor, on both walls. One is to be on the side wall not more than 12" (30cm) off the back wall and a minimum 42" (107cm) long. The second one is to be a maximum 6" (15cm)

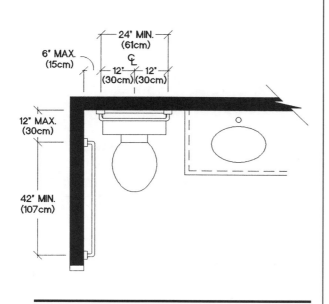

Figure 83 - Grab bar locations at toilet.

off the side wall and a minimum 24" (61cm) long. This grab bar on the back wall must be a minimum 12" (30cm) on either side of the toilet center line.

Often the side wall does not in fact extend far enough to allow for a 42" (107cm) grab bar. While this would not meet code requirements, there are options that would improve the safety and function of the area.

First a grab bar that folds down off the back wall on the opposite side of the toilet may be used. This would be particularly useful if a bidet is adjacent.

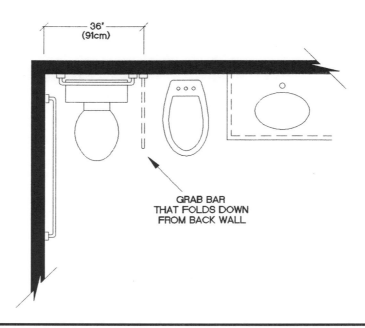

GRAB BAR
THAT FOLDS DOWN
FROM BACK WALL

Figure 84 - Optional grab bar location.

Another option might be to install a seat with integral bars on the toilet (*see Chapter 7, Accessories, for examples of options*).

When possible, extending the grab bar length on the back wall will improve safety and transfer options. In any case, providing support throughout the area at 33" - 36" (84cm - 91cm) off the floor will allow for the addition of desired grab bars.

The toilet tissue holder and the towel storage for the bidet should be placed within the universal reach range of 15" - 48" (38cm - 122cm). The preferred location for the toilet tissue holder is slightly in front of the seat, 8" (20cm) is ideal, and 26" (66cm) off the floor.

When locating a towel holder, care must be given not to obstruct the use of the grab bar. Placement a minimum of 1 1/2" (4cm) below the grab bar will avoid any interference.

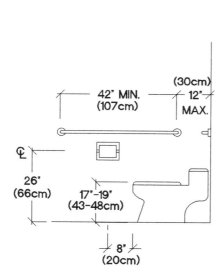
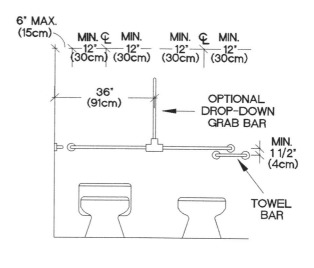

Figure 85 - Accessories/grab bars at toilet/bidet area.

THE FIXTURE

Style and installation of the toilets and bidet have much more impact on universal use than material which is typically vitreous china. This section will look first at the toilet and then the bidet in terms of universal design and its impact on style and installation.

There are three main styles of toilets:

- floor-mounted

- wall-hung

- wall-hung with concealed tank

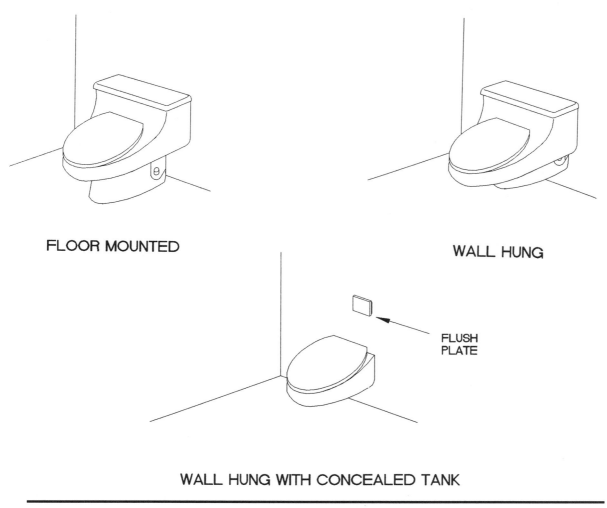

FLOOR MOUNTED

WALL HUNG

FLUSH PLATE

WALL HUNG WITH CONCEALED TANK

Figure 86 - Styles of toilets.

Floor-Mounted Toilets

Floor-mounted toilets are by far the most common. They adhere to universal design principles if the toilet seat is at the right height and the clear floor space around them is sufficient.

Figure 87 - Floor-mounted toilet.

Wall-Mounted Toilets

Wall-mounted toilets, while less common, have more advantages in terms of universal design. They can be mounted to create the appropriate seat height, and they provide greater clear floor space and easier maintenance.

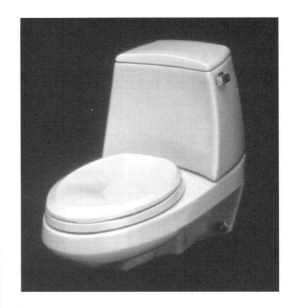

Figure 88 - Wall-mounted toilet.

Wall-Mounted Toilet with Concealed Tank

The wall-mount toilet with concealed tank is the most universal design choice. In this style, the tank is designed to be concealed in a 4 3/4" (12cm) space in the wall. The average toilet extends into the room 27" - 30" (69cm - 72cm) off the back wall. This type of unit extends only 22 1/2" (57cm), depending on the model, saving around 6" (15cm) of clear space. In addition, it may be installed at the appropriate height and it provides total clear floor space below it as it is off-the-floor, easing cleaning and maneuvering. Finally, this design creates a quieter flushing action which is particularly desirable as hearing abilities decrease.

There are not many models of this style to choose from and it is somewhat pricey, but the benefits may well outweigh the price.

Figure 89 - Wall-mounted toilet with conceled tank.

Toilet Seat Height

After clear floor space, the seat height on a toilet is the main universal design concern. No single height is right for all users.

- Low seats are not good for anyone, with the exception of small children, and there are portable seats to address their changing needs.

  Low seats are difficult for people with mobility impairments who have trouble standing from a low position. They are also difficult for people using wheelchairs, as they may transfer on easily, but have trouble transferring from the lower seat to their higher wheelchair seat.

  Finally, anyone with back strain (pregnant women for example), reduced strength or joint conditions (like arthritis) will have more difficulty standing from a low position.

- High seats are better for most people who can stand, with or without mobility aids. If they are too high, they will be difficult or impossible for people using wheelchairs to transfer to without assistance.

  In addition, too high a seat will be difficult and uncomfortable for shorter people because their feet won't touch the floor.

The range of heights specified for toilet seats in residential spaces is 15" - 19" (38cm - 48cm). The compromise recommended by most experts is 18" (46cm), the same as many wheelchairs.

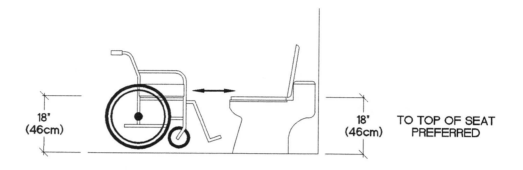

Figure 90 - Optimum toilet seat height for most users.

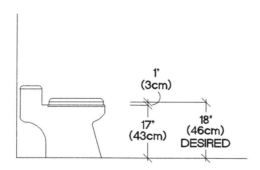

Figure 91 - Measure toilet height to top of seat.

Few toilets are designed with a seat height of 18" (46cm). The vast majority are the traditional 15" (38cm) height. There are a few *"designed for people with special needs"* that unfortunately end up at 19" - 20" (48cm - 51cm) high, which is too high.

In examining the product offerings from two major manufacturers, there were many toilets with a 15" (38cm) seat height, three toilets at 19" - 20" (48cm - 51cm) seat height, two wall hung fixtures that would allow for an 18 seat height, and two floor models with 18" (46cm) seat heights. Of 50 toilet models, four could provide the desired seat height without further alteration.

In defense of manufacturers, people want what they are accustomed to, and that is 15" (38cm) high toilet seats. The truth is that able-bodied adults can use these toilets because they have adapted to them. But a higher seat would be more appropriate, even for those able-bodied people. Perhaps this is an area for the bathroom designer to break with tradition and begin to incorporate the higher toilet seat as a matter of course.

Because there are so few products designed for the 18" (46cm) seat height, it is important to look at alternative ways to accomplish this. The first is to mount the standard height toilet on a raised base to bring the seat to the desired height.

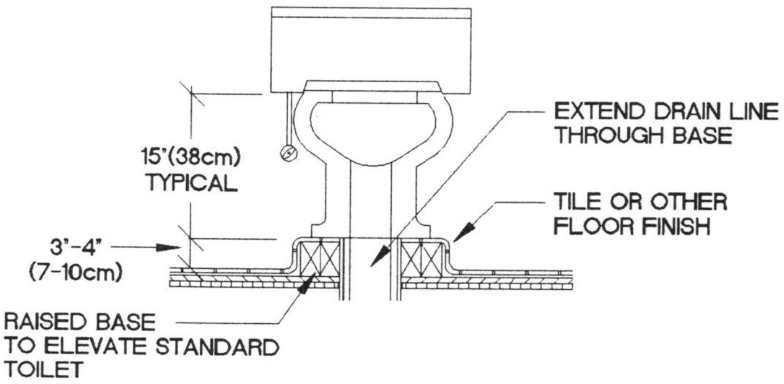

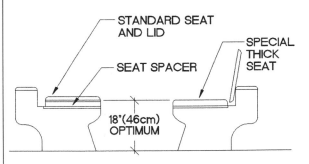

Figure 92 - Elevated base for toilets.

Figure 93 - Elevated seats on traditional height toilets.

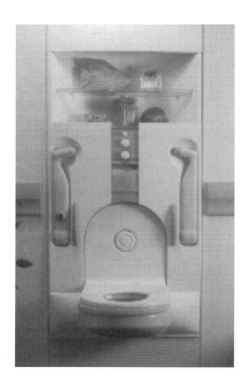

Figure 94 - Modular toilet system adjusts in height.

Second, special thick toilet seats or spacers that fit between the toilet seat and the rim of the toilet bowl will adjust the height up from the standard 15" (38cm). While these usually have a more institutional look, they have the advantage of flexibility in that they can be easily changed as needs change. Care must be given to selection and installation to be sure these seats are stable.

A toilet module has been designed that adjusts easily and instantly to accommodate the height of a standing or seated user. Hand rails fold down for use by those who desire them.

The entire system folds up against the wall when not in use for easy cleaning and flexible maneuvering. This system is wonderfully flexible and truly universal. It is not yet on the market and will have to pass some plumbing and cost hurdles before we can easily use it.

Another product, readily available and easily installed is the electric powered toilet seat elevator. This mechanism actually tilts and raises or lowers the seat to assist a person in moving from a standing position to a seated position, and again to a standing position.

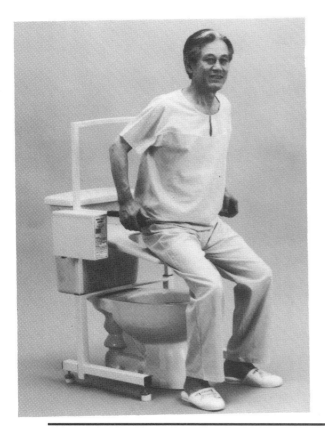

Figure 95 - Powered toilet seat elevator.

A more low-tech assistive device for standing and sitting are seat mounted grab bars which work well for many people who can stand but are a barrier for people in chairs who slide to transfer.

The bidet is a wonderful option for self-care, particularly for people whose physical disabilities make independent personal hygiene difficult. The standard bidet will be a challenge for those who have trouble sitting or standing, but problems will be reduced by adding support (grab bars) and storage within reach of the seated user. Building up the base or using wall-hung models will make height adjustment possible, but the lower position is more appro-

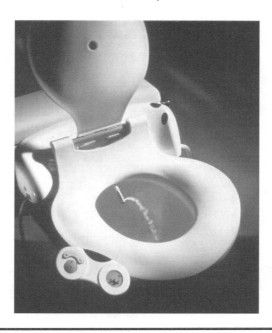

Figure 96 - Personal hygiene system at toilet.

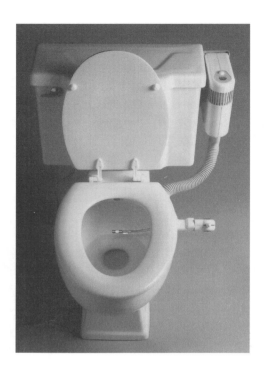

Figure 97 - Personal hygiene system at toilet.

Figure 98 - Bidet.

Figure 99 - Wall hung bidet.

priate for personal cleaning. The real boon to personal hygiene for people with mobility impairments is the toilet mounted bidet. These systems attach behind and under the toilet seat or replace the toilet seat and supply a warm water cleaning spray and a warm air drying spray. Traditionally, the bathroom has been a place where people adapted to existing fixtures and systems. Lately, though, the bath fixture industry has begun to put the needs of people first. As universal bathroom designers, we must work carefully to stimulate and promote these changes, breaking our own patterns and habits along with those of our clients and the manufacturers.

chapter 7

FITTINGS, CONTROLS AND ACCESSORIES

Universal design principals impact both the selection process and the design for installation of faucets and controls, support systems, and accessories in the bathroom.

As manufacturers respond to consumer needs, new features are appearing to make accessories and the space safer and more accessible. In addition, the designer must think in terms of universal principles when creating the centers of the bathroom, including installations that sometimes break with tradition.

FAUCETS AND CONTROLS

The single lever faucet is the most universal in design. It allows temperature and flow adjustment with one control, easier for one-handed use or for use when both hands are occupied.

A pull-out hand shower adds flexibility. Several models are available with a loop-type lever handle that make use easier for a person with grip or dexterity limitations.

Figure 100 - Single lever faucet.

Figure 102 - Single lever faucet.

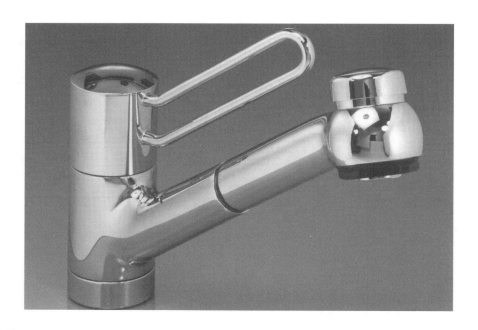

Figure 101 - Single lever faucet.

UNIVERSAL BATHROOM PLANNING

Lever or wrist blade handles also allow for ease of use. Round or square handles that require grasping and twisting are the most difficult to use.

Figure 104 - Touchless electronic controls.

Touchpad controls are also available that allow for control of water temperature and flow from a remote location. These are relatively new on the market and are much higher in cost.

While there are many faucet styles that lend themselves to universal use, the drain control is often a problem, especially when it is a tiny round knob or button on the back of the faucet. A large or remote lever is more accessible. Another alternative is to install a separate drain plug that can be manually put in place.

The controls for the shower and/or bathtub, including the shower-

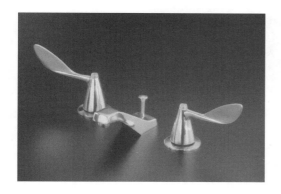

Figure 103 - Faucet with lever or wrist blade handles.

Touchless electronic faucets are available that automatically turn on when they sense motion. For the most part, temperature and flow rate are preset. Models are available now that include handles for manual override control and prototypes exist for a retrofit system that allows temperature adjustment through sensors in the front of the sink. These options require no hand dexterity and may be worth their expense in certain situations.

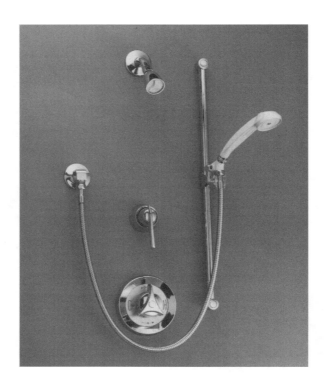

Figure 105 - Controls and hand held sprays.

head, the hand-held spray and the diverter (when required) should follow the same guidelines as faucets. First, controls, whether for flow and temperature, for diverting, or to release a sliding spray head, should be assymetrical and preferably a lever design. Push plates and electronic touch or voice-activated controls will also provide accessibility.

Mentioned previously, a handheld spray unit on a sliding bar must have its lowest position no higher than 48" (122cm) off the floor. If it is to double as a showerhead, its highest position should be close to 78" (198cm). The hose on a hand-held spray should be a minimum 72" (183cm) long. Button or

push-pull diverters should be avoided. Products are available with the hose of the hand spray attached at the fixed showerhead. This concept is acceptable as long as the diverter is not at the connection point on the arm of the shower head, but in a location within the universal reach range of 15" - 48" (38cm - 122cm). Likewise, the push-pull diverter often located on the top of the bathtubfill spout is very difficult for many people to grasp.

Sometimes a desirable option is to have more than one control, one for use from outside the bathtub or shower and one that controls the hand-held spray for use while in the bathtub/shower.

Antiscald temperature control and pressure-balance systems should be used. These features mix and regulate the water so that it cannot exceed a pre-set temperature. In addition, the pressure-balance system adjusts the flow of hot and cold water to ensure no dramatic temperature changes occur because of sudden changes in pressure in the system.

Visual cuing on controls is desirable, including high contrast, color-coding or raised characters to identify temperature adjustments.

SUPPORT SYSTEMS

Grab Bars and Other Supports

Grab bars or railings placed in the bathroom must be capable of supporting 300 pounds (136kg) and must be 1 1/2" (4cm) from the wall. This clearance must be exact as it allows ample space for the user's hand and not enough for the user's arm to slip through.

Grab bars should be 1 1/4" - 1 1/2" (3cm - 4cm) in diameter (or less than 2" (5cm) at the largest point if their shape is other than round) and should have a slip-resistant surface.

The recommended height for grab bars is usually 33" - 36" (84cm - 91cm) off the floor. A simple solution to the question of appropriate placement for a specific client is to plan and install plywood reinforcement throughout the bathroom. This allows the client to actually test the space and determine exact locations. It also allows for a minimum amount of rails or grab bars at the time of the project and easy installation of additional grab bars as needed or desired.

Horizontal grab bars are the basic and most useful choice. In addition, vertical grab bars can sometimes be helpful to a standing person for entry/exit from the bathtub/shower. Some experts discourage the use of vertical or diagonal grab bars because of a concern that a hand is more likely to slip along bars in this position. **NKBA** guidelines require at least one bar in the bathtub/shower area and recommend additional grab bars at each workstation in the bathroom as well as reinforcement for future additions.

Grab bars come in all shapes, sizes, materials and colors. One interesting design option is to use a continuous bar around the entire room as a functional and decorative feature. Hanging towels (or anything else) should not interfere with use of grab bars. There is a risk that anything within reach may be grabbed by someone in need of support. Proper wall support and installation of grab bars as towel bars will eliminate the risk of a person mistaking a towel bar for a grab bar.

Along with the familiar grab bar, other support systems exist, also in many colors and materials. Grab bars that fold down off a back wall are useful where support is needed and there is no side wall.

Figure 107 - Ladder support.

Figure 106 - Fold-down grab bar.

Ladder or triangle supports can be ceiling installed, with proper reinforcement, for assistance where there are no adjacent walls or where greater flexibility is required.

Grab bars are available from adaptive equipment manufacturers that attach to the bathtub or toilet, requiring no alterations in construction. Although these are not usually

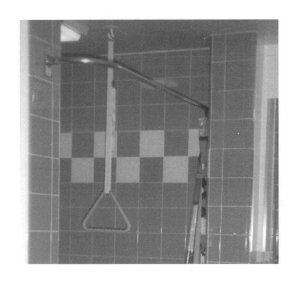

Figure 108 - Triangle support.

specified by the bathroom designer, it is good to be familiar with them. These items are relatively inexpensive, easy to install or remove, and cumbersome to store. Unfortunately, they have not, as yet, been designed with a residential appearance. They are the answer in certain situations.

When selecting a grab bar that attaches to a fixture, it is important to examine the method of attachment for its strength and stability.

Bathtub and Shower Seats

Portable or removable bathtub and shower seats provide the options of sitting when desired or needed and standing or soaking upon their removal. The concept of sitting is relaxing and provides assistance to people with limited strength, endurance, or balance. The flexibility of a removable seat is often desirable, but requires storage space when not in use.

SEAT TYPES

Several types of seats are available. The following examples from the **Center for Inclusive Design and Environmental Access at SUNY Buffalo**, will provide an awareness of them allowing the designer to guide each client to the best choice.

Bathstool

With no backrest, the bathstool is suitable for a person of slight to medium build. Compact in size and economical, it works well in narrow tubs and can be stored easily. It is available with a hard or padded seat, can be contoured, and may have hand grips on the sides of the seat. Careful attention must be given to its intended use as it is less stable than other options.

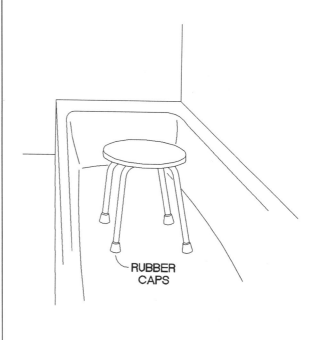

Figure 109 - Bathstool.

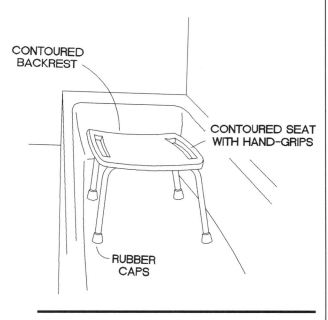

CONTOURED BACKREST

CONTOURED SEAT WITH HAND-GRIPS

RUBBER CAPS

Figure 110 - Bathstool hand grip.

Bathchair

The bathchair provides improved stability, greater support and more comfort. It is available with firm or padded contoured seat, hand grips, and is adjustable in height. The backrest improves bathing for a person with back conditions and the padding is easier on those with sensitive skin. The bathchair may not fit in narrow bathtubs, requires more storage space, and hinders easy access to a person's back and lower body.

The hand grip bathchair is ideal for leisurely bathers who need assistance in maintaining an upright position. The hand grips are useful to provide support while reaching various parts of the body. The contoured seat and backrest provide comfort to the bather.

With variable seat and backrest heights, the height adjustable chair accomodates persons of different stature and provides custom seating conditions. While there are various mechanisims for adjusting seat and backrest heights, the most common is the twist mechanism. Located on each of the legs, these mechanisms are easily locked and unlocked by hand. Constant adjustment, however, tends to loosen them, which can cause the chair to collapse unexpectedly.

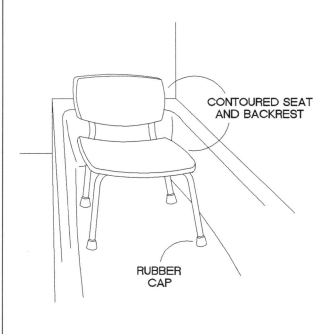

CONTOURED SEAT AND BACKREST

RUBBER CAP

Figure 111 - Bathchair.

Horseshoe Bathstool

The horseshoe bathstool or seat has a unique shape that is helpful to a person who has difficulty accessing and cleaning themselves while sitting on the bathtub floor. One style is designed at a 6" (15cm) height which allows a person to soak in the bathtub. This style is not good for a person who has difficulty sitting down and getting up. Other styles are available with adjustable height, contouring, padding, and backrests to provide for a variety of support.

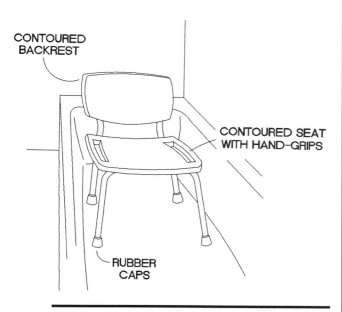

CONTOURED
BACKREST

CONTOURED SEAT
WITH HAND-GRIPS

RUBBER
CAPS

Figure 112 - Hand grip chair.

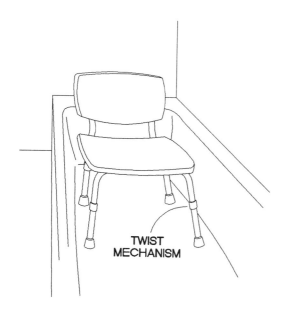

TWIST
MECHANISM

Figure 113 - Height adjustable bathchair.

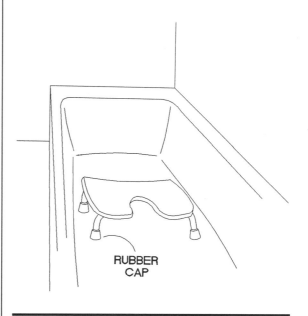

RUBBER
CAP

Figure 114 - Horseshoe bathseat.

Bathtub Board

The bathtub board is suitable for people with strong backs who wish to sit to bathe. It is made from two pieces of vinyl-coated steel that slide into one another to fit a variety of bathtub sizes, and is padded on the underside to prevent scratching. Easily moved and stored, this option must be used with care as it can be unsteady.

Figure 115 - Horseshoe bathstool.

VINYL-COVERED STEEL BOARD

Figure 117 - Bathtub board.

Transfer Bench

Using the handrest for support, the bather transfers into the bathtub by gradually sliding across the seat. The slatted seat allows water to drip into the bathtub and the slot at the bathtubs edge enables the person to draw the curtain for privacy. While the bench is portable, its size makes it difficult to store.

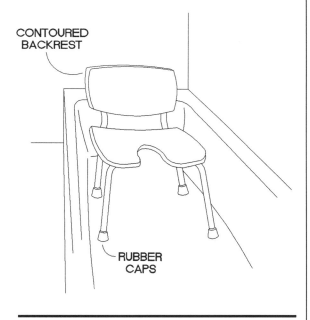

CONTOURED BACKREST

RUBBER CAPS

Figure 116 - Horseshoe bathchair.

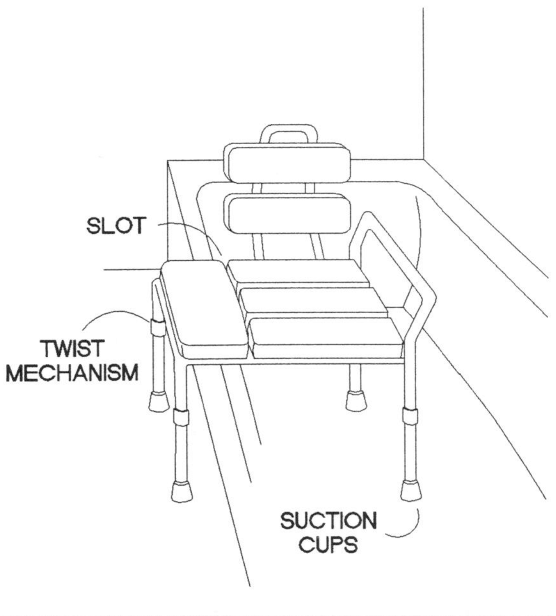

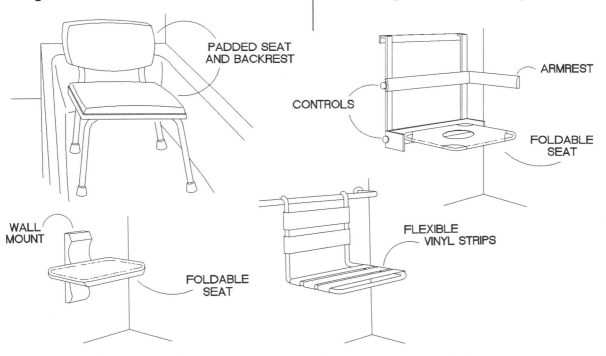

SLOT

TWIST
MECHANISM

SUCTION
CUPS

Figure 118 - Padded transfer bench.

Showerseats

Showerseats are available that are removable or that fold up when not in use, with or without armrests, in a variety of styles and materials. Models are available that are adjustable in height, padded, and with easy access to body parts for cleaning. The shower seat is desirable for those who wish to sit for part or all of a shower.

For further assistance in safe transfer into and out of the bathing fixture, chair designs and other equipment exist that allow a person other means of access into a shower or bathing fixture. These options

PADDED SEAT
AND BACKREST

CONTROLS

ARMREST

FOLDABLE
SEAT

WALL
MOUNT

FOLDABLE
SEAT

FLEXIBLE
VINYL STRIPS

Figure 119 - Showerseats - adjustable, portable, foldable.

should be explored through a medical health care professional.

Shower Wheelchair

The shower wheelchair transports non-ambulatory persons into the shower. It is lightweight and is constructed completely from rust-resistant hardware. The seats horseshoe shape enables easy cleaning of ones underside. The swing-back arms simplify transfers in and out of the wheelchair, and swing away footrests adjust to various positions. The chair is usable only in shower stalls accessible to wheelchairs.

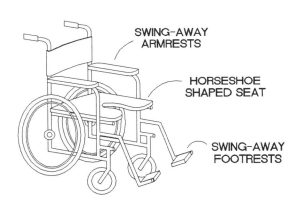

Figure 120 - Shower wheelchair.

BATHTUB LIFTS

Although not typically thought of as standard usage equipment of the bathroom designer, lifts may be specified through a doctor or occupational therapist. A basic understanding of the types and their function will help a bathroom designer in planning the overall space and in discussing options with the client and therapist.

Inside Bathtub Lifts

Bathtub lifts typically function with a special hose and hardware that connect the lift to the bathtub faucet. These lifts are portable, but their size and weight make them difficult to store. Usually these lifts will transfer people up to 200 pounds (91kg), but water pressure must be adequate and consistent.

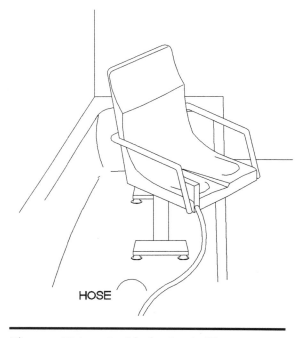

Figure 121 - Inside bathtub lifts.

Outside Bathtub Lifts

Outside bathtub lifts may be permanently installed, with hose and hardware that connect to the water supply. Typically they will allow a person to move lower into the bathtub, desirable for soaking. Consistent and adequate water pressure is also imperative.

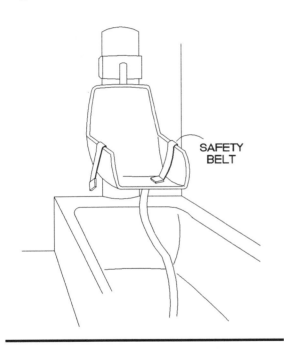

Figure 122 - Outside bathtub lifts.

Hydro-Cushion

The hydro-cushion attaches via a hose to the bathtub filler. The bag or cushion is filled with water to elevate. A person sits on the cushion and empties it to be lowered into the bathtub.

To exit, the cushion is refilled, again raising the seat. This product usually will support 300 pounds (136kg) and again relies on constant water pressure.

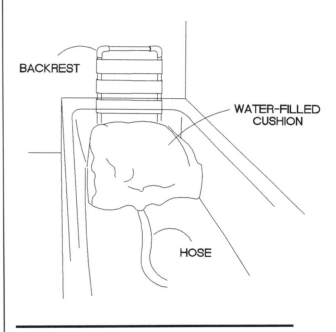

Figure 123 - Hydro-cushion.

Bathchair Lift

The bathtub or floor mounted bathchair lift usually requires assistance from a care provider. The user sits on the seat and is rotated up and over the bathtub rim. The floor-mounted version takes considerable space in the bathroom, and the bathtub-mounted version takes less.

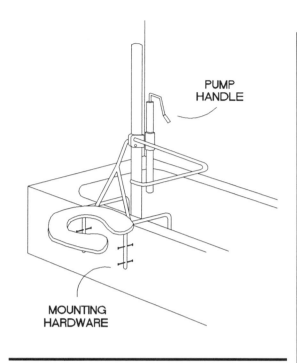

Figure 124 - Bathchair lift - bathtub mounted.

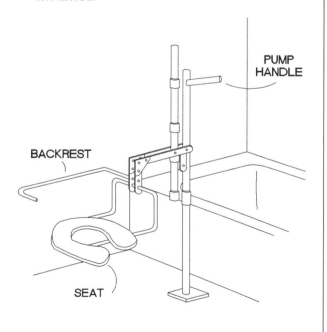

Figure 125 - Bathchair lift - floor mounted.

Hoyer Lift

Floor Mounted, the Hoyer Lift is a portable lift that assists people who need a caregiver to help in transfer. The person is transferred into a suspended cloth sling. A hydraulic or mechanical system lifts and supports the person, rotating to allow for easy bathtub entry and exit. This type of lift is heavy and requires large clear floor spaces and storage areas. However, it carries up to 400 pounds (182kg) and provides for transport as a person can be lifted from a bed, transported to the bathtub and lowered in. It is a great assistive device for trained caregivers.

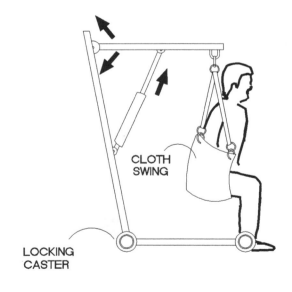

Figure 127 - Hoyer lift.

Electrically Powered Lift

The electrically powered lift can provide independence for people with mobility impairments. The person sits in a harness that is moved along a track with motion controlled by a low-voltage remote control. This lift can be used by a caregiver or in some cases, by the person needing assistance.

All lifts require planning, installation, and operation by skilled professionals.

CHAIN

VINYL AND STEEL HARNESS

Figure 127 - Electrically powered lift.

ACCESSORIES

Many simple adaptive devices or adaptive designs of existing accessories are available to make the bathroom safe and accessible. The selection and installation of accessories should be based on their ease of reach and operation as well as their aesthetic value. Any accessory that frees one's hands is good.

- Shampoo and soap dispenser, installed in the bathtub/shower within the reach of the intended user, is good.

- Wall-mounted hair dryers that require one or no hands are also available.

- Mirrors are available that tilt so that they can be positioned for people of any height.

- Lighted magnifying mirrors are available that can be pulled into position for use by people of varying heights to improve function for people with visual, height or mobility differences.

- Reachers, graspers and aids for dressing oneself are examples of the types of products available through assistive products catalogs.

Items such as toothbrushes, hand-sprays, or comb and brushes with handles that are a comfortable size (use recommended grab bar size of 1 1/4"-1 1/2" (3cm - 4cm) as a guide) will be easier for those who have less gripping ability.

While some of these things will be specified by others, a familiarity with them will help the bathroom designer to overcome traditional barriers in the bathroom.

As accessories are chosen, attention should be given to cuing for people with visual, hearing and cognitive differences.

- A white grab bar on a white wall might be difficult to see. It will be more effective if it is accented with a bright color.

- An assistive device that sounds or flashes a light when the curling iron is left on will improve its safe use.

- A faucet and counter edge in high contrast to the counter and lavatory will reinforce safe and easy usage.

Manufacturers are beginning to respond to these criteria, and bath designers must take the time to find the right accessories for each space.

chapter 8

STORAGE

Reach range parameters, varying height counters, and knee spaces make adequate amounts of storage a key issue in the universal bathroom. Because of the nature of activity in the bathroom, storage must be planned to house needed supplies and equipment in close proximity to each of the centers. Often, the space is small, which makes careful consideration of needs and options imperative.

Goals/Considerations to Keep in Mind

- One main goal is to plan the maximum amount of storage within the 15" - 48" (38cm - 122cm) universal reach range and to make it as safe and easy to access as possible.

- Another goal is to make stored items easy to see. As always, storing items near their point of first use is a good guide, or in several locations if they are used in several places. Because overall storage in the bathroom is limited, these goals should be applied first to items used frequently, such as toothbrushes or hair dryers, with items used less frequently, such as back-up bathroom tissue, stored in the remaining spaces.

- If a client has particular storage needs for assistive equipment or personal hygiene supplies, these must be measured and planned for in convenient locations.

- Drawers on full extension slides and open shelves eliminate the need to maneuver around a drawer to access the stored items.

- An open shelf also allows for easy view of stored items, helpful when memory fails or vision is impaired.

- Lighting the interiors of storage areas will also improve visibility.

- Tall storage takes advantage of the full universal reach range - 15" - 48" (38cm - 122cm).

- Because many items used in the bathroom will fit in a small space, wall cabinets or storage systems 12" (30cm) deep or less will meet many needs.

- In some cases, recesses created between studs will allow for storage that does not use clear floor space or create a protrusion.

- Rolling storage has several advantages in the universal bathroom because of its flexibility. It can be moved out of an area to give more clear floor space and it allows for stored items to be moved into place easily when in use.

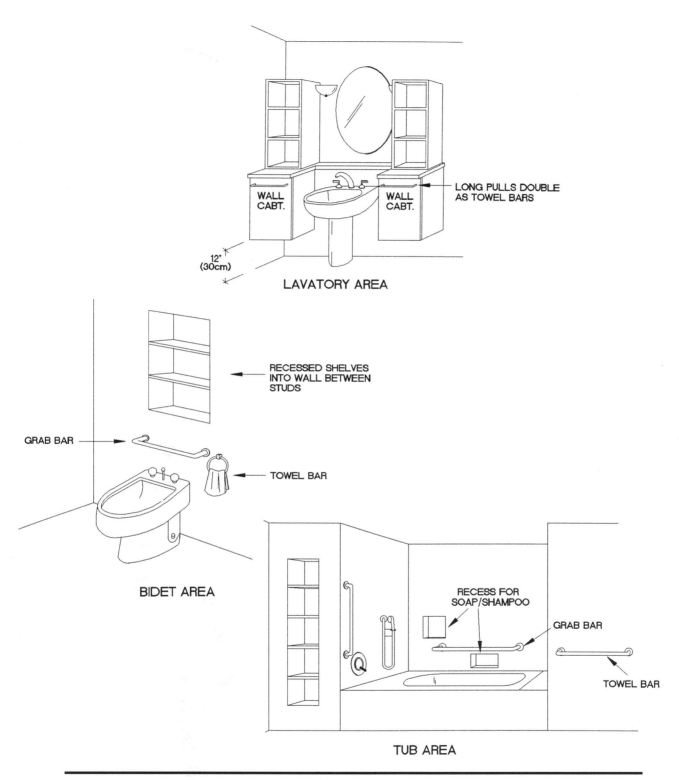

LONG PULLS DOUBLE AS TOWEL BARS

WALL CABT.

WALL CABT.

12" (30cm)

LAVATORY AREA

RECESSED SHELVES INTO WALL BETWEEN STUDS

GRAB BAR

TOWEL BAR

BIDET AREA

RECESS FOR SOAP/SHAMPOO

GRAB BAR

TOWEL BAR

TUB AREA

Figure 128   - Examples of storage.

Figure 129 - Examples of storage.

CABINETRY CONSTRUCTION AND HARDWARE

Several options in cabinetry or storage and hardware selection have impact on universal design.

Frameless Cabinetry

A benefit of frameless construction is total accessibility to the interior of the cabinet, and the same is true with much of today's framed construction.

Raising toekicks to 9" - 12" (23cm - 30cm) high provides clearance for wheelchair footrests and other walking aids. This option is available on most custom lines and some stock lines as well.

Door Options

A variety of options are available for moving doors out of the way.

- Hinges that allows doors to swing completely open to 180° are helpful.

- In addition, a hinge is now available that folds the doors back against themselves and flat against adjacent cabinets, making the doors less obstructive.

- Doors can also be hinged to be retractable, but this option takes up as much as 6" (15cm) on each side, which translates to needing 42" (107cm) for a 30" (72cm) knee space.

- Doors mounted on removable face frames can be used for adapting to knee space by removal of the door and frames.

- Tambour doors or doors that slide or open upward on wall cabinets also eliminate the concern for moving safely around them.

Hardware Considerations

Decorative hardware should be easy to use and should not require strength or dexterity to operate.

- Pulls should be chosen in place of knobs. Pulls that are integral and are easy to grasp are ideal because they do not protrude.

- Touch latches eliminate the need for any grasp or strength.

Material Selection

Finally, material selection should consider durability in terms of finish.

- Particularly at 12" (30cm) above the finished floor and below, cabinetry may be exposed to tremendous wear from repeated impact from mobility aids.

- High-gloss or finishes that create glare should be avoided.

Beyond this, selection of cabinetry is not impacted by universal design. For a more thorough study of cabinetry and bathroom storage, refer to the **NKBA Bathroom Industry Technical Manuals #3 and #4 as well as NKBA's Universal Kitchen Planning, Design That Adapts To People.**

chapter 9

FINISHING THE SPACE

To finish the universal bath, several key factors must be considered: lighting and electrical, including ventilation and heating, and flooring and wall surfaces.

LIGHTING

Lighting is crucial to the universal environment, particularly for those with visual impairments. As we age, our vision changes. The quality of light in a bathroom is determined not only by the light source, but also by the colors, amounts of contrast and reflective quality of surfaces in the room.

Light Adjustability

It is important to provide adjustability and increased available ambient and task lighting without glare or harsh shadows. People with visual impairments and aging eyes typically benefit from increased light, but this is not always the case. Consultation with qualified professionals (medical, lighting designer) is recommended.

LIGHT SOURCES

Natural Light

Natural light sources are best and should be generous in the plan. Avoid glare from natural light sources with shades or blinds or glass surface treatments that deflect glare but allow light to come through.

Incandescent/Fluorescent Light

To supplement natural light, lamp fixtures should be chosen that produce a high-accuracy color rendering. A color rendering accuracy rating of 85 or higher for either incandescent or fluorescent is desirable. Though it is true that the eye yellows with age, changing how we see color, lighting experts suggest that as long as there is good color rendering, either type of lamp may be used.

Halogen Light

Halogen is another option, although the amount and intensity of heat produced by a halogen lamp may be less than ideal in terms of safety. The fixture should be designed to conceal the light source and diffuse light in an effort to reduce glare. **Glare creates hazards** as it can be blinding, and research shows that it contributes to confusion associated with aging.

Lighting Plan

The lighting plan in the universal space should include generous ambient and task lighting and offer flexible controls. One eye condition might need greater general lighting, but another might benefit from reduced ambient lighting and increased task lighting.

Flexibility in controls allows for a variety of users to function in the bathroom. In addition, the plan should take into account reflectant qualities in the room surfaces and eliminate harsh shadows.

For example, side lights added to down lights in a vanity area will eliminate shadows. Another example would be to direct a light into the cabinet space from outside or above and use transparent shelves to cut down on harsh shadows in the storage area.

Surfaces

- In choosing surfaces in the room, avoid glossy and harsh white surfaces that will reflect light and can create glare.

- Consider the size of the space and the color and reflectant quality of surfaces when planning the amount of light needed.

- A room with dark cabinetry will require more light than one with light surfaces.

Along with reflection, consider color and contrast. They have a major impact on how practical a room is for a person with vision impairments.

- Because of the yellowing and thickening of the eye's lenses that occurs with age, it becomes difficult to differentiate colors that do not contrast.

- Navy, black and brown might look similar, or pastel colors might blend together. For this reason, contrast judiciously and with safety in mind.

- Placing light objects against darker ones, or vice versa, makes them stand out.

- Contrast can be used effectively in counter edges, flooring, control locations, on/off indicators, etc. **This same benefit can become a hazard if overused.** A black and white checked floor becomes a hazard as it affects depth perception.

Lighting design requires intense review of the parameters of each project. A more thorough review of the technical aspects of lighting is found in the **NKBA Bathroom Industry Technical Manual #2**. Consider a team approach with a lighting designer.

FLOORING

Goals/Considerations

There are several goals in choosing flooring for the universal bathroom.

- The floor should be low-maintenance and durable.

- It should be resilient to allow for minimum injury or breakage from drops or falls, and it should be a fairly smooth or regular surface for ease of use by persons with mobility or balance impairments.

- It should be matte finish, as highly polished surfaces can create glare and are usually slippery.

- The most important goal in selecting flooring is to choose flooring that can be as slip-resistant as possible.

While no flooring choice is ideal in every respect, most flooring materials can be used effectively if these goals are considered in the selection process.

Slip-Resistant Flooring

Slip-resistance in bathroom flooring, always the key concern, becomes even more important when universal design concepts are applied.

The floor that is somewhat slippery and less safe for an able-bodied person is even more of a hazard when the person is a toddler or has difficulty with balance or uses crutches.

Flooring manufacturers use a slip-resistance rating called the **coefficient of function**, with higher numbers indicating greater slip resistance. When using a **COF rating** to evaluate a floor surface, it is important to determine the rating when wet for bathroom use.

Research at **Pennsylvania State University** estimated that 88% of the population would be protected by a COF of .6 (.8 for ramps). There are a number of ceramic and vinyl surfaces available with ratings at least this high.

In addition, slip-resistant strips or coatings are available to reduce the risk of falls in particular areas, but heavy use, water, and continual cleaning can reduce the practicality of their usefulness.

Ceramic Tile

The appropriate ceramic tile can be a good choice.

- First, check manufacturers recommendations for use, durability, and slip resistance. A slip-resistant glazing can be of help.

- Choose tiles that are smooth or even-surfaced with a minimum of grout to create a level floor.

- Choose tile and grout that is stain and moisture resistant.

- Mosaic tiles provide added insurance against slipping.

Although tile is not resilient, the value of tile in a universal bathroom is its durability in wet situations, its easy maintenance and the opportunities for patterns to create the desirable contrast.

Stone Flooring

When considering a stone floor, pay attention to the surface and the porosity. Often stone is highly polished, making it a slippery surface, or tumbled, making it an irregular surface. For the universal bathroom, a matte finish level surface and a denser stone that will be more resistant to stains is the better choice.

Vinyl Flooring

Vinyl flooring products, including sheet goods, solid tiles and composition tiles, are another good option.

They are durable, low-maintenance and somewhat resilient, and they are available in a variety of patterns and colors. With certain products, the designer can create a pattern that allows for effective contrast to help with *way-finding*. A surface with less sheen will reduce glare and may be more slip-resistant.

If choosing either type of vinyl tiles, pay attention to the amount and depth of grout lines. A fairly smooth and minimal grout line is best, chosen with attention to levelness.

- Vinyl composition tiles perform much like vinyl sheet goods and allow the designer to create patterns and color schemes.

- Solid vinyl tiles usually have more of a matte finish, which can help in slip resistance.

With any vinyl flooring, consider the finish and the maintenance requirements.

Wood Flooring

Wood floors have good resilience and require varying degrees of care. Given the characteristics of wood in regard to moisture, a strong or penetrating sealer should be used. Wood floors should also be designed to be slip-resistant.

Carpet

Although carpet is frequently avoided in the bathroom because of concerns for maintenance, it has some merit in the universal bathroom.

A firmer, more industrial carpet with minimal or no padding is generally more stain resistant. This carpet provides warmth, resilience and a smooth surface for ease of travel. In addition, patterns can be created with carpet for contrast for *way-finding*.

Contrast/Way-Finding Considerations

When choosing floor patterns and finishes, consider contrast as a way-finding detail. A light tile floor with contrasting tiles around the perimeter of the bathroom and its major components will help to indicate area and edges. On the other hand, an all-over pattern can create problems in terms of depth perception. A matte surface on the floor will most likely be more slip-resistant and will reduce glare.

Thresholds should be flush and level, and again, there should be no irregularities in the floor.

FLOORING MATERIALS/UNIVERSAL CONSIDERATIONS

Material	Maintenance /Stain Resistance	Slip Resistance	Resilience	Level	Low-Glare
Ceramic Tile	choose non-porous, careful on grout, very easy care	mosaics, slip-resistant glaze, slight texture, can be slippery when wet, but above will help, check rating	hard surface	choose only level tiles	honed color, matte finish
Stone	choose denser stone, non-porous, can be easy care	no polished stone texture	hard surface	choose only level tiles, minimum grout no tumbled stone if surface is irregular	no polished stone
Vinyl Sheetgoods	no wax, very easy care	matte or low gloss, slight texture	consider underlay very resilient	very level	no high gloss finish
Vinyl Composition Tiles	review manufacturers care and installation guide on seams, otherwise, easy care	matte or low gloss, slight texture, minimum grout helps	fairly resilient	very level	no high gloss finish
Solid Vinyl Tiles	easy care, check manufacturers for stain resistance	matte finish and grout, good for slip resistance	very resilient	minimum grout, very level	matte finish
Wood Flooring	easy daily care, more long term maintenance	slippery when wet	resilient and warm	very level, no grooves in seams	low-gloss finish
Carpeting	choose tight industrial type/stain resistant	firm, resistant to slip, no padding	very resilient and warm	very level	no glare
Cork Flooring	easy maintenance, caution with seams	similar to vinyl sheetgoods	resilient, warm, sound insulator	very level	non-glare

WALL FINISHES

The selection of wall surfaces in the universal space requires only that established parameters be reviewed and emphasized.

- Ambient sound can become more of a problem for a person with hearing impairments.

- Wall and window treatments that absorb some of this room's noise include cork, carpet and fabrics.

- Surfaces that reduce glare enhance the space for everyone, particularly those with vision impairments.

- The natural sunlight that creates warm ambient light can also create glare, and there are glass and window treatments to eliminate the glare while allowing the light and the view.

- Wall colors and patterns should be chosen with consideration of the total room in terms of contrast and light.

- Consider the possible rigorous wear on the lowest 12" (30cm) of wall surface from mobility aids. One solution is to continue the flooring right up the wall 12" (30cm) and trim it at the top.

CONTROLS, ELECTRICAL AND VENTILATION SYSTEMS

Controls for ventilation, lighting, and any electrical systems in the bathroom should be mounted within the universal reach range of 15" - 48" (38cm - 122cm).

In addition, controls must follow codes and safety guidelines.

The possible addition of a security system, a safety alarm system, or a telephone will allow a person in need of help in the bathroom to call for assistance. The type and location of the system should be discussed with each client to ensure effectiveness.

chapter 10

SAFETY

Safety, created by ease of use, is a main principle of universal design. That same improved accessibility may be seen as a hazard in some situations. *"Keep medications out of reach of children"* is a well-known rule of home safety.

Universal design guidelines would provide a safe access to a high space via a stepstool or a system that lowers that high storage into the universal reach range, where everyone can access it.

Improved accessibility minimizes bending, reaching, stretching and using undue force, making safer and more independent use possible. Yet designers and clients must recognize the relative risks in a space to be used by many people.

Careful consideration must be given to those who will be operating in the bathroom. **Barriers must be eliminated and safety checks must be created as a part of the design process.**

In most cases, safety concerns relating to increased access have to do with improper use by children or those who are confused or forgetful.

Safety Aids

Aids include redundant cuing such as sound and flashing light to indicate when an appliance is left on or when water is running. Automatic shutoff is another safety check and is commonly available on curling irons and hair dryers. In addition, locking away those items that are unsafe for a particular user will help.

Home Control Systems

There are home control systems that allow a person to check on the status of the household via a control panel or even by calling in on the telephone. From these remote locations, a user can adjust room temperature or shut off appliances. Or with a preselected program, a user can execute the usual morning operations, such as turning up heat, starting coffee and lighting the path to the bathroom.

These devices respond to commands by visual and auditory cuing. When the right button is pushed or the time arrives, a voice says *"Good Evening"* and the heat and lights are turned down, appliances are checked and shut off and the doors are locked.

While this is definitely high tech, it goes a long way as a safety check.

Way-Finding

Way-finding is a simple concept normally achieved by using high tactile or visual contrast borders such as a dissimilar colored countertop edge or a border tile pattern which follows a path of egress.

Way-finding techniques are an excellent way to assist those who may be forgetful or who have a visual disability.

Fire Safety

Safety relating to fire may include extinguishers that are easy to reach and use, and should include a clear means of leaving the space should a fire occur.

Security Systems in the Bathroom

The addition of a security system can add to the safety of the bathroom in that it provides an easy method of calling for help should a problem arise.

Security systems can be activated by the typical means with the control in the universal reach range and supplemented by controls throughout the baseboard to allow a person who falls to call for help. Another control option is one that the user wears, which is within reach all the time.

Other Safety Considerations

What can be easily seen and understood is more apt to be used safely.

- Lighting that eliminates glare and harsh shadows and components that are self-evident in their use reduce the risk of misuse by anyone.

- Safety related to reducing the risk of falling has several components. The use of slip-resistant flooring, as discussed in the section on flooring, is first.

- In addition, hand-holds or grab bars can be used wherever there is a concern about slipping.

- Items stored within reach will eliminate unnecessary leaning, stretching or climbing.

- Spatial design that requires the least maneuvering and that provides for easy draining of excess water on the floor will also help.

Whenever possible, discuss each decision with the intended user to make the safest choices.

Safety concerns should guide, not limit the design of universal bathrooms.

chapter 11

BATHROOMS

THAT

WORK

The bathrooms featured in this chapter attempt to tie together many of the design and planning techniques discussed in this book. Here, you will see how bathrooms can be planned utilizing creative common sense applications of universal thinking.

Several of the ideas you'll discover are totally non-traditional, others expand on commonly thought of concepts and some are not new at all, just good design.

As you explore the photos and drawings featured on these pages, attempt to mentally identify the use of the individual and overall work center spaces which you will see accommodate people of varying sizes and abilities.

RACHEL'S BATHROOM

This remodeling project includes a kitchen and a bathroom, designed by **Mary Jo Peterson** for the Burgess-Goldberg family. This story and the space that evolved, provide designers with not only the *"how-to"*, but equally important the *"why bother"* of universal bath design.

The Burgess-Goldberg family includes a working widowed mother, a teenage son, and Rachel, a 13 year old girl who uses a wheelchair and has multiple physical disabilities. As we approach the project, their house has a number of barriers for Rachel.

In the kitchen for example, only one cabinet is within her reach and the space is so cramped that most movement in her wheelchair results in banging or bruising a wall or cabinet surface.

In the bathroom Rachel's mother has to lift her into and out of the bathtub, a task that is becoming difficult and dangerous as Rachel grows. The rest of the space is limiting for Rachel and difficult for other family members as Rachel's assistive devices occupy more of the already limited space. In the family room is a small second bathroom that Rachel cannot access at all.

Project Goals

The main goal of the project is to create kitchen and bathroom spaces without unnecessary barriers, allowing Rachel optimum safe levels of activity. As Rachel reaches adulthood, one way to provide her with maximum independence would be for her mother to move out of the house, allowing Rachel to live with a care-giver and thus be truly independent.

With this in mind, the team that made this goal a reality was formed. Members of the team include Rachel, Rachel's mother and sister (a physical therapist), Rachel's own occupational therapist, Mary Jo as designer, and an outstanding contracting team led by **Dale Zimmerman**.

The New Plan - Meeting the Requirements

The new plan involves relocating both the kitchen and bathroom. The kitchen is now moved into what had been the family room and second bathroom. A new bathroom is now where the old kitchen had been.

Existing conditions predetermined that the new kitchen and the new bathroom would be elevated 6" (15cm) from the existing grade to accommodate the transition.

- The new space plan is more open, with the existing living room flowing into the kitchen, incorporating what was a small dining room into this more flexible space.

- Vaulted ceilings, sky lights, and window expand the space.

- The change from smaller separate spaces to one larger and more open space also translates to ease of movement for Rachel and reduces wear and tear on walls and doors exposed to the exuberant movements of a young girl in a wheelchair.

The Plan Implementation

The new bathroom is a space that is not only safer and more accessible to Rachel and those assisting her, but also a space that reflects the high levels of energy, activity, and pleasure that are the personality of this household.

- To begin, the bathroom is entered through an oversized pocket door. The door is actually the maximum size opening that allows for its pocket and the pre-existing location of the utility space.

- Grab bars continue through the room, functioning as support and as a decorative detail.

- A countertop extending over the lavatory area knee space and the adjacent toilet, allow for resting space for frequently used items.

- The sink itself is relatively shallow with a rear drain to allow for optimum knee space, and the single lever faucet is easy to use and is familiar.

- The actual 32" (81cm) height of the knee space is based on Rachel's wheelchair arm height, so that she can roll up close for grooming.

- In the toilet area, Rachel and her mother opted for a standard height toilet with an elevated seat and integral grab bars. Past experience has taught them that this setup is most conducive to Rachel making best use of her strengths and abilities for transfer and stability.

- In addition the ceiling is re-enforced for hanging assistive triangle supports installed at the lavatory and toilet area.

- Adjacent to the toilet, the roll-in shower increases access to the toilet for transfer and provides for Rachel and a care giver for grooming and hygiene.

- Grab bars surround the area and an added adjustable support drops down from the ceiling.

- Controls include the hand-held spray with an extended hose for ease of use by everyone.

- The walls of the shower are kept to a minimum, extending only, as far as necessary to retain water, so that Rachel's entry, movement, and exit can occur without interference.

- Continuing around the room, there is a ramp and a second exit. The ramp is necessary due to the change in floor levels. The door exists because typical traffic patterns would allow her mother to assist Rachel from the shower to her bedroom in the evenings. This route would be the most direct. Exiting through the secondary door provides a direct route out the front door in case of emergency.

- To combine safety and aesthetics, the floor tile was patterned in this area to emphasize the ramp, with a contrasting arrow at both ends of the slope.

- The fourth wall of the bath includes some storage space that is fixed and some that is movable. Closed area storage is provided for typical bath products as well as personal hygiene supplies.

- The rolling storage basket allows access to the utilities through a pre-existing panel. Rachel can roll her stored grooming items to where she needs them and again, out of the way, as needs for the clear floor space change.

Aesthetics and Finishes

Aesthetics of this bathroom, chosen with Rachel's guidance, definitely reflect the personality of the family.

- Gray and white wall tiles with a mottled gray floor tile were her mothers choice for their ability to look clean under any circumstances.

- Red accents in the grab bars, window treatment and accessories call out safety features and brighten the space.

- Bright yellow in the hanging support system ties into the overall theme as Rachel's choice, Mickey Mouse, ties together the colors of red, yellow, black and white.

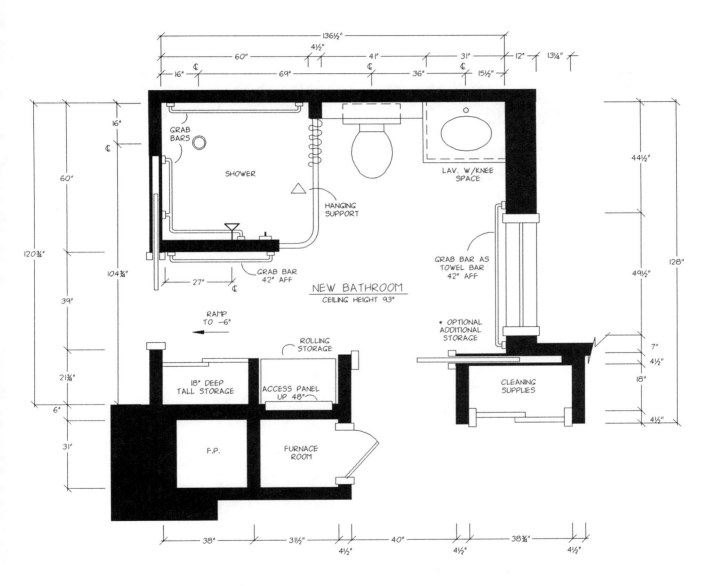

Figure 130 - Burgess-Goldberg Bathroom.

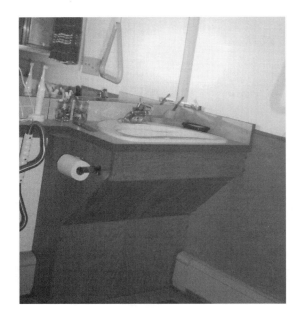

Figure 131 - Burgess-Goldberg Bathroom.

THE DOBKIN BATH

This master suite was and is a labor of love, created by designer **Irma Dobkin, ASID**, for herself and her husband. The plans, along with Irma's descriptions will inform and inspire bathroom designers to incorporate universal design concepts as an integral part of the beauty and function of every bathroom space.

Irma, a design student in her early forties, now faced with the reality of the aging process, gained considerable insight from her own mothers aging. The aging process creates inevitable changes in physical as well as mental abilities. Accommodations for these changes are reflected in the design she has created.

Floor Plan of Original Suite

The Dobkins sat down and evaluated the strengths and weaknesses of the existing bedroom and compiled a wish list of how a remodeled room would work and look. The list included concerns for accessibility should a wheelchair ever be needed. Independence was of paramount consideration as an acceptable solution.

The Users and Their Needs

An empty-nest, professional working couple, they are art collectors who entertain frequently. Their desire was to create a dramatic and romantic bedroom, bathroom and dressing area using the following criteria.

- A self-contained living environment, eliminating the need to travel through the house and negotiate steps to the kitchen and the laundry room.

- The space would be universally designed and wheelchair accessible (to some degree).

- A shower without a curb and threshold in case a wheelchair, crutches or other walking aids would be needed.

- A separate area for the toilet and bidet close to the sleeping area would be convenient for middle of the night visits.

- An organized, dramatic and compartmentalized suite.

- Separate grooming areas would provide convenience when both users were in the space.

- A bed facing the entry door and angled fireplace wall provided a fabulous view.

- Sensitivity toward cost dictated the reuse of the existing toilet and bidet. However since each stood 14 1/4 inches (37cm) AFF to the seat, they would be built-up.

- Acoustics were a concern (difficulty discerning foreground from background sound). So the architectural finish materials selected had to be evaluated in light of their acoustical properties.

The Design

The new master suite restores romance, integrating safety, accessibility, and beauty. The space anticipates the physiological changes of aging.

- Special assistive devices are woven into the tapestry of the compartmentalized space.

- Judicious selection of materials assures safety and operational ease.

- Automated draperies, mechanical beds, and lighting now require little strength or dexterity.

- A soaring architecture elevates the spirit, neutrals and niches provide surrounds for art and sculpture.

The Details

- A curbless shower, using large-scaled floor tile, led to the design of a trough for water management.

- Grab bars, used as a rail detail, are integrated throughout.

- *Way-finding* is logical. Multiple routes avoid congestion, as do the wide passages and doorways.

- Frequently used, the toilet is the space's hub.

- The bumper designed for the pocket door permits effortless operation regardless of dexterity or strength.

- The physical separation of sink areas permits individualized solutions; one being fully wheelchair accessible.

- The custom nightstands puts light and bed controls along the bedside for safety and convenience

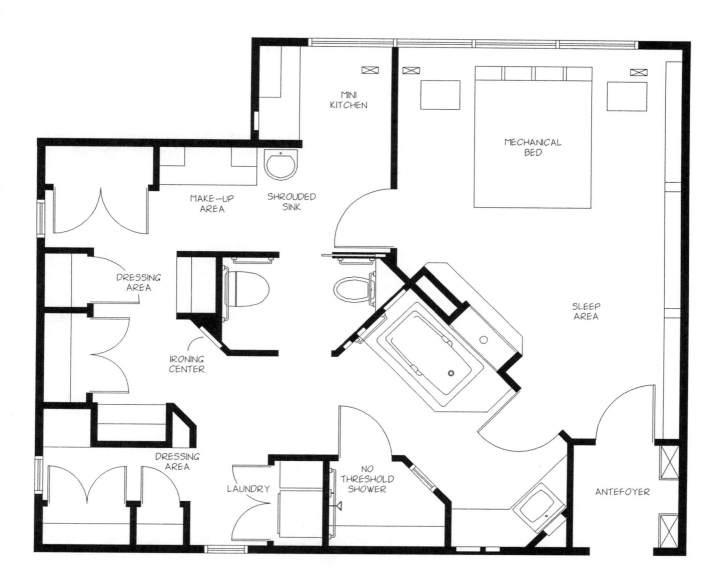

Figure 132 - Dobkin Bathroom

Figure 133 - Dobkin Bathroom

UNIVERSAL BATHROOM PLANNING

THE KLINE BATH

The client profile for this universal bathroom project, designed by **Annette DePaepe, CKD, CBD, ASID,** is not unlike the profile for many custom bathroom projects.

The Klines are a couple in their late forties looking to create a master bath that will be both functional and beautiful, an environment that will feel like a sophisticated spa retreat and flow naturally with their bedroom's contemporary Japanese influence. John Kline is 5' 7" (170cm) and Harriet is 5' 3" (160cm) and they want a space that suits their physical characteristics.

Recent attention to *"the aging boomer"* has helped them to appreciate design details that while subtle, will allow them to enjoy their space for as long as they wish.

Design Requirements

The space to be utilized is an addition on the east end of the bedroom. Parameters include:

- Access to the bedroom and to an exterior patio to be built on the north wall.

- An open roll-in shower with large seat, stool or bench area adjacent to the shower, toilet with space for side transfer, lavatory with kneespace, storage closet and a 60" (152cm) wheelchair turning space.

The New Plan - Meeting the Requirements

The new plan responds to the client's desires and offers more.

- With doors on east and north walls, a clear floor space of 60" (152cm) is maintained, creating the flow the Klines had requested while providing the clearance needed for a wheelchair to turn 360°.

- A custom 31 1/2" (80cm) high pedestal sink accommodates both standing and sitting use and provides kneespace.

- The shower is designated by four columns that frame the 36" (91cm) wide seat and window areas.

- Controls are placed at the entrance, with a hand-held showerhead on the seat deck for easy access.

- All glass used is tempered for safety.

- The 1/2" (4cm) high beveled curb is easy to roll-over with a wheelchair and adds to the open flow of the space.

- The floorspace at the shower entrance provides the 90° turning space required for a wheelchair.

- The vertical towel warmer allows towels to be hung at a wide range of heights above the floor.

- A solid surface bench opposite the shower provides for towel drying and aids in transfer.

- The remaining floor space accommodates the toilet and side transfer space.

- All corners are eased to eliminate any sharp edges and surfaces are of tile and solid surface for easy maintenance.

- In order to provide the spa retreat feeling requested, a special reflecting pool for floating candles and potpourri lies between the shower and lavatory and drains into the shower.

- The semi-circular protrusion of the lavatory front is mirrored in the back splash and mirror top.

- The square motif, picked-up from a shoji screen in the bedroom, is used throughout the bathroom to create a unified theme.

- Squares are found in the molding, cabinet door style, lighting, floor and bench/lavatory supports.

- The neutral with black accent colors help to create a feeling of understated sophistication.

The finished space is remarkable for its beauty and more subtly for its foresight and flexibility, providing for a longer lifespan.

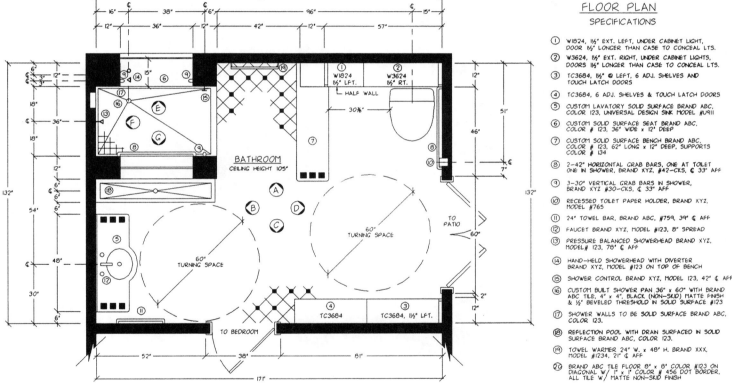

FLOOR PLAN
SPECIFICATIONS

1. W1824, 1½" EXT. LEFT, UNDER CABINET LIGHT, DOOR 1½" LONGER THAN CASE TO CONCEAL LTS.
2. W3624, 1½" EXT. RIGHT, UNDER CABINET LIGHTS, DOORS 1½" LONGER THAN CASE TO CONCEAL LTS.
3. TC3684, 1½" @ LEFT, 6 ADJ. SHELVES AND TOUCH LATCH DOORS
4. TC3684, 6 ADJ. SHELVES & TOUCH LATCH DOORS
5. CUSTOM LAVATORY SOLID SURFACE BRAND ABC, COLOR 123, UNIVERSAL DESIGN SINK MODEL #U911
6. CUSTOM SOLID SURFACE SEAT BRAND ABC, COLOR # 123, 36" WIDE x 12" DEEP
7. CUSTOM SOLID SURFACE BENCH BRAND ABC, COLOR # 123, 62" LONG x 12" DEEP, SUPPORTS COLOR # 134
8. 2-42" HORIZONTAL GRAB BARS, ONE AT TOILET ONE IN SHOWER, BRAND XYZ, #42-CKS, ₵ 33" AFF
9. 3-30" VERTICAL GRAB BARS IN SHOWER, BRAND XYZ #30-CKS, ₵ 33" AFF
10. RECESSED TOILET PAPER HOLDER, BRAND XYZ, MODEL #765
11. 24" TOWEL BAR, BRAND ABC, #759, 39" ₵ AFF
12. FAUCET BRAND XYZ, MODEL #123, 8" SPREAD
13. PRESSURE BALANCED SHOWERHEAD BRAND XYZ, MODEL #123, 78" ₵ AFF
14. HAND-HELD SHOWERHEAD WITH DIVERTER BRAND XYZ, MODEL #123 ON TOP OF BENCH
15. SHOWER CONTROL BRAND XYZ, MODEL 123, 42" ₵ AFF
16. CUSTOM BUILT SHOWER PAN 36" x 60" WITH BRAND ABC TILE, 4" x 4", BLACK (NON-SKID) MATTE FINISH & ½" BEVELED THRESHOLD IN SOLID SURFACE #123
17. SHOWER WALLS TO BE SOLID SURFACE BRAND ABC, COLOR 123.
18. REFLECTION POOL WITH DRAIN SURFACED IN SOLID SURFACE BRAND ABC, COLOR 123.
19. TOWEL WARMER 24" W. x 48" H. BRAND XXX, MODEL #1234, 21" ₵ AFF
20. BRAND ABC TILE FLOOR 8" x 8" COLOR #123 ON DIAGONAL W/ 1" x 1" COLOR # 456 DOT BORDER, ALL TILE W/ MATTE NON-SKID FINISH

BATHROOM
CEILING HEIGHT 105"

TURNING SPACE
60"

TO PATIO

TO BEDROOM

Figure 134   - Kline Bathroom

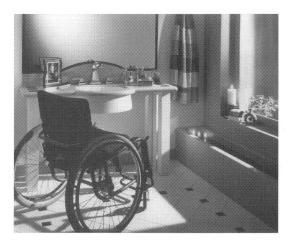

Figure 135 - Kline Bathroom

THE HEATHER BATHROOM

Lorraine and George Heather are in their fifties and wish to update and change their home to accommodate their changing lifestyles. George is 6' 2" (188cm) tall, a large man and Lorraine is 5' 4" (163cm), operating from a power wheelchair as an injury from a car accident has resulted in the loss of the use of her legs.

Design Requirements

Having retired from teaching, Lorraine still has an interest in helping young people and has decided to offer her home and herself as a source of rehabilitation for young people who are recovering from injuries similar to hers.

In addition, because George is involved in town politics and their home is often a place where varieties of people congregate, they have decided to make one bathroom on the main floor a flexible and accessible space where people of varying size and ability can function.

To accommodate the Heathers' desire for flexibility in their guest bathroom, the new space allows for adjustment in the major work areas and in the storage areas.

The New Plan - Meeting the Requirements

- As you enter the bathroom, storage and mirrors are located on either side of the door.

- In both corners fixed storage is 18" (46cm) deep and just 66" (168cm) high, placing most of the storage within the universal reach range. Between the units and the door are full length mirrors to allow for full view for a person who is seated or standing.

- In front of each mirror is a rolling storage unit with a hinged top and drawers. These units allow a person to move stored items easily and the surface doubles as a counter when needed.

- Moving into the shower area, a sloped floor to the drain and a 60" x 48" (152cm x 122cm) curtained area help to retain water.

- The seat can be adjusted, both horizontally and vertically, or folded out of the way for varied preferences in showering.

- The control wall includes a hand-held spray which can be adjusted in height or used in-hand.

- Water temperature can be pre-set or adjusted with the pressure balanced valve eliminating the risk of scalding. A separate on/off lever allows for volume control.

- The lavatory area is flexible as well, with a sink that can be adjusted vertically or horizontally by pushing a lever up, and using one hand, easily positioning the fixture, then pushing the lever down to lock into place. this adjustability lends itself to people of varying size, age and ability. The ability to move the sink left or right changes the clear floor space as desired for showering and toileting.

- In the toilet area, flexibility in surrounding grab bars and the adjacent lavatory provide clear floor space for a variety of approaches and transfers. Grab bars can be raised, lowered, or folded out of the way to suit the abilities and preferences of the user.

- The gray and white theme in the bathroom is accented by bright red. The room has generous task and ambient lighting, including natural light. Adjustability in switches allows for differences in visual needs. The overall effect is light and spacious.

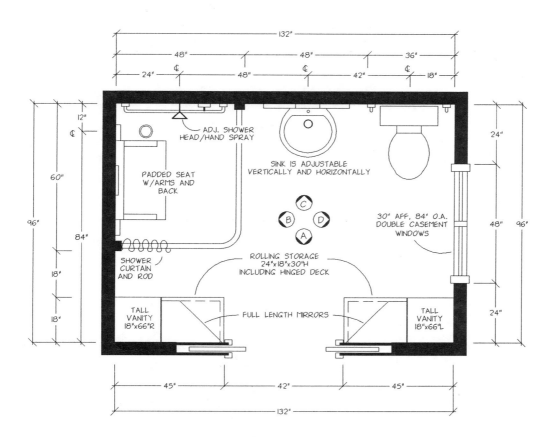

Figure 136 - Heather Bathroom.

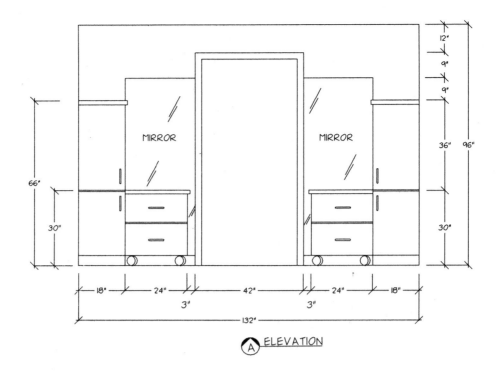

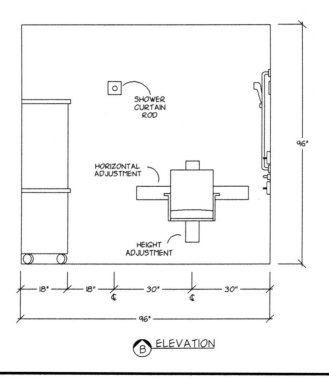

Figure 137 - Heather Bathroom.

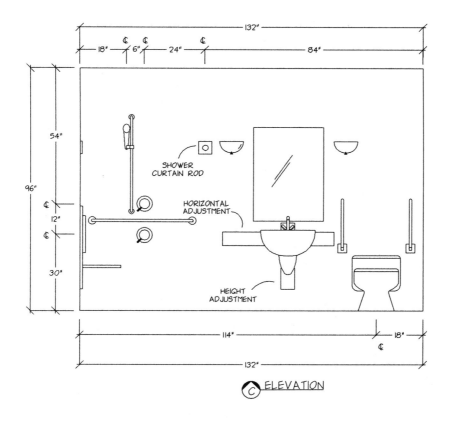

SHOWER
CURTAIN ROD

HORIZONTAL
ADJUSTMENT

HEIGHT
ADJUSTMENT

ⒸELEVATION

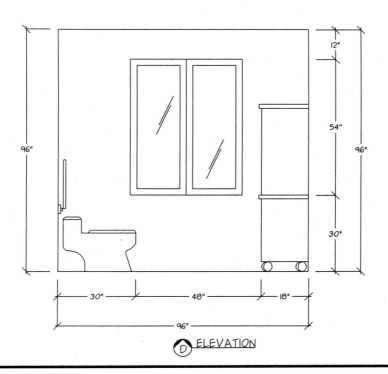

ⒹELEVATION

Figure 138 - Heather Bathroom.

Figure 139 - Heather Bathroom.

chapter 12

UNDERSTANDING

DISABILITIES

AND

FUNCTIONAL

CONSIDERATIONS

FUNCTIONAL ASSESSMENT OF BATHROOM SKILLS

When planning bathroom modifications for an individual with an injury or disability it is imperative to start with a full assessment of the person's functional capabilities. In other words, it is important to consider the total person and the environment, not just his or her component parts.

To do this comprehensively, the team of an occupational therapist and bathroom designer, can assess the person and the environment respectively while considering each others expertise. Although most injuries or disabilities have a common set of symptoms, it is often true that each person's particular set of symptoms varies widely.

Analysis of the Individuals Needs

How a person *"lives"* with and tolerates these symptoms will vary with the individual. It is also true that some conditions present themselves differently or have an unpredictable course. Lifestyle in terms of roles, responsibilities and desires must be explored.

A comprehensive assessment of a person's capabilities would include looking at the physical, sensory, perceptual, cognitive and emotional components of function.

An **Occupational Therapist** is a trained professional educated to assess these components as they relate to functional abilities in order to make recommendations which would result in optimizing each person's independence.

- By considering medical history, prognosis and skill level the therapist analyzes one's ability to complete grooming and hygiene skills.

- Specific activities such as oral hygiene, shaving, toileting, bathing, cosmetic application and the ability to complete hair care are assessed.

- Strengths and areas of concern are determined. A treatment plan is developed which would include techniques, strategies, environmental modifications and adaptive equipment.

While some of these recommendations are universal, some are specific to the individual.

The teaming of skills of a bathroom designer and an occupational therapist will provide the optimal solution.

MOBILITY

Mobility is the ability to move around an identified space safely and efficiently. A person's ability to move may be impaired due to many factors. Relative to the purpose of bathroom design, the cause of the impairment and how movement and function are affected are essential to the success of the design choice.

Mobility Impairments

Impairment of mobility may mean the person can freely and easily move around the bathroom but needs to sit at certain intervals of time perhaps due to decreased endurance.

At the other end of the spectrum, impaired mobility may mean reliance on a wheelchair. Each of these individuals can successfully function in the bathroom if given the *"right"* setup.

If mobility is impaired due to conditions involving joint inflammation and resulting degeneration, techniques known as *"joint protection"* and *"energy conservation"* are employed. This approach is utilized in such conditions as osteo and rheumatoid arthritis (inflammation of joints) and ankylosing spondylitis to reduce the strain on joints. Joints feel painful, swell and get red resulting in lack of movement.

Convenience Considerations

Grooming and hygiene activities can be completed with less effort if done after gathering all items in one location.

- Ideally, an all purpose work surface at a comfortable sitting height adjacent to a lavatory should be planned.

- Close access to a mirror and electrical outlets will greatly enhance that individual's ability to function in a pain free workspace.

- Storage should be designed to reduce unnecessary walking and lifting so energy can be conserved for grooming and hygiene.

- A built-in vanity area with access to drawers and a water source will accomplish this need. An open kneespace at

the vanity would allow for wheelchair accessibility as well.

For individuals in need of walking aides (e.g. canes, walkers, wheelchairs), the ability to carry things is often compromised.

- Cabinet and countertop arrangements which allow the sliding of items is oftentimes an inexpensive yet safe solution.

- Caution should be taken in making such a recommendation, with attention to a person's balance and how he/she lifts and moves their feet. Judgment must be assessed by a trained professional.

- Clients with spinal cord injuries, multiple sclerosis, or amputations can be easily accommodated to allow for independent access and use of the bathroom. Wheelchair accessible space for safe and independent transfers from wheelchairs to the toilet and bathtub or shower could mean dignity for the individual as well as relief for the care provider.

- Consideration of wheelchair heights is essential to the success of any person who is operating from a wheelchair.

Design That Adapts To People

- A solution as simple as a raised toilet seat or raised toilet seat height may mean the ability to toilet oneself thereby perserving the individual's dignity and prevent the possibility of falls.

- Many types of adaptive seats and lifts are available for bathtubs and showers *(See chapters 5 and 6)*.

- Many assistive devices are also available.

- For specific types of transfer, *(refer to Appendix 5)*. Safe independent use of these devices requires proper selection and training through the services of a therapist.

BALANCE

Balance and mobility are closely aligned and should be assessed together. Balance or a state of equilibrium can be compromised by many injuries or illnesses.

Neurological conditions such as Multiple Sclerosis and Parkinson's Disease as well as orthopedic conditions which relate to bones, muscles and joints (e.g. hip or other leg fractures, leg length discrepancy, arthritic conditions, leg amputations,) are only some of the conditions which may result in balance problems.

Design Concerns

The functional considerations would include; walking and carrying things, bending over to obtain objects from a low height, reaching up to access items from above shoulder height to bring them safely to the countertop or lavatory, getting in and out of a bathtub or shower and getting on and off a toilet seat safely.

Design Solutions

Solutions includes a lavatory with open kneespace and rearrangement of cabinetry so storage is within easy reach, (e.g. approximately waist height). This reduces the chance of slips or falls and should be strongly considered. Individuals with decreased balance and/or mobility need greater security.

COORDINATION

Coordination or the ability to control movement can be assessed by observing the ability to move around the environment in a smoothly executed manner and to use various bathroom items and tools safely and efficiently.

Motor control can be affected by many different injuries and disabilities. For example, many neurological conditions such as Cerebral Vascular Accidents (stroke), Multiple Sclerosis, Parkinson's Disease, Traumatic Brain Injury and Cerebral Palsy as well as Peripheral Nerve Injuries (i.e. Carpal Tunnel Syndrome) result in a decrease in motor control. Symptoms such as spasticity, tremors, weakness and impaired sensation can result in incoordination.

Safety and Convenience

The most pressing issue for someone with incoordination in the bathroom is safety. Positions which foster better motor control such as sitting may help an individual gain control over their muscles.

When the use of both sides of the body at the same time is compromised, adaptive equipment that stabilizes objects may be extremely helpful. Items such as a suction denture or nail brush allow for independence with the use of one arm and hand.

Tremors or incoordination may result from fatigued muscles so energy conservation and work simplification techniques discussed earlier would again be essential. Individuals with incoordination may find an increase in ability when provided with a different handle (i.e., built-up, weighted, or curved) or a universal cuff to attain items they would otherwise have to do without.

Assistive technology that eliminates and simplifies steps such as faucets with preset water temperatures on the shower will help provide independence for a person with incoordination.

STRENGTH

Strength is the ability of a muscle or a muscle group to produce or resist a physical force.

This concept is often mixed up with **endurance, which is the ability to continue an activity despite increasing physical or psychological stress**.

It is true however that weaker muscles tend to have decreased endurance. Conditions in which muscle strength is impacted may include: Multiple Sclerosis, Spinal Cord Injury, Muscular Dystrophy, and Cerebral Vascular Accident (stroke).

Other conditions such as those related to cardiac (heart) and pulmonary (lung) conditions (e.g. heart arrhythmias and Congestive Obstructive Pulmonary Disease - C.O.P.D.), depression and pain can result in decreased endurance versus loss of muscle strength.

Strength Solutions

In terms of functional outcome, it does not matter if the issue is strength, endurance or both. The key is for the individual to learn how to pace themself so energy can be devoted to those components of activities determined to be essential. In addition to pacing, energy conservation and work simplification techniques should be employed.

Adaptive equipment is available to reduce energy drains and allow that person to redirect their effort for the best result - independence.

SENSATION

Sensation is the ability by which stimuli are perceived and conditions outside and within the body are distinguished and evaluated.

Sensation requires one to be able to take in stimuli, process it (by itself as well as with other input) and then respond appropriately. The processing of sensory information and a person's response to it will be discussed in more detail in the next section on perception and cognition.

Consider all the Senses

When looking at sensory stimuli and processing in a bathroom, there is not one sensory input which can be excluded.

We need to be able to see, hear, feel, taste, smell and know our posi-

tion in that environment. If any of these are compromised due to injury or illness, compensatory strategies and environmental modifications can allow for functional independence.

Design Solutions

Sensory losses such as impaired vision can be accommodated for by the use of enlarged visual cues (e.g. colors on faucets) or Braille.

Diminished touch needs to be closely assessed by a trained professional to determine the extent of the impairment. *For example*, the loss of ability to determine hot and cold can be devastating for someone as she may not realize the water is too hot until after the fact. Sensory retraining to help people learn to use other senses to compensate for the loss of a particular sense can make the difference between independence and devastation. The case in point would be to train the person with diminished hot/cold to rely on vision to a far greater extent especially when adjusting water temperature for bathing.

In addition, a person may have diminished (light or depth) sensory pressure which functionally may translate to not feeling a severe cut. In this instance, the cut would go unattended after shaving. We see this type of sensory loss in the feet and possibly the hands of diabetics. The result can be a devastating infection.

Impaired sensation may result in many issues pertinent to bathroom skills; however, compensatory techniques to assist the person in using other cues from their body or the environment have proven to be very useful and improve safety consciousness. When there is reduced sensation, mirrors to check difficult to see areas can be of greater help in preventing other problems such as skin breakdown or infections.

PERCEPTION/COGNITION

Perception and cognition are easily defined; however, their boundaries are nebulous.

Perception can be viewed as the conscious recognition and interpretation of sensory stimuli through unconscious associations.

On the other hand, **cognition** can be seen as the mental process characterized by knowing, thinking, learning, and judging.

In simplistic terms, we take information in from the environment and about ourselves through our senses. This information is then processed and associated with other information so we form our own perceptions. These perceptions are part of the formation of our knowledge base which is what we use to think, learn and judge our world and ourselves. How many times have you seen three or four different people call the same color tile by three or four different names: blue, green, aqua or teal. Each person, based on their color perception and knowledge of color labels will argue his or her answer as being correct.

Perceptual and cognitive dysfunction can be seen as the result of some type of injury or change to the brain. Traumatic brain injury, cerebral vascular accident and brain tumor are a few of the possible diagnoses which can cause problems in this area of function.

Perception Types

The area of perception can be divided by type of sensory input. *For example*, perception may include:

- visual,

- auditory,

- tactile, etc.

Each of these can then be subdivided into more specific areas. Visual perception can include:

- figure-ground (the ability to distinguish foreground from background)

- depth perception (ability to determine how far away one object is as compared to another)

- visual memory (the ability to remember what you have seen)

- visual sequential memory (the ability to remember a visual sequence)

- visual closure (the ability to see the whole from parts of the whole)

- spatial relationships (the ability to see an object orientation in space), etc., etc.

A similar type of subdivision can be made for each area of perception as well as the complex addition of a motor or movement response, i.e. visual-motor integration.

Understanding Perception Problems

A person with figure-ground perception problems might have difficulty finding a brush or a comb in a drawer full of brushes or combs. An organizer of some type may help the person scan and find the particular object more easily.

Color choice and use of contrasting materials can play an integral part in relieving this type of perceptual issue throughout the bathroom space without compromising beauty and design.

Cognition

Cognition is a complex component to function as it includes:

- attention

- memory (short and long term)

- planning

- organization

- problem solving

- decision making

- judgment

Most individuals who would be using a bathroom independently may have minimal cognitive dysfunction. Attention, memory loss or confusion related to multi-step tasks are the areas which can be most easily addressed by a bathroom designer/Occupational Therapist team.

- Environmental devices such as dual cues (i.e. blinking light and soft bell) will serve to keep a person focused.

- Single function controls on faucets would be another consideration.

Cognitive concerns can have a strong impact on safety. A trained health care professional can assess the level to which a person can function independently and safely.

ADAPTATIONS AND MODIFICATIONS

There are many adaptive bathroom devices available commercially. The market has seen tremendous growth in both high and low tech solutions available for institutional and residential applications.

Care needs to be given to choices made recognizing beauty, design and function. The key to success is listening to and observing the client. Selection must be matched not only to the desired function, but to the specific abilities of the individual.

Consideration of other variables such as prognosis (whether a particular injury or disability will get better, stay the same or get worse), current and future roles and responsibilities (i.e. care for others, career) and personal motivation for use of the space in question (a person who wants or is ready to be independent versus one who is not motivated at a given point in time).

Many adaptations are not commercially available. These need to be fabricated by the team of client, family, bathroom designer, Occupational Therapist, and sometimes a rehab engineer.

chapter 13

The Client

In any designer/client relationship, understanding the client and establishing mutual respect is critical to the success of a design project. This need for trust is even more important when the client has a disability that limits his or her opportunities to collect information about the project.

- You must speak comfortably to the client.

- You must establish what the client needs and wants and whether or not you can meet those requirements.

Approaching the Client

This chapter presents some additional information to better enable you to show respect and collect information to confirm and solidify the relationship when the client has a disability.

A respectful approach to the client with a disability requires observance of certain etiquette and attitudes. People with disabilities need to be recognized as people first, in thought and words. They don't wish to be thought of as sick or as objects of pity or even admiration. Also, as Joseph Shapiro states in *No Pity*, politically correct euphemisms like *"the vertically challenged"* or *"differently abled"* are not popular.

Avoid negative terms like *"confined to a wheelchair"*. In other words, positive references and direct honest conversation works best. The following conversational guidelines and examples will help. If you aren't sure how to refer to a disability, ask your client. If you feel you have spoken out of turn, acknowledge it and apologize.

Attitude	Negative	Positive
• Avoid negative description	afflicted with polio	person who has had polio
	crippled with arthritis	person with arthritis
	confined to a wheelchair	person who uses a wheelchair, or a wheelchair user
	victim of M.S.	person who has M.S.
	Disabled and Normal people	people with disabilities and people without disabilities
• Put people first and avoid grouping	the disabled	people with disabilities
	the blind	people with blindness or visual impairments
	the deaf	people with deafness or hearing impairments
• Emphasize abilities, not limitations	confined to a wheelchair	uses a wheelchair
	can't climb stairs	stairs are an obstacle or a barrier
• Use appropriate terminology for specific disabilities	the blind	boy who is blind, girl who has low vision, man who is visually impaired
	birth defect	congenital disability
	the deaf	person who is hearing-impaired
	crippled	person with mobility impairment

Conversation Guidelines

These guidelines for conversation with a client who has a disability are universally appropriate.

- Position yourself to speak at eye level.

- Respect your client's privacy. You need to know certain things to better serve her, but it is her decision what she chooses to share with you.

- Respect the client's assistive devices and don't interfere with his use of them.

- Ask specific questions about the client's needs and abilities as outlined in **NKBA's Universal Design Survey**.

- Listen and record what is said. Remember that while you may have more awareness of design options, your clients have the awareness of their needs.

There is a tendency to get caught up in terminology. These guidelines are intended to help you avoid that.

If you focus on the person and not the disability, you will most likely have positive results.

THE CLIENT SURVEY

The client survey included on the following pages is expanded from the **NKBA Business Management forms** to incorporate appropriate questions regarding disabilities. It is a checklist from which you will determine the questions to ask your client. From time to time, you will find the need to customize this survey to fit various projects.

A Helpful Hint

An occupational or physical therapist or a doctor who works with your client will have an understanding of your client's present and expected future abilities that you as a bathroom designer probably don't have. If your client agrees, include these professionals in completing the survey and collecting information.

Set up a home consultation or a conference call to provide the opportunity for input from the therapist, or visit the rehabilitation center with your client.

The ideal teaming of a bathroom designer with an occupational therapist and perhaps a rehab engineer can truly make a difference in the success of a project.

Form #4025

UNIVERSAL BATHROOM PLANNING CLIENT SURVEY

Name: _____ Date: _____

Address: _____

City, State, Zip: _____

Phone: _____ Work: _____

Jobsite Address: _____

City, State, Zip: _____

Directions: _____

_____

Appointment: _____

Date: _____ Address: _____

Time: _____ City/State/Zip: _____

Phone: _____ Comment: _____

_____

Allied Professional: _____

_____

_____

Pertinent Information: _____

I. THE CLIENT - PHYSICAL PROFILE

Sight:

Do you wear glasses for reading? _____ for distance? _____

Any visual impairments that influence the type/amount of lighting needed? _____

Are you taking any medications that affect your sight? _____

Hearing:

What issues regarding your ability to hear will affect the design process?_____

Tactile/Touch:

Can you feel hot and cold?_____ texture?_____

Taste/Smell:

Do you know of any change in your sense of taste? ___ smell? _____

Strength & Function:

What can you lift? _____ carry? _____

Do you have more strength on one side than the other? _____

Do you use both hands fully?_____ palms only?_____

How is your grip?_____Left Side? _____ Right Side? _____

How is your balance? _____Standing? _____ Bending?_____

Areas of Physical Limitation:

Does your mobility or balance vary by time of day? _____

Is there an assistant who helps sometimes?_____ All the time? _____

What adaptive equipment do you use?_____

Weight?_____Height?_____

Prognosis: (Is condition stable? Is further deterioration anticipated? Is improvement anticipated?)

_____

SAMPLE

Consultants:

Physician _____ telephone: _____

Occupational Therapist _____ telephone: _____

Comments from Physician and Occupational Therapist:

_____

Transfer Information: (Prefer right, left, or forward?)

_____

Special Safety Concerns:

_____

Reach and Grasp Profile:

Have your client position themselves as shown where applicable, fill in the appropriate reach/grasp measurements.

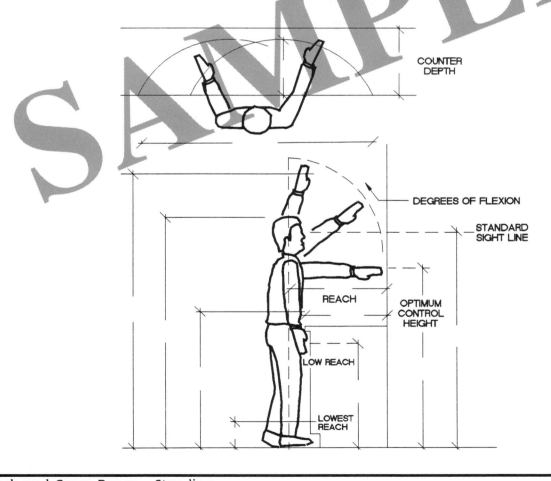

Reach and Grasp Range - Standing

FORWARD REACH

SIDE REACH

MAX. REACH

SIGHT LINE

0°

Reach and Grasp Range - Seated

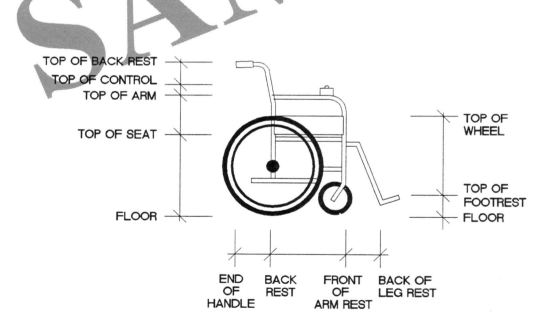

TOP OF BACK REST
TOP OF CONTROL
TOP OF ARM

TOP OF SEAT

FLOOR

TOP OF WHEEL

TOP OF FOOTREST

FLOOR

END OF HANDLE   BACK REST   FRONT OF ARM REST   BACK OF LEG REST

Wheelchair Profile

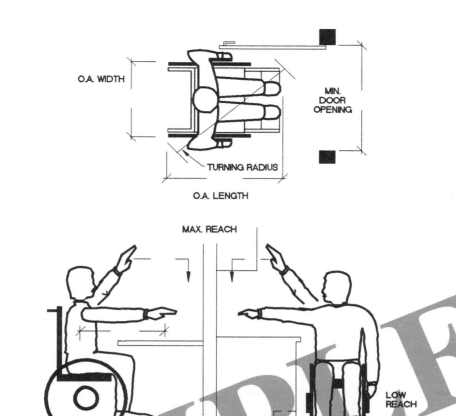

SAMPLE

Wheelchair Profile - Reach Range

What activities in the bathroom would you like to do that you are not able to do now?

_____

_____

_____

Bathroom

1. Sink/Lavatory Area

Are there any access concerns? _____sink?_____

Is the present height/depth of the sink/lav comfortable for you? _____

present height _____preferred height_____

What height range is best for storage?_____

_____

Design That Adapts To People   207

Is there a need for open space below the sink and vanity? _____

_____

Does the present faucet operate easily for you?_____

      preferred location & style _____

Do you wish a knee space at the sink/lav area? _____

Comments/Concerns _____

_____

2. Bathtub/Shower Area

Do you prefer a bath? _____ or shower? _____

Is your bathtub easy and safe to get into and use? _____

Is there a bathtub/shower seat? ____should one be included in the plan_____

Is there a hand-held spray? _____should one be included in the plan_____

Can the controls be reached from both a sitting and standing position? _____

Are the controls easy to use?_____

      present style and location _____

      preferred style and location_____

Is the bathtub/shower floor non-slip? _____

How will you approach/transfer to the bathtub/shower? _____

_____

_____

Comments/Concerns_____

_____

SAMPLE

3. Toilet Area

Is the present toilet at a height that is safe and comfortable for your approach/transfer?

_____

Do you prefer a standard height toilet or a raised height toilet? _____

Will you use an elevated seat? _____

What height must the seat be? _____

Present clearances

    left _____

    right _____

    front _____

Preferred clearances

    left _____

    right _____

    front _____

TOILET			
#	A	B	C	D
1				
2				
3				
4				

Is the toilet paper dispenser within your reach? _____

    present location _____

    preferred location _____

Is the flush lever easily and safely used? _____

    present location _____

    preferred location _____

4. Support System

Where do you need grab bars in the toilet area? _____

_____

Where do you need grab bars at the bathtub/shower? _____

_____

Do you need any other grab bars or railings? _____

_____

5. Storage

Is there adequate storage within your reach?_____

_____

Are the medicine cabinet and shelves within your reach? _____

_____

Are the storage areas safely and easily opened? _____

_____

For what items do you need storage? _____

_____

Any unusual sized items? _____

_____

Do you have any supportive or hygiene equipment that requires storage? (list items and

dimensions) _____

_____

6. Counter Heights

current height_____ preferred height _____

Is there enough work space? _____ knee space?_____

7. Accessories and Controls

Are towel racks easily and safely used? _____

_____

Are towel racks likely to be used as grab bars? _____

_____

Are the light/fan switches easy to use? _____

present height and style_____

preferred height and style _____

Are the electrical outlets GFCI?_____

_____

Are outlet locations safe and easy to use? _____

      present height _____

      preferred height _____

8. Moving Around

What problems exist in entering and moving around in the bathroom? _____

_____

What style door do you prefer? pocket _____ hinge_____ other _____

What is your door swing preference? (check clear floor space outside door) _____

Where would you like the door handle located? _____

9. Lighting and Ventilation

Is there enough lighting

      for bathing _____

      in the lav/mirror area _____

      in the toilet area _____

      for general illumination _____

Is the bathroom well ventilated? _____

10. Other Concerns/Comments

Is there a safe and easy exit in case of fire? _____

Are the windows operable? _____

Comments _____

_____

MARKETING UNIVERSAL DESIGN SERVICES

Given that universal design needs to be part of all good bathroom design, designers with these skills should market them as part of the expertise that they bring to the drawing board.

Just as a thorough understanding of fixtures and equipment or spatial considerations is part of your background, universal design should become part of your knowledge base as well.

It is important to understand that this is not design that is different for people who are different, but design that is expanded to better serve a more diverse target clientele.

In a given advertising or promotional campaign, you might choose to emphasize universal design skills. When doing so, traditional marketing concepts apply, with the target possibly changing or broadening. Also, certain marketing strategies may be emphasized more.

APPLYING MARKETING SOLUTIONS

STEP 1 - IDENTIFY TARGET MARKET

Applying general marketing solutions to universal design - the first step is to identify the target. In addition to your standard business target, you may wish to focus marketing efforts on people with specific disabilities or people who are middle-aged or older or people with young children. Keep in mind that universal design skills benefit everyone, so while you may focus on one group in one marketing effort, you will want to remember the others.

For example, universal design concepts make independent living more possible for people who are older, but these same benefits apply to people in the so-called prime of life, for their parents, for their own future and for their children, allowing the bathroom to work better and safer for more of the people in it.

People who benefit directly from universal design are part of your market already. The key may be to more thoroughly identify with the universal design aspects of your client's needs. In addition to your usual avenues for marketing, you may reach this population through hospitals and rehabilitation centers, home-health care equipment stores, independent living centers and advocacy groups focusing on a particular aspect of aging or disability. Other contacts include lawyers and real estate agents.

STEP 2 - UNDERSTAND YOUR TARGET

The next traditional marketing step is to understand your target in terms of motivation, priorities and buying trends. Usually, this can be done through NKBA surveys, magazine surveys or consumer news.

You will want to expand your sources to research and publications that deal with the specific target. These might be special interest groups like the **American Association for Retired Persons (AARP)** or local and national magazines and newsletters or papers that target your same clientele.

Networking

Even more than with traditional bathroom design, networking is a key aspect of marketing universal design services and design for people with specific disabilities. The greatest single source of business is referral from past clients or from other professionals. If a person's occupational therapist or a friend or family member with a similar disability refers the person to you, there is a confidence or trust initiated.

Team Approach

A team approach may be the key to expanding your penetration to this market and to the total success of each project. Beyond the familiar allied professionals, consider medical people, particularly occupational and physical therapists and rehabilitation engineers who are experts in adaptive devices and assistive technology. They will add to your credibility, expand the information available to you and open new avenues for networking.

To help you understand the nature of the role an occupational and physical therapist plays in the life of your clients, a description is listed for you here. These non-traditional, allied professionals are among new resources you can use.

Occupational Therapists

Occupational therapists help individuals with mentally, physically, developmentally or emotionally disabling conditions to develop, recover or maintain daily living and work skills. They not only help patients improve basic motor functions and reasoning abilities, but also compensate for permanent loss of function.

Their goal is to help patients have independent, productive and satisfying lifestyles.

Occupational therapists use activities of all kinds ranging from using a computer to caring for daily needs, such as dressing, cooking and eating.

For those with permanent functional disabilities, such as spinal cord injuries, cerebral palsy or muscular dystrophy, therapists provide such adaptive equipment as wheelchairs, splints and aids for eating and dressing. They also design or make special equipment needed at home or at work. Therapists develop and teach patients to operate computer-aided adaptive equipment, such as microprocessing devices that permit individuals with severe limitations to communicate, walk, operate telephones and television sets and control other aspects of their environment.

Physical Therapists

Physical therapists improve the mobility, relieve the pain and prevent or limit the permanent physical disabilities of patients suffering from injuries or disease. Their patients include accident victims and disabled individuals with conditions such as multiple sclerosis, cerebral palsy, nerve injuries, burns, amputations, head injuries, fractures, low back pain, arthritis and heart disease.

Therapists evaluate a patient's medical history; test and measure their strength, range of motion and ability to function; and develop written treatment plans. These plans, which may be based on physician's orders, describe the treatments to be provided, their purpose and their anticipated outcomes. As treatment continues, they document progress, conduct periodic re-evaluations and modify treatments, if necessary.

The Networking Concept

Professional networking can take place through professional and community involvement. Attending, participating and speaking at **NKBA** events, speaking to rehabilitation centers, visiting nursing associations or independent living centers, or participating in local advocacy and support groups are a few examples. These activities will give you contacts and information and allow you to promote yourself and get a clear picture of the group you are serving.

STEP 3 - FOCUSED ADVERTISING

The last step in the marketing process is to reach your target through focused promotions. You can write articles for newsletters or write your own newsletter and send it to past clients and professional contacts. Sometimes the advertising budget favors spending time instead of money, so speak to and write to these groups.

Maintain a mailing list and follow up on your contacts. Keep in mind that repeat business is more common in clients with disabilities or clients who are aging.

Remember that universal design skills will not only enable you to better meet the needs of a client with a particular disability, these skills will also enable you to design a bathroom that is safe and accessible to all people.

Use and sell these skills with your entire target market as one aspect of what makes your bathroom design services superior.

POST OCCUPANCY EVALUATIONS

One way to become better at what you do is through the **Post Occupancy Evaluation (POE)**.

Many firms conduct Post Occupancy Evaluations in an effort to broaden not only their own knowledge of design, but to expand their marketing potential. A Post Occupancy Evaluation is simply a way to evaluate whether or not your design solution actually solved your client's problems.

A systematic evaluation of your completed bathroom projects can tell you things you never imagined and prepare you for the next job you do.

Conduct the Post Occupancy Evaluation **four to nine months after the client begins using the room** on a full-time basis. This allows time for the client to use the storage, fixtures and equipment and for the room and the design concepts to be experienced under the demands of various usage.

Using the Design Survey

The Post Occupancy Evaluation is performed in person using the design survey you used to obtain the design criteria when you began the project. However, it is a good idea to plan for the Post Occupancy Evaluation at the time you close the sales portion of the job. **Explain what you would like to do, why you are doing it and why the clients' participation will be important.**

With the original design survey in front of both you and the client, read through the survey and re-direct the questions to your client. Client comments should be tape recorded (ask permission first) or recorded through note taking. This exercise will allow you and your client to re-examine the success of the project. You should add some additional questions that are unique to the job and that will assist you the next time you design a similar project.

These particular questions should address design features and the products used. *Did they like the special-height cabinets? Or the universally accessible features?*

Be sure to pay particular attention to what the clients say with regard to doing something differently if they could do it over again. Whenever possible, include all of the family members who use the space.

Learning the Impact of Your Design

During the Post Occupancy Evaluation process, you will receive information on the design, the products used and your clients' reaction to their new space. There is no better way to learn how your work impacts people's lives. You will learn if your design solved the problem and obtain qualitative information on specific products and features you find yourself using on a regular (or not-so-regular) basis. You'll be able to document user acceptance of design guidelines, colors, lighting techniques, new equipment and materials and more. If they had to choose those products or that design feature again, would they? This is what you really want to know. This information will be most valuable the next time a client wishes to use that product or incorporate that design element. Your professionalism will be

---

perceived as a real asset to a client through the decision-making process.

Through Post Occupancy Evaluations, bathroom firms that market themselves as service-oriented companies can expand their professional expertise while gaining important marketing information. By using Post Occupancy Evaluations in the planning process, you can justify your thought process through previous project documentation and experience. When information is documented, it instantly becomes credible. It is logical; it can be verified by others; and it is extremely difficult to dispel. Such experiences can yield rewards that advertising could never accomplish. Post Occupancy Evaluations will expand your expertise, involve your clients in the process and create repeat business for the future.

Over time, complete marketing strategies will become evident based on the types of work that you perform. You will be amazed at the uses for this information as you plan spaces and become known as the firm who specializes in service.

UNIVERSAL BATHROOM DESIGN CHECKLIST

GENERAL BATHROOM DESIGNER TIPS:

☐ Use *"Easily accessed"* storage - visible storage is good except where privacy is desired.

☐ Use non-glare finishes, especially for older eyes.

☐ Provide non-glare, adaptable lighting throughout the space to make area comfortable for younger and older eyes.

☐ Lower mirror and wall storage for people with limited reach range.

☐ Lighter colors are especially beneficial for older eyes, with contrast at fixtures or edges. There are iridescent inlay materials available.

☐ Lower windows allow a seated user to see outside.

☐ Non-skid floors are safer for people using walkers and crutches.

- A flush or nearly flush threshold is safer for visually/mobility impaired users.

- Use drawers and tambour units instead of doors to make access easier.

- Adjustable-height sinks are available for use by all.

- Use full-extension locking drawer glides for maximum accessibility, strength and safety.

- Have timers installed to insure that any fixtures or grooming equipment that should not be running will be automatically shut off.

- Automatic doors that open and close based on a pressure pad, or pocket doors improve mobility.

- Voice activated lights: *"ON"*, *"OFF"*, *"DIM"*.

- Lowered light switches controls, and outlets make it easier for children and people in wheelchairs to reach.

- Touch- latch cabinet doors eliminate the need to grasp knobs or pulls, especially a problem for arthritic fingers.

- Use wire or architectural pulls in lieu of knobs.

- Use lighted interiors on cabinets to aid in visibility.

- Install repairable surfaces in areas where surfaces may be scarred or scorched accidentally.

- Store heavy objects at the safest and most convenient height.

- Design your projects so that they do not appear to be clinical. Like anyone, people with disabilities deserve beautiful design and function.

- Provide a built-in step stool in the toe space to create a step for users of shorter stature.

- Lower accessories , towel bars, toilet paper holder, etc, to be within a more universal reach range.

- Always plan reinforcment in the walls around bathtub/shower and toilet for the possible later installation of addional grab bars.

- A cabinet on wheels can meet additional bathroom storage needs.

- Add a seat to help in transfer and dressing.

TOILETS

- [ ] A board or bench seat may help in transferring to the toilet.

- [ ] Choose a toilet with a seat at wheelchair height for easy transfer.

- [ ] Add a base under the toilet to raise the seat to wheelchair height.

- [ ] Elongated toilets are easier for aligning with a wheelchair.

- [ ] The flushing lever should be on the approach side of the toilet.

- [ ] A toilet in the shower is easily cleaned and doubles as a shower seat.

- [ ] Use a padded or non-slip toilet seat with a shower toilet.

- [ ] Plan the sink and mirror outside of the shower area.

- [ ] Add a flush lever extension to the toilet.

- [ ] Use a toilet paper holder with a controlled flow.

- [ ] Mount the toilet paper holder at 26" (66cm) high in front of the toilet.

- [ ] A recessed holder won't interfere with approach.

BATHTUBS AND SHOWERS

- [ ] Consider showers with curtains, not doors.

- [ ] Shower curtains should be longer than floor length to help retain water in the shower area.

- [ ] Padded vinyl shower seats can be slatted for drainage.

- [ ] Wood or textured vinyl backs on shower seat prevent sticking.

- [ ] Consider a fold-away shower seat for transfer from wheelchair.

- [ ] Choose an adjustable-height hand-held shower with a single-lever mix valve.

- [ ] Specify a pressure-balancing mix valve to prevent hot water surges.

- [ ] Insure that the diverter is a lever and within the universal reach range.

- [ ] The hand-held shower should detach from a wall mount with vertical adjustment.

- ☐ The flexible shower hose should be at least 72" (183cm) long.

- ☐ Some hand-held showers have a water volume control button.

- ☐ Make sure that the shower-head bar does not interfere with grab bars.

- ☐ For free hands, install a safety belt in the shower.

- ☐ Bathtubs with a flat bathtub bottom may offer more stability.

- ☐ Insure that the floor of the bathtub is slip resistant.

- ☐ Choose a lever type bathtub drain control.

- ☐ Choose a lever-type faucet.

- ☐ To wash your back, choose a pistol grip bath brush.

- ☐ Consider difficulty of transfer over deck mounted shower doors on a bathtub.

- ☐ Glass doors, even when tempered, can break easily.

LAVATORIES

- ☐ Recognize the impact on clear floor space of sinks with legs and pedestals.

- ☐ Insulate pipes under approachable sinks to prevent burns.

- ☐ Pressure-balancing levers prevent a sudden change in water temperature.

- ☐ Consider adding a spray at the lavatory for washing hair.

- ☐ Start your mix valve at a temperature of 115°F (46°C).

- ☐ Identify the edge of the lavatory with a colored strip.

- ☐ Use red on the hot water control and blue on the cold.

GRAB BARS

- ☐ Grab bars are generally located 33" - 36" (84cm - 91cm) high on back and side walls of bathtub/shower.

- ☐ Grab bars are generally located behind the toilet and on each side.

- ☐ Angled grab bars are very dangerous.

- ☐ Grab bars should not break or chip or have sharp or abrasive edges.

- ☐ They must not rotate within their fittings.

- ☐ The bar should contrast from the wall to ensure accurate vision.

- ☐ Use flat finishes, as glare may visually distort shiny grab bars.

- ☐ Special finishes are available for a sure grip.

Appendix 2

ACCESS

BATHROOMS

As part of a research and training development project, the Access Bathrooms were created by two teams of certified designers.

THE DESIGN TEAM MEMBERS

The designers were given a space, a client profile and the assignment to create an accessible bathroom within those parameters. The teams were made up of the following Certified Bathroom Designers.

- **Mary Jo Peterson**, CKD, CBD, Mary Jo Peterson Design Consultants, Brookfield, CT;

- **Ken Smith**, CKD, CBD, National Kitchen & Bath Association;

- **Jim Krengel**, CKD, CBD, Kitchens by Krengel, St. Paul, MN;

- **Joy Piske**, CKD, CBD, Winnipeg, MB, Canada.

These two project descriptions and the resulting design solutions are featured here for your review. You will notice that not all of the *" 41 Bathroom Planning Guidelines"* were met in every instance. It is important to remember that the guidelines are there for you as a designer to use as a *"measurement"* to assimilate a competency. **It is not always possible to meet every guideline.**

ACCESS PROJECT #1
JASON'S BATH

CLIENT PROFILE

Sally and Tom Edwards have three children, the oldest being Jason, age 18, who was involved in a car accident and has no use of his legs. As a family, they have decided to remodel the main floor bedroom and bathroom to be Jason's room. Jason intends to go on to college in a year and may move away from home, but this plan will provide him with a room whenever he is home.

Jason uses a wheelchair and has full use and strength in his upper body. He is able to transfer using his tremendous upper body strength and coordination, and enjoys most moving in generous spaces.

The family would like the new bathroom to be spacious and contemporary, and to include bathtub and shower options, either as one unit or as separate units. There is a need for closed storage of some equipment that Jason uses for personal hygiene, and open storage for the usual bathroom gear.

The intended space is the existing bathroom and closet. The walls separating the closet from the existing bathroom and surrounding the shower may be removed. The wall between these spaces and the bedroom may be moved as far as the bedroom window, and somewhere in that space, a new closet must be provided. Any plumbing can be moved, but it would be best not to move the toilet.

The Shower Area

The 36" x 36" (91cm x 91cm) transfer shower provides easiest use for Jason. He will roll next to the shower, adjust the controls (set off center towards the room) and then backup to make a parallel transfer onto the shower seat. This will be done using his wheelchair and the shower grab bars for support. The decorative shower curtain then is pulled for his shower.

The shower may also be used by standing persons by flipping up the seat, or if desired they may flip it down and shower in a seated position. The pressure balanced temp control will prevent any risk of burning.

Bathtub Area

Offset controls (set closer to room) allow for ease in filling the bathtub with water. If assistance is desired, the dignity bathtub allows Jason or others to transfer to the built in transfer seat. Once on the seat, Jason would rotate into the bathtub and lower himself hydraulically.

Once in the bathtub, Jason can activate the whirlpool by the air switch located in the front side of the bathtub. A second control and hand-held spray allows for refilling or warming of the bathtub during use.

The beauty of this particular bathtub is that in a lowered position the seat is totally flush with the bottom of the bathtub, unusual in lifts and providing ease of use and comfort for anyone wishing to bathe.

In the bathtub area grab bars and hand rails are provided for safe and easy maneuvering. An additional grab bar is to be used as a towel bar. The windows in the bathtub area open by remote control, convenient for anyone given the bathtub location. The deck area provides convenient towel storage/display.

From the bathtub, moving towards the toilet and personal hygiene area, grab bars in brass, non-slip finish line the walls, creating a chair rail effect and allowing for assistance at any point. The rolling storage provides for Jason's personal hygeine needs and can be moved easily to be adjacent to the toilet with built-in bidet. This toilet was chosen for its height which suits Jason. A second grab bar mounted below the standard grab bar serves as a tower bar. This application eliminates the risk of Jason using an accessory installed to hold towels as a grab bar. In other words, **every horizontal bar in the room, whether intended for towels or support has been installed to support Jason's weight.**

In the vanity area, storage includes drawers on full extension slides and open shelves within Jason's reach range. The higher section of the tall vanity cabinet provides additional storage behind a door.

The vanity counter has been placed at 32" (81cm), a universal height with an apron and a decorative protective panel to house the plumbing.

The sink is 6 1/2" (17cm) deep with a rear drain and lever faucets to facilitate universal access. The counter extends and angles back to provide generous work space, contributing to the rich and open feeling of the room while providing 51" (130cm) of clear kneespace for grooming.

Controls and switches are installed 44" (112cm) off the floor to the left of the entry allowing for separate controls of lighting in the shower (1) bathtub area (dimmer), vanity area (dimmer), toilet area (1), and general illumination (dimmer) as well as auxiliary heat/fan and a remote control for the windows in the bathtub area.

UNIVERSAL BATHROOM PLANNING

The floor, shower, bathtub area and counters are made of solid surface material for ease of care and slip resistance, as well as a rich look. The contrast borders add a decorative detail while also enhancing *way-finding* in the space.

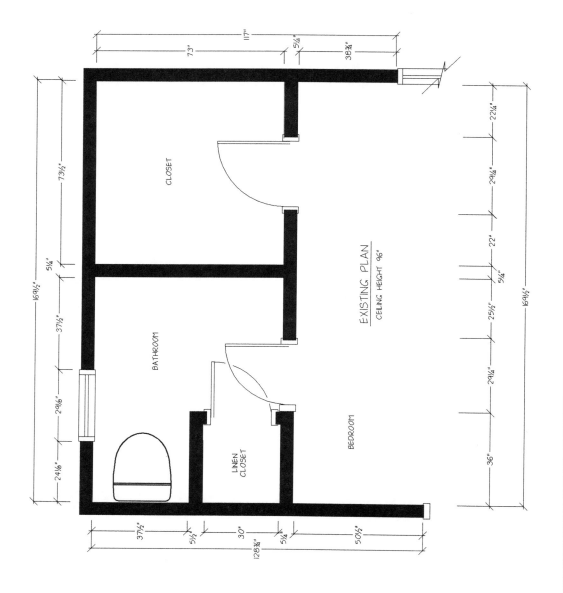

EXISTING PLAN

CEILING HEIGHT 96"

CLOSET

BATHROOM

LINEN CLOSET

BEDROOM

ACCESS Project #1 - JASON'S BATHROOM - Peterson/Smith, Designers

UNIVERSAL BATHROOM PLANNING

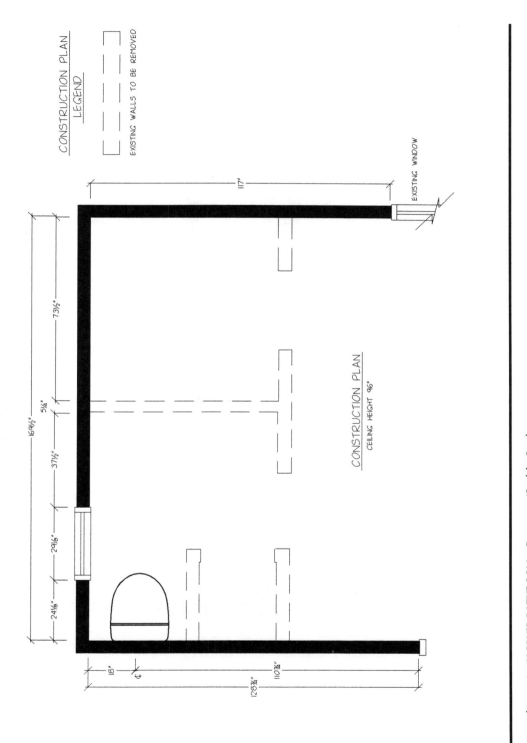

CONSTRUCTION PLAN
LEGEND

EXISTING WALLS TO BE REMOVED

117"

EXISTING WINDOW

73½"

5¼"

169½"

37½"

CONSTRUCTION PLAN
CEILING HEIGHT 96"

29⅛"

24⅛"

18"
₵

128¾"

110¾"

ACCESS Project #1 - JASON'S BATHROOM - Peterson/Smith, Designers

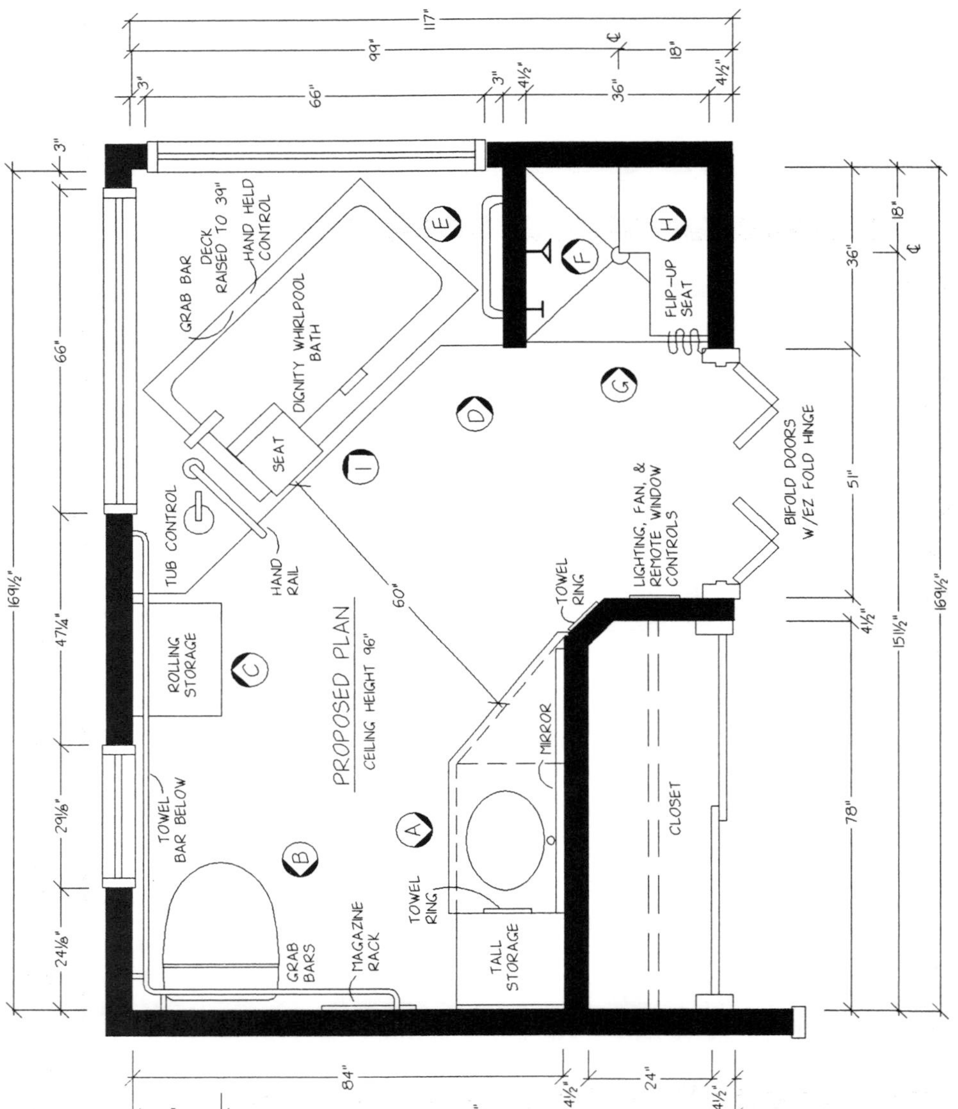

GRAB BAR
DECK RAISED TO 39"
HAND HELD CONTROL
DIGNITY WHIRLPOOL BATH
SEAT
TUB CONTROL
HAND RAIL
ROLLING STORAGE
TOWEL BAR BELOW
GRAB BARS
MAGAZINE RACK
TOWEL RING
TALL STORAGE
MIRROR
TOWEL RING
CLOSET
LIGHTING, FAN, & REMOTE WINDOW CONTROLS
BIFOLD DOORS w/EZ FOLD HINGE
FLIP-UP SEAT

PROPOSED PLAN
CEILING HEIGHT 96"

A B C D E F G H I

117"
99"
66"
3"
3"
4½"
36"
18"
4½"
169½"
3"
66"
47¼"
29⅛"
24⅛"
60"
36"
18"
51"
15½"
169½"
78"
4½"
18"
84"
99"
117"
4½"
24"
4½"

ACCESS Project #1 - JASON'S BATHROOM - Peterson/Smith, Designers

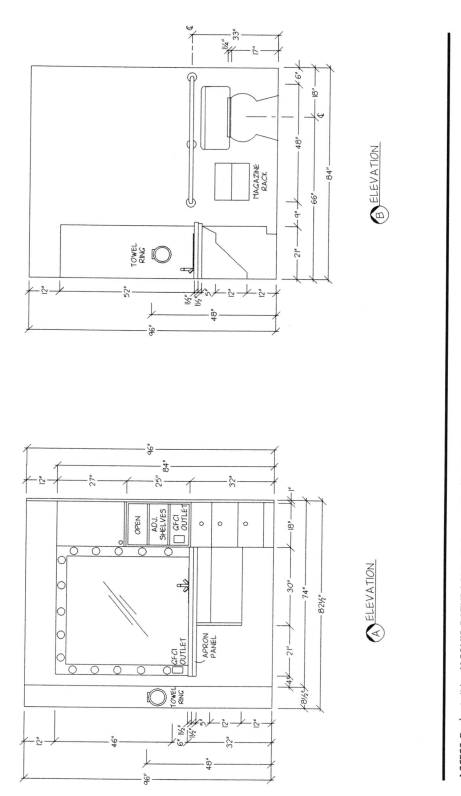

ACCESS Project #1 - JASON'S BATHROOM - Peterson/Smith, Designers

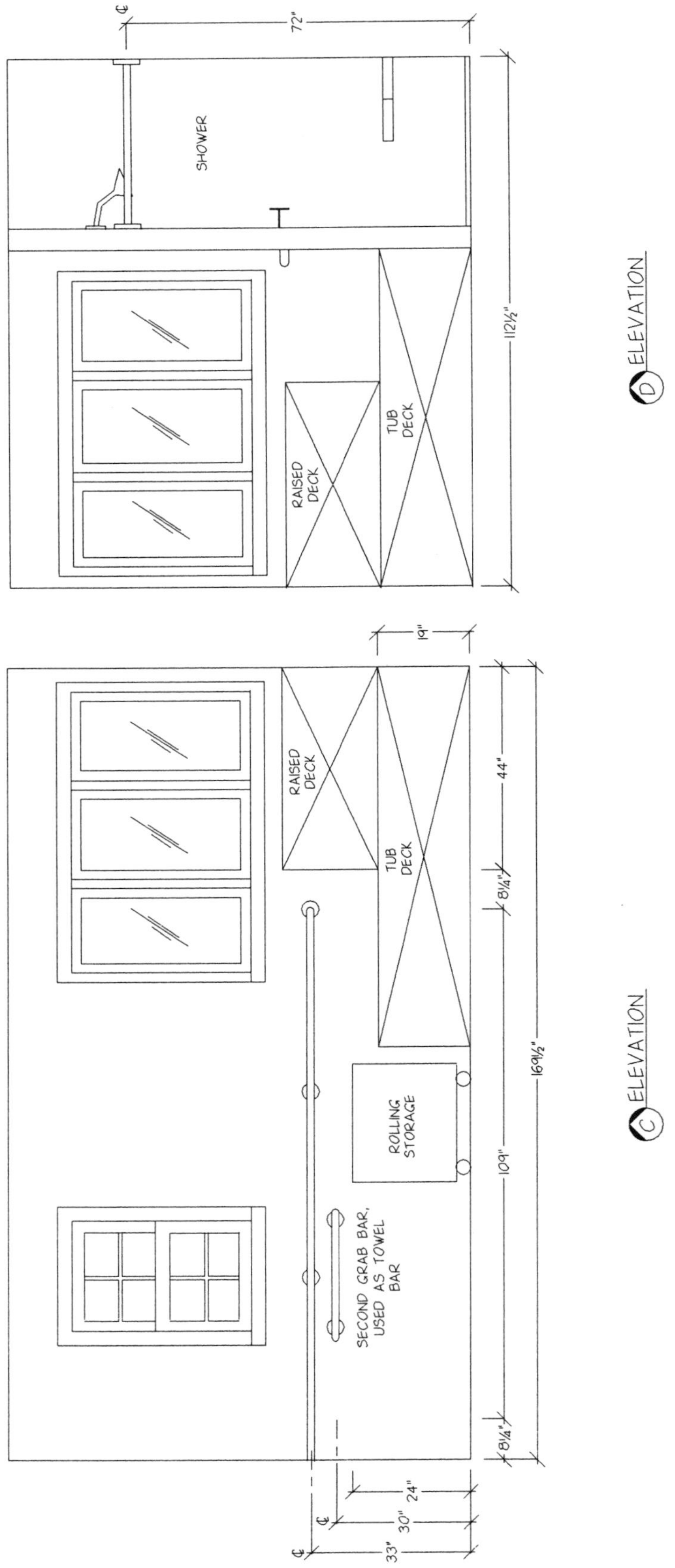

SHOWER

RAISED DECK

TUB DECK

72"

112½"

D ELEVATION

RAISED DECK

TUB DECK

SECOND GRAB BAR, USED AS TOWEL BAR

ROLLING STORAGE

19"

44"

8¼"

169½"

109"

8¼"

33"

30"

24"

C ELEVATION

ACCESS Project #1 - JASON'S BATHROOM - Peterson/Smith, Designers

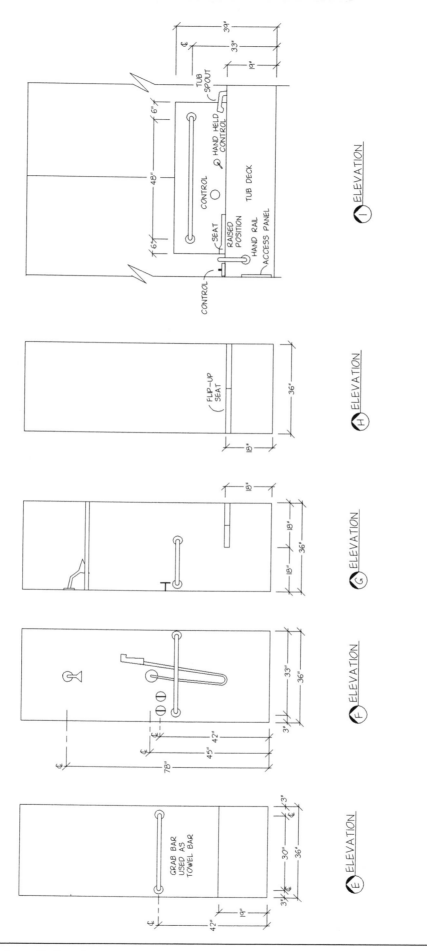

ACCESS Project #1 - JASON'S BATHROOM - Peterson/Smith, Designers

ACCESS PROJECT #2
THE SCHULZE BATHROOM

Client Profile

Howard and Nancy Schulze, age 60 and 54 years, respectively, are remodeling the hall bathroom and the master bathroom in their home. After living in their home since it was built 30 years ago, they are ready for a change, and as they have decided to remain in this home indefinitely after retirement, they want bathrooms that will meet their current and future needs.

They are happy to see the space gutted - in fact, the more change the better. They would like to borrow space from the hall bathroom to enlarge the master bathroom. They want the hall bathroom to provide a combination bathtub/shower, one sink and the water closet. They would like a fresh look and a smaller, safer space.

The focus of this project is the master bathroom. Howard would like a huge and wonderful shower and a whole new look. Nancy feels the same and does not look for more storage in the bathroom but stresses wanting a bigger and more open feel to the room. The basic needs are a water closet, one sink with minimum storage and no bathtub, but a fun shower.

Because the Schulze's plan to live here indefinitely and because Howard has recovered from a hip replacement and Nancy has the beginnings of arthritis, universal and accessible features are important, particularly in the master bathroom.

Increased lighting, decreased background noises, universal controls, safe surfaces, space for maneuvering and easy access to the shower must be incorporated.

While Howard and Nancy are truly fit and without limitations today, they wish to plan a space that is without barriers, not only for their present needs, but for varying needs of others and themselves in the future.

Design Statement

Howard and Nancy Schulze were easy to work with. We were able to achieve nearly all of their requirements due to their flexibility and positive attitudes toward life.

Since the master bathroom was the most important to both of them, we focused on this area, making certain to give them each of the items requested and provide them with a fun, functionally and aesthetically pleasing space.

The doorway was enlarged to accommodate a future wheelchair

when and if it should become necessary and a large floorspace (which isn't usually possible in a bathroom) to allow for a comfortable turn around of a wheelchair. The shower has been designed to allow a wheelchair to roll right into the space, and the vanity features an attractive open space below it so that a future wheelchair can be used if necessary.

Due to Howard's hip replacement and also for the sake of good universal design, a sit down area has been planned in the shower. The large space will accommodate both Howard and Nancy as they still enjoy intimate time together. The shelf in the shower will hold items frequently used without bending, and the glass block will allow additional light into the shower space.

Both the shower and toilet areas feature grab bars in new, fun colors. Both Howard and Nancy like the idea of something other than chrome because chrome looks too institutional to them.

The floor is non-slip tile that will be maintenance free. The cabinets have pulls and also are in a light finish. There is both general lighting in the bathroom, a light above the toilets for reading, a light in the shower and lighting on both sides and above the mirror.

The biggest controversy was removing part of the closet. Howard finally agreed that the smaller closet would become his in order to have a larger bathroom.

The shower features several showerheads as well as pressure-balancing valves to eliminate the possibility of scalding.

The hall bathroom has been reduced dramatically in size, but since the children are gone there is little need for the additional space. Howard hardly ever uses a bathtub, but Nancy likes to luxuriate in a bathtub from time to time, and they both agree that a bathtub is important when they are not feeling well. The bathtub and toilet feature grab bars and the bathtub fittings have anti-scald controls.

Both vanities have been specified as 34" (86cm) finished height for ease of use. Pocket doors will be used in both areas to conserve space and provide for additional safety because many bathroom accidents involve a person falling against a door.

These bathroom modifications will enable them to live both comfortably and safely in the home that they have grown to love.

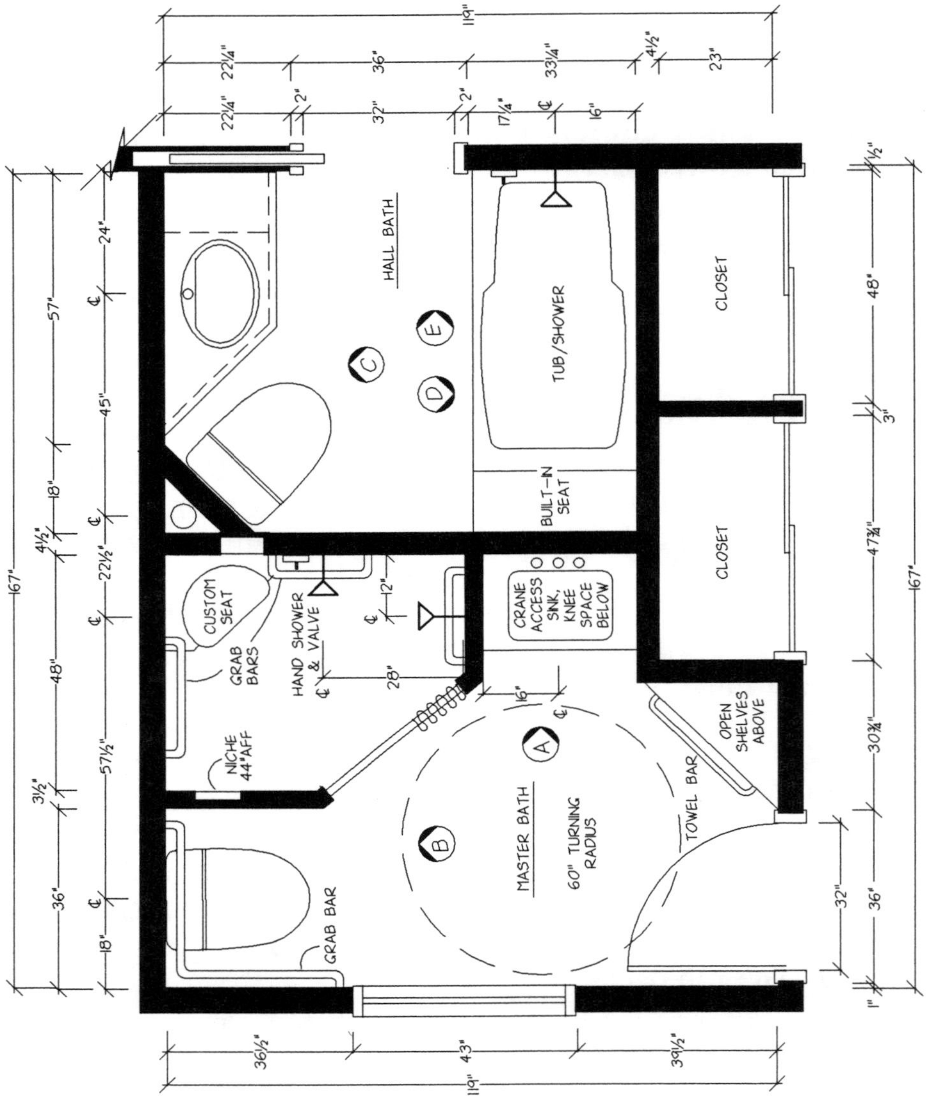
HALL BATH
TUB/SHOWER
CLOSET
CLOSET
BUILT-IN SEAT
CRANE ACCESS SINK, KNEE SPACE BELOW
CUSTOM SEAT
GRAB BARS
HAND SHOWER & VALVE
NICHE 44"AFF
MASTER BATH
60" TURNING RADIUS
TOWEL BAR
OPEN SHELVES ABOVE
GRAB BAR
A
B
C
D
E
167"
119"

ACCESS Project #2 - THE SCHULZE BATHROOM - Krengel/Piske, Designers

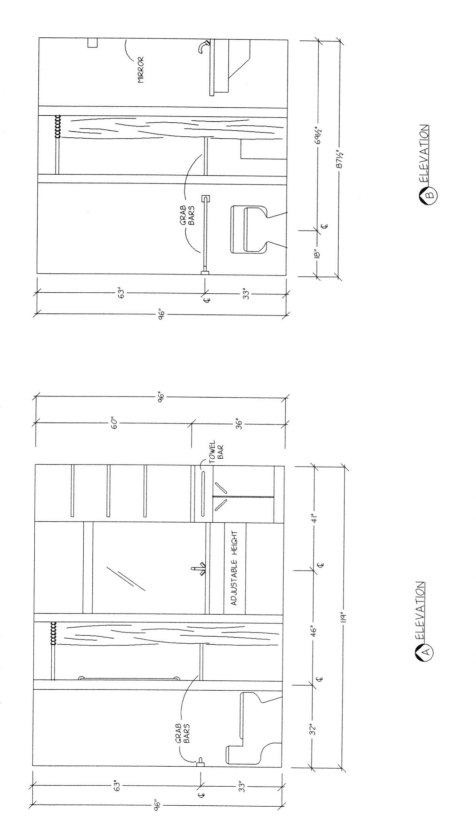

ACCESS Project #2 - THE SCHULZE BATHROOM - Krengel/Piske, Designers

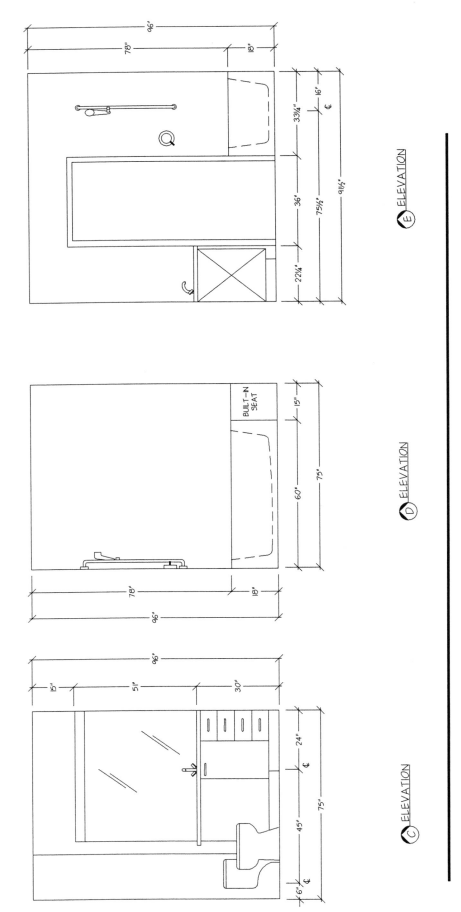

E ELEVATION

D ELEVATION

C ELEVATION

ACCESS Project #2 - THE SCHULZE BATHROOM - Krengel/Piske, Designers

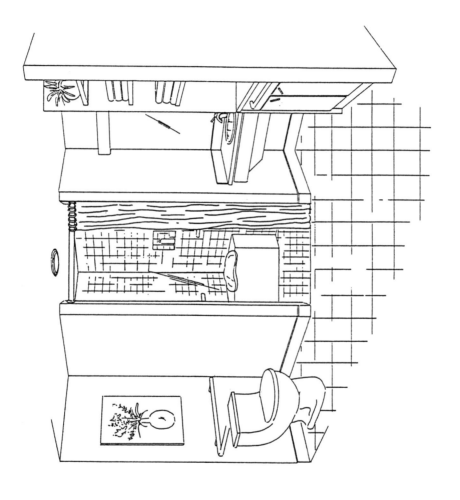

ACCESS Project #2 - THE SCHULZE BATHROOM - Krengel/Piske, Designers

LAWS

AND

STANDARDS

At this time there are no laws regulating universal design in private, single-family homes. There are, however, laws and standards that serve as a starting point in designing universal spaces, plus local and state codes that impact residential construction. The main laws and standards are outlined here.

ARCHITECTURAL BARRIERS ACT

In 1968, the **Architectural Barriers Act** was passed to regulate buildings used or funded by the federal government. The **Uniform Federal Accessibility Standards (UFAS)** were published in 1984. The purpose of UFAS was to set *"uniform standards for the design, construction and alteration of buildings so that physically handicapped persons will have ready access to and use of them in accordance with the **Architectural Barriers Act**."* UFAS represented the most comprehensive standard to that date and was a good effort to minimize the differences among the federal standards and the access standards recommended for facilities that did not fall under the **Architectural Barriers**

Act. The technical provisions of UFAS were for the most part the same as the 1980 edition of the **American National Standards Institute A117.1**, *"Specifications for Making Buildings and Facilities Accessible to and Usable by Physically Handicapped People."*

FAIR HOUSING AMENDMENTS ACT

In 1988, the **Fair Housing Amendments Act** was passed into law as an amendment to the **Civil Rights Act** of 1968. The **Civil Rights Act** prohibited discrimination in sale, rental, or financing of dwellings based on color, religion, sex or national origin. The **Fair Housing Amendments Act (FHA)** added people with disabilities and people with children to the list. In 1991, the **Final Fair Housing Accessibility Guidelines** were published to *"provide builders and developers with technical guidance on how to comply with the specific accessibility requirements of the Fair Housing Amendments Act of 1988."* This standard and law applies to multi-family construction where there are four or more units under one roof. While the requirements of the law are mandatory, these precise guidelines are not: *"Builders and developers may choose to depart from the Guidelines and seek alternate ways to demonstrate that they have met the requirements of the Fair Hous-*

ing Act." The Act provides that *"compliance with ANSI 117.1 or with local laws that required accessibility, would be adequate."*

AMERICANS WITH DISABILITIES ACT

In 1990, the **Americans with Disabilities Act (ADA)** was passed into law, requiring non-discrimination in many areas of life against people with disabilities. Title II of the Act relates to places of state and local governments (federal continues to be regulated by UFAS) and Title III relates to places of public accommodation and services operated by private enterprises. In 1991, the **ADA Accessibility Guidelines (ADAAG)** were produced to set *"guidelines for accessibility to places of public accommodation and commercial facilities by individuals with disabilities."* At this time ADAAG does not cover private residences.

AMERICAN NATIONAL STANDARD FOR ACCESSIBLE AND USABLE BUILDINGS AND FACILITIES

First issued in 1961, the current **ANSI Standard for Accessible and Usable Buildings and Facilities (A117.1)** was revised in 1992. This standard was created as a model code *"for adoption by government agencies and for organizations set-*

ting model codes to achieve uniformity in the technical design criteria in building codes and other regulations." It is also intended to provide technical design guidelines to make buildings and facilities accessible to and usable by persons with physical disabilities. It is in compliance with or is the basis for much of the information given in the other standards. And it includes information relating to the kitchen and the bathroom, among other things.

This brief overview on most of the major laws and guidelines regarding accessibility should help clarify how they relate to bath design. Tremendous research and involvement on local, state and national levels have led to these guidelines, and it is not the intent of this chapter to create *"experts"* on these laws and codes. If a situation arises that may be covered, contact the appropriate agency and work from their guidance. In most cases, information and some amount of technical assistance are free.

In addition, these laws and codes and the organizations that developed them provide minimum guidelines and space requirements. It is important to note that these standards are minimums and not hard-and-fast rules. They will serve as a basis

from which to expand and create truly universal bathrooms.

ARCHITECTURAL AND TRANSPORTATION BARRIERS COMPLIANCE BOARD

The **Architectural and Transportation Barriers Compliance Board**, known as the **Access Board** was established to ensure compliance with the **Architectural Barriers Act**. In addition, the **Access Board** was given authority to develop minimum standards of accessibility and to provide technical assistance. It is a great source of information and clarification on standards relating to accessibility. In addition, sources for obtaining and gathering information about the laws and guidelines are cited in *Appendix 4*.

Today there is a trend toward greater and greater uniformity among the various codes and guidelines, and the **ANSI** code is referred to most often. It is again in the review process for possible revision. The **Access Board** states as a goal that the **ADAAG** will be constantly revised and improved to insure its effectiveness. Proposed changes to **ADAAG** include a section on residential housing, including bathrooms for public housing covered under Title II.

Appendix 4

PRODUCTS SOURCES AND RESOURCES

In designing a universal bathroom, some new and some existing products will be used. The single-lever faucet is an example of an existing product that has always worked well in terms of universal use. Sometimes an existing product can be worked into a design in a non-traditional way. To be universal in use, the same faucet located to one side of a sink instead of at the back will put it within reach of more users. Finally, there are a number of products new to the market that have been designed for universal use.

The Importance of Reliable Sources

To maintain a complete and current file of the new products on the market would be nearly impossible. Technology and a growing awareness of universal design are bringing new products and new twists on existing products on an almost daily basis. Because of this, it is important to have good sources for information and a method for evaluating new products.

To become aware of new products relating to universal design, there are several existing sources of information listed later in this appendix. Among them, three are particularly useful.

- **Abledata** is a database on products for people with disabilities. Information is available by purchasing the program or for a small charge by calling Abledata directly. When you provide them with a description of needs or the desired product, they will give you information on the manufacturers in their databank who produce such a product along with general pricing.

- The **1995 Accessible Building Product Guide** is a current listing compiled by Universal Designers and Consultants.

- **NKBA's Enabling Products II - A Sourcebook** lists current products that are universal in design. The information in this book is compiled by an organization, ProMatura, that does market and product research relating to the mature market with clients including consumer product/service companies and senior housing developers. While no single source can encompass this con-

stantly changing product base, this book offers a tremendous amount of specific product information.

Listed at the back of this chapter are business and educational research service centers focusing on universal design. They can help to first identify new products and equally important, to help evaluate them.

Once a possible product has been identified, it must be evaluated. This becomes particularly important with products that are new to the market and somewhat untested or unfamiliar. Along with the obvious, consider the level of technology involved.

Although technology can provide amazing options, the less complex a product, the easier it will be to use and maintain. If a client lacks a comfort level with a product, it will not be used. To that end, provide opportunities for the client to test-use the product when possible. If this is not possible, network to find others who have used the product. They may be other designers, referrals from the manufacturer or distributors, or other related professionals. Manufacturers may have independent market research on the product.

The following product evaluation guide lists points to consider in the evaluation process.

PRODUCT EVALUATION GUIDE

I   **The Process**

    A.   Determine the task to be done

    B.   Assess client abilities (use survey)

    C.   Evaluate Product/Technology

        1.   What does it do and what can't it do?

        2.   How complicated is it?

        3.   How does it compare to its competitors?

        4.   Ask opinion of others on your team (doctor, therapist, supplier)

        5.   Ask other designers

        6.   Ask for formal evaluation results

        7.   Ask where the product is sold

II.   **Points to Consider**

    A.   Installation (can it be installed to meet client needs)

    B.   Safety (general and added checks - auto shutoff)

    C.   Design (least amount of energy used)

    D.   Cuing (size of graphics, dual cuing)

    E.   Color and Contrast for Visibility

    F.   Maintenance (who, what, how often, how expensive)

    G.   Reach Range and Line of Sight

    H.   Comfort Zone (appearance, location, ease of use)

    I.   Time on Market, warranty, reliability of manufacturer

    J.   Specifications (match with client

RESOURCES

There are numerous resources, in print and through people and agencies specializing in universal design and design for people with various disabilities.

This resource list is divided into printed materials, other sources of information, and suggestions for obtaining information in your area.

SECTION 1
Books and Printed Materials

☐ Accent on Living, Directory of Products, Sources, Organizations and Dealers. Available from Cheever Publishing, Inc., RR2 Gillum Road and High Drive, P.O. Box 700, Bloomington, Il, 61704. 309-378-2961

☐ The Accessible Bathroom. Host. Jablonski, Lori, and Nickels, Karen, 1991. Available from Design Coalition, Inc., 2088 Atwood Ave., Madison, WI, 53704. 608-246-8846

☐ Access Information Bulletins. Available from National Advocacy Program, Paralyzed Veterans of America, 801 18th Street, NW, Washington, DC 20006. 202-872-1300

☐ Accessible Environments: Toward Universal Design. Mace, Ron, Graeme Hardie and Jaine Place. Available from Center for Universal Design, NCSU, Box 8613, Raleigh, NC 27695. 800-647-6777

☐ Accessibility Reference Guide, An Illustrated Commentary on U.B.C. Chapter 31 and CABO/ANSI A117.1-1992. International Conference of Building Officials (IBCO). Available from the ICBO Order Department at, 5360 Workmenmill Road, Whittier, CA 90601. 310-692-4226

☐ The Accessible Housing Design File. Barrier Free Environments, Inc., New York: Van Nostrand Reinhold, 1991. Available from International Thomson Publishing, 7625 Empire Drive, Florence, KY 41042. 800-842-3636

☐ Adaptable Housing. U.S. Department of Housing and Urban Development, 1987. Available from HUD User, P.O. Box 6091, Rockville, MD 20850. 301-251-5154 or 800-245-2691

☐ Aging in the Designed Environment. Christenson, M., New York: Haworth Press, 1990. Available from Haworth Press, 10 Alice Street, Binghamton, NY 13904. 800-342-9678

☐ American National Standard - Accessible and Usable Buildings and Facilities (ANSI A117.1-1992). Available from Council of American Building Officials, 5203 Leesburg Pike, #708, Falls Church, VA 22041. 703-931-4533

☐ Americans with Disabilities Act Guidelines for Buildings and Facilities, 1992. Available from Architectural and Transportation Barriers Compliance Board, 1331 F Street, NW, Suite 1000, Washington, DC 20004. 800-872-2253 or 202-514-0301

☐ The Arts and 504: A 504 Handbook for Accessible Arts Programming. Available from Office for Special Constituencies, National Endowment for the Arts, 1100 Pennsylvania Ave., NW, Washington, DC 20506. 202-682-5531

☐ Assistive Technology Sourcebook. Enders, A. & M. Hall, 1991, Available from RESNA Press, Washington, DC.

☐ Bathroom Industry Technical Manuals. Cheever, Ellen M., McDonald, Marylee, and Geragi, Nick, 1996. Available from the National Kitchen and Bath Association, 687 Willow Grove St., Hackettstown, NJ, 07840. 1-800-THE-NKBA

☐ Bathroom Lifts. Mullick, Abir. Available from Center for Inclusive Design and Environmental Access, School of Architecture and Planning, University of Buffalo, 390 Hayes Hall, Buffalo, NY, 14214. 716-829-3485

☐ Beautiful Barrier-Free: A Visual Guide to Accessibility. Leibrock, C., & Behar, S., 1993. Available from International Thomson Publishing, 7625 Empire Drive, Florence, KY 41042. 800-842-3636

☐ Benches and Seats. Mullick, Abir, Available from Center for Inclusive Design and Environmental Access, School of Architecture and Planning, University of Buffalo, 390 Hayes Hall, Buffalo, NY, 14214. 716-829-3485

☐ Building for a Lifetime. Wylde, M., Adrian Barron-Robbins and Sam Clark, 1994. Available from Tauton Press, Inc., 63 S. Main St., Newtown, CT 06470. 203-426-8171

☐ The Complete Guide to Barrier-Free Housing: Convenient Living for the Elderly and the Physically Handicapped. Branson, G.D., Available from Betterway Books, 1507 Dana Avenue, Cincinnati, OH 45207. 800-289-0963

☐ CAH Selected Readings List. Available from Center for Universal Design, North Carolina State University, Box 8613 Raleigh, NC 27695. 919-515-3802

☐ A Comprehensive Approach to Retrofitting Homes for a Lifetime. NAHB Research Center for HUD. Available from NAHB Research Center, 400 Prince George Blvd., Upper Marlboro, MD 20774. 301-249-4000

☐ A Consumer's Guide to Home Adaptation, 1989. Available from Adaptive Environments Center, 374 Congress St., Suite 301, Boston, MA 02210. 617-695-1225

☐ Design for Aging - An Annotated Bibliography, 1980-1992. Available from Aging Design Research Program, AIA/ACSA Council on Architectural Research, 1735 New York Ave., NW, Washington, DC 20006.

☐ Design for Independent Living: Housing Accessibility Institute Resource Book, 1991. Available from Center for Accessible Housing, North Carolina State University, Box 8613 Raleigh, NC 27695. 919-515-3802

☐ The Do-Able Renewable Home. Salmen, John P.S., 1991. Available from AARP, 601 E Street, NW, Washington, DC 20049. 202-434-2277

☐ E.C.H.O. Housing: Recommended Construction and Installation Standards. Available from American Association of Retired Persons, 1909 K Street, NW, Washington, DC 20049. 202-434-2277

☐ Enabling Products II - A Sourcebook. Wylde, M., 1995, Available from National Kitchen and Bath Association, 687 Willow Grove Street, Hackettstown, NJ 07840. 908-852-0033

☐ Fair Housing Accessibility Guidelines, US Department of Housing and Urban Development, 1991. Available from Fair Housing Information Clearing House, P.O. Box 9146, McLean, VA, 22102. 800-343-3442

☐ Fair Housing Design Guide for Accessibility. Davies, T.D., & Beasley, K.A., 1992. Available from Paradigm Design Group, 801 8th St. N. W., Washington, DC 20006. 202-416-7645

☐ The First Whole Rehab Catalog: A Comprehensive Guide to Products and Services for the Physically Disadvantaged. Abrahms, A.J. & M.A., Abrahms, 1991. Available from Betterway Books, 1507 Dana Avenue, Cincinnati, OH 45207. 800-289-0963

☐ Handbook for Design: Specially Adapted Housing, VA pamphlett 26-13, April 1978. Available from: Assistant Director for Construction and Valuation (262), Veterans Administration, 810 Vermont Avenue, NW, Washington, DC, 20420; 202-273-5400

☐ Harris Communications, Inc., 1995. Catalog products for people with hearing impairments. Available from: Harris Communications, Inc., 6541 City West Parkway, Eden Prairie, MN 55344-3248. 800-825-6758

☐ Home Safety Guide for Older People: Check it out, fix it up. Pynoos, J. and E., Cohen, 1990. Available from Serif Press, Inc., Attn: Melissa Junior, 1331 H Street, NW, Suite 110 Lower Level, Washington, DC 20005, 202-737-4650

☐ Housing Accessibility Information System. Available from NAHB Research Center, 400 Prince George Blvd., Upper Marlboro, MD 20774. 301-249-4000

☐ Housing as We Grow Older. Barner, P. (Ed.), 1992. Available from NRAES Cooperative Extension, 152 Riley-Robb Hall, Ithaca, NY 14853-5701.

☐ Housing Disabled Persons, 1990. Available from Canada Mortgage and Housing Corporation (CMHC), 700 Montreal Road, Ottawa, Ontario K1A OP7. 613-748-2068

☐ Housing Interiors for the Disabled and Elderly. Raschko, B., 1982. Available from International Thomson Publishing, 7625 Empire Drive, Florence, KY 41042. 800-842-3636

☐ Independence in the Bathroom, May, 1992. Available from The Rehab Engineering Center at the National Rehab Hospital and ECRI. 102 Irving Street N.W., Room 1068, Washington, DC 20010-2949. 202-877-1932

☐ Kitchen Industry Technical Manuals, Cheever, Ellen M.; DePaepe, Annette; Geragi, Nick; McDonald, Marylee, 1996. Available from National Kitchen and Bath Association, 687 Willow Grove Street, Hackettstown, NJ 07840. 908-852-0033.

☐ Lighting Kitchens and Baths. Grosslight, Jane, 1993. Available from Durwood Publishers, Box 37474, Tallahassee, FL, 32315.

☐ Low Vision Information, 1993. Available from The Lighthouse, Inc., 111 East 59th Street, New York, NY 10022. 800-334-5497.

☐ Mobile Homes: Alternative Housing for the Handicapped, 1976. Available from Barrier Free Environments, Inc., Highway 70 West, Water Garden, PO Box 30634, Raleigh, NC 27622. 919-782-7823.

☐ Open House Guidebook. Available from Canada Mortgage and Housing Corporation (CMHC), 700 Montreal Road, Ottawa, Ontario K1A OP7. 613-748-2068.

☐ Paraplegia News. Available from PVA Inc., 2111 East Highland, Suite 180, Phoenix, AZ 85016. 602-224-0500.

☐ The Perfect Fit: Creative Ideas for a Safe and Livable Home. Available from American Association of Retired Persons, 1909 K Street, NW, Washington, DC 20049. 202-434-2277.

☐ The Planner's Guide to Barrier Free Meetings, 1980. Available from Barrier Free Environments, Inc., Highway 70 West, Water Garden, PO Box 30634, Raleigh, NC 27622. 919-782-7823.

☐ Resources for People with Disabilities and Chronic Conditions. Available from Resources for Rehabilitation, 33 Bedford Street, Suite 19A, Lexington, MA 02173. 617-862-6455.

☐ The 1995 Accessible Building Product Guide. Salmen, John P.S. and Julee Quarve-Peterson, 1995. Available from John Wiley and Sons or from Universal Designers and Consultants, Inc., 1700 Rockville Pike, Ste. 110, Rockville, MD 20852. 301-770-7890.

☐ The Safe Home Checkout: Easy Assessment, Simple Solutions. Lisak, J., Culler, K., & Morgan, M., 1991. Available from Geriatric Environments for Living and Learning, 230 West North Ave., Suite 122, Chicago, IL 60610. 708-850-3195

☐ Transgenerational Design: Products for an Aging Population. Pirkl, James, 1994. Available from IOnternational Thomson Publishing, 7625 Empire Drive, Florence, KY 41042. 800-842-3636.

☐ Senior Housing News. Available from National Council on Senior Housing, NAHB, 1201 15th Street NW, Washington, DC 20005. 800-368-5242, x220.

☐ Staying at Home, Available from American Association of Retired Persons, 1909 K Street, NW, Washington, DC 20049. 202-434-2277.

☐ UFAS Retrofit Guide: Accessibility Modifications for Existing Building, 1993. Available from International Thomson Publishing, 7625 Empire Drive, Florence, KY 41042. 800-842-3636.

☐ Universal Design Newsletter. Available from Universal Designers and Consultants, 1700 Rockville Pike, Rockville, MD 20852. 301-770-7890.

☐ Universal Kitchen Planning Design that Adapts to People. Peterson, Mary Jo, 1995. Available from the National Kitchen and Bath Association, 687 Willow Grove St., Hackettstown, NJ, 07840. 800-THE-NKBA.

☐ Wheelchair Bathrooms. Schweiker, Harry A. (Jr.), 1971. Available from Paralyzed Veterans of America, 801 18th Street NW, Washington, DC, 20006. 800-424-8200.

☐ Wheelchair House Designs, 1989, Available from Easter Paralyzed Veterans Association, 75-20 Astoria Boulevard, Jackson Heights, New York 11370-1178. 718-803-3782

SECTION II
Other Sources

☐ **Abledata,** 8455 Colesville Rd., Suite 935, Silver Spring, MD 20910. 800-227-0216

☐ **Adaptive Environments,** 374 Congress Street, Suite 301, Boston, MA 02210. 612-695-1225

☐ **American Association of Retired Persons,** 601 E Street, NW, Washington, DC 20049. 202-434-2277

☐ **American Deafness and Rehabilitation Association,** P.O. Box 251554, Little Rock, AR 72225.

☐ **American Foundation for the Blind,** 11 Penn Plaza, Suite 300, New York, NY 10001.

☐ **American OT Association, Inc.,** 1383 Piccard Drive, Rockville, MD 20850

☐ **American National Standards Institute (ANSI),** 1430 Broadway, New York, NY 10018. 212-868-1220

☐ **Association for Safe and Accessible Products,** 1511 K Street, NW, Suite 600, Washington, DC 20005. 202-347-8200

☐ **Barrier Free Environments, Inc.,** P.O. Box 30634, Raleigh, NC 27622. 919-782-7823

☐ **Center for Accessible Housing,** North Carolina State University, School of Design, Box 8613, Raleigh, NC 27695-8613. 919-515-3802

☐ **Center for Inclusive Design and Environmental Access,** School of Architecture and Planning, University of Buffalo, Buffalo, NY 14214-3087. 716-829-3485

☐ **Disabled American Veterans National Service Headquarters,** 807 Maine Ave., SW, Washington, DC 20024. 202-554-3501

☐ **Disability Rights Education Defense Fund,** 1633 Q Street, NW, Suite 220, Washington, DC 20009. 202-986-0375

☐ **Eastern Paralyzed Veterans Association,** 7520 Astoria Blvd., Jackson Heights, NY 11370-1178. 718-803-3782

☐ **Hear You Are, Inc.,** 4 Musconetcong Ave., Stanhope, NJ 07874. 201-347-7662

☐ **Independent Living Research Utilization Project,** 2323 S. Shepard Street, Suite 1000, Houston, TX 77019.

☐ **Lifease,** 2451 15th St. N.W., Suite D, New Brighton, MN 55112. 612-636-6869

☐ **The Lighthouse, Inc.,** 111 East 59th Street, New York, NY 10022. 212-821-9200

☐ **Maddock, Inc.,** Catalog for orthopedic and ADL products, 800-443-4326

☐ **National Center for Disability Services,** 201 I.U. Willets Rd., Albertson, NY 11507. 516-747-5400

☐ **National Council on Independent Living,** 2111 Wilson Blvd, Suite 405, Arlington, VA 22201. 703-525-3406

☐ **National Eldercare Institute on Housing and Supportive Services,** Andros Gerentology Center, USC, University Park, MC-0191, Los Angeles, CA 90089.

☐ **National Institute on Disability and Rehabilitation Research,** US Department of Education, 400 Maryland Ave., SW, Washington, DC 20202.

☐ **National Rehabilitation Engineering Center on Aging,** 515 Kimball Tower, University at Buffalo, Buffalo, NY 14214-3079.

☐ **National Rehabilitation Information Center,** 8455 Colesville Rd., Suite 935, Silver Spring, MD 20910, 800-346-2742

☐ **North Carolina Assistive Technology Project,** 1110 Navaho Drive, Suite 101, Raleigh, NC 27609-7322. 919-850-2787

☐ **ProMatura,** 428 N. Lamar Blvd., Oxford, MS 38655. 601-234-0158

☐ **Sammons 1994 Catalog for Orthopedic and ADL products,** Sammons, PO Box 5071, Bolingbrook, IL 60440. 800-323-5547

☐ **Trace Research and Development Center,** 1500 Highland Ave., Madison, WI 53705.

☐ **Universal Designers and Consultants, Inc.,** 1700 Rockville Pike, Suite 110, Rockville, MD 20852. 301-770-7890

☐ **Volunteers for Medical Engineering,** 2201 Argonne Drive, Baltimore, MD 21218. 410-243-7495

SECTION III
Suggestions for Local Sources of Information

☐ Independent Living Centers

☐ Local chapter of advocacy groups. Easter Seals, Paralyzed Veterans, American Association of Retired Persons, etc.

☐ State Office of Disabilities - sometimes called Governors Commission or Council on the Rights of People with Disabilities, or Protection and Advocacy Program

TRANSFER

TECHNIQUES

Understanding how a person will approach and transfer to a bathtub, a shower, or a toilet/bidet will help the bathroom designer to make the best use of clear floor space in the bathroom.

The following information on transfer is taken from the **Accessible Housing Design File**.

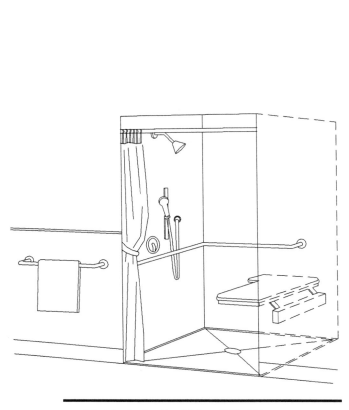

Molded plastic 36" x 36" (91cm x 91cm) Transfer Shower.

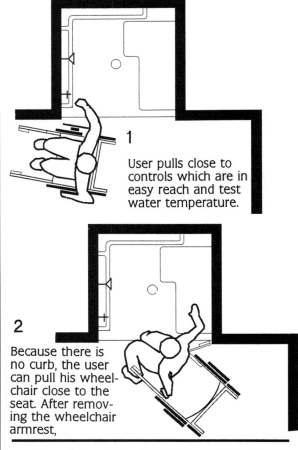

1
User pulls close to controls which are in easy reach and test water temperature.

2
Because there is no curb, the user can pull his wheel-chair close to the seat. After remov-ing the wheelchair armrest,

Use of the 36" x 36" (91cm x 91cm) Transfer Shower by wheelchair users.

3
the user transfers from his wheelchair to the shower seat. Trans-ferring is made easier and safer because the shower seat is gener-ally mounted at the same height as the wheelchair seat.

4
Using the grab bar for support, the user slides over to the corner where the shower walls provide lateral support. The size of the shower places the controls within easy reach. The grab bar pro-vides a place to rest the arm for those who can-not easily reach forward and backward.

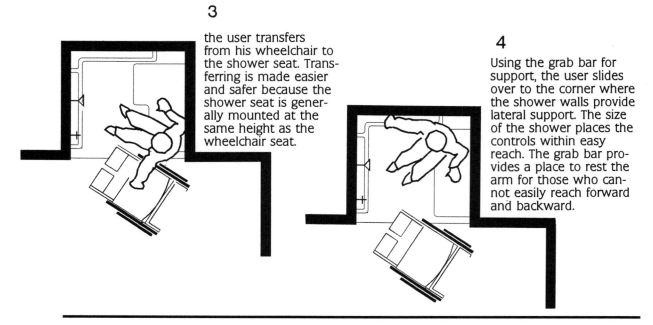

Use of the 36" x 36" (91cm x 91cm) Transfer Shower by wheelchair users.

PARALLEL TRANSFER ONTO A BUILT-IN TRANSFER SEAT FROM A WHEELCHAIR

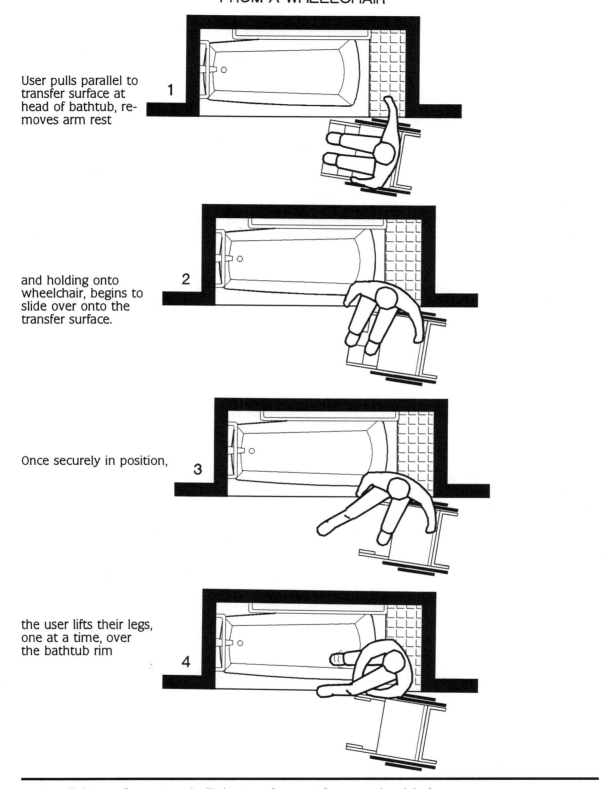

User pulls parallel to transfer surface at head of bathtub, removes arm rest

1

and holding onto wheelchair, begins to slide over onto the transfer surface.

2

Once securely in position,

3

the user lifts their legs, one at a time, over the bathtub rim

4

Parallel transfer onto a built-in transfer seat from a wheelchair.

and places them into the bathtub.

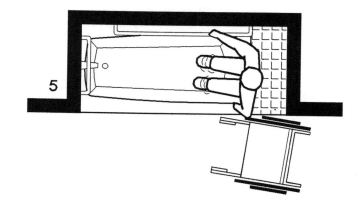

Gripping the grab bar and the
wheelchair for support, the
user slides forward on the
transfer surface.

Using the grab bar and the
bathtub rim, she lowers herself into the water

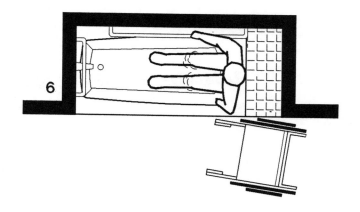

transfer from a wheelchair into a bathtub (continued).

FORWARD TRANSFER FROM A WHEELCHAIR INTO A TUB

User pulls close to bathtub, swings footrests to side, lifts legs over bathtub rim, and pulls chair tight to wall of bathtub.

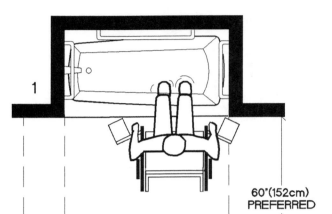

1

60"(152cm)
PREFERRED

12"–18"
(30–46cm)

60"(152cm)
MINIMUM

After sliding forward in his chair and onto the bathtub rim, the user reaches for the grab bar in preparation for transferring.

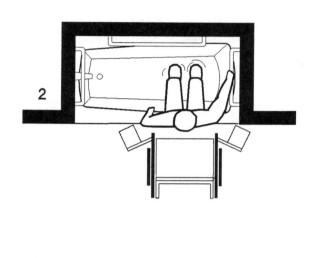

2

Grasping both the bathtub rim and the grab bar on the back wall, the user slides off the bathtub rim and lowers himself into the water.

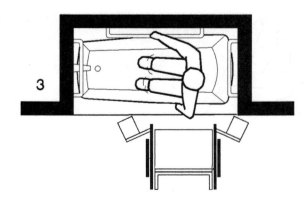

3

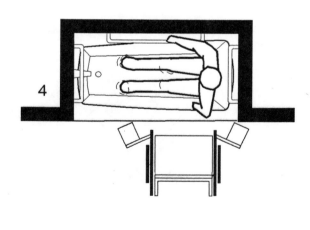

4

Forward transfer from a wheelchair into a bathtub.

DIAGONAL APPROACH

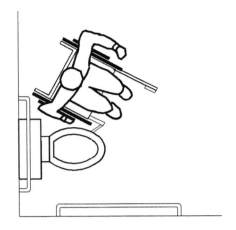 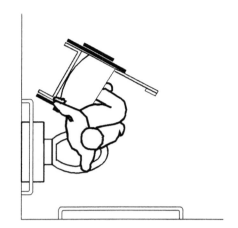

The user parks at a comfortable angle with the chair seat against the toilet.

After swinging the footrests out of the way and possibly removing the armrest, the user makes a sliding transfer using the grab bars and chair for support.

Common wheelchair to toilet transfer techniques. Diagonal approach.

REVERSE DIAGONAL APPROACH

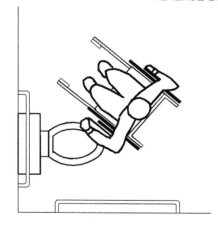 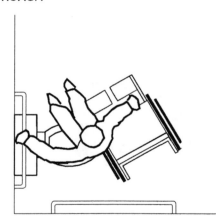

This method may be used to achieve a left-handed transfer in a right-handed room or vice versa.

Common wheelchair to toilet transfer techniques. Reverse diagonal approach.

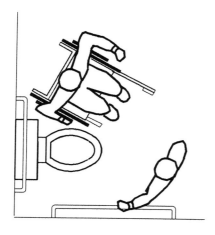
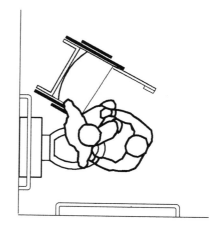

The user is positioned diagonally with the wheelchair seat close to the toilet. The attendant stands in front.

After swinging the footrest to the side, the attendant lifts the person to a standing position, rotates them, and places them on the toilet seat.

Common wheelchair to toilet transfer techniques. Diagonal approach with attendant assistance.

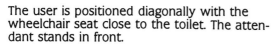

PERPENDICULAR APPROACH

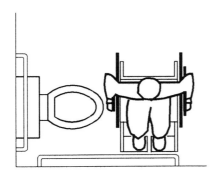

The user positions their chair at a 90 degree angle to the toilet, locating the wheelchair seat as close as possible to the toilet seat.

After removing one armrest and using the grab bar and toilet for support, the user makes a sliding and pivoting transfer onto the toilet seat.

Common wheelchair to toilet transfer techniques. Perpendicular approach.

Table of Illustrations

Bibliography

■ American Association of Retired Persons. <u>Understanding Senior Housing for the 1990's</u>. AARP, 1992.

■ American Association of Retired Persons and ITT Hartford, <u>The Hartford House - A Home for a Lifetime</u>, 1994.

■ American Foundation for the Blind. <u>Building Bridges</u>, 1993.

■ American Foundation for the Blind. <u>Aging and Vision</u>, 1987.

■ American National Standards Institute, <u>American National Standard - Accessible and Usable Buildings and Facilities (ANSI A117.1-1992)</u>, Council of American Building Officials, 1992.

■ <u>Americans with Disabilities Act - Questions and Answers</u>. US Equal Employment Opportunity Commission and US Department of Justice Civil Rights Division, 1992.

■ <u>Americans with Disabilities Act Title III Technical Assistance Manual</u>. US Department of Justice.

■ <u>Americans with Disabilities Act Accessibility Requirements</u>. US Architectural and Transportation Barriers Compliance Board (Access Board), 1991.

■ Barrier Free Environments, Inc. <u>Adaptable Housing</u>. U.S. Department of Housing and Urban Development, 1987.

■ Barrier Free Environments, Inc. <u>The Accessible Housing Design File</u>. Van Nostrand Reinhold, 1991.

■ Barrier Free Environments, Inc. <u>UFAS Retrofit Guide.</u> VanNostrand Reinhold, 1993.

■ Beasley, Kim, AIA. "Home Sweet Home." <u>Paraplegia News</u>, September, 1994.

■ Boyce, Peter, lighting designer, <u>Lighting Research Center, Renesslaer Polytechnic Institute</u>, Troy, New York. Interview.

■ Branson, G.D. <u>The Complete Guide to Barrier-Free Housing: Convenient Living for the Elderly and the Physically Handicapped</u>. Betterway Publications, Inc., 1991.

■ <u>Bulletin #5: Using ADAAG.</u> The Access Board, February, 1993.

■ Bureau of the Census, Housing and Household Economic Statistics Division. (statistics), November, 1994.

■ Bureau of the Census, Population Division, Age and Statistics Branch. (statistics), November, 1994.

■ Center for Accessible Housing. Fact Sheets.

■ Cheever, Ellen M.; McDonald, Marylee; Geragi, Nick; and DePaepe, Annette. Kitchen Industry Technical Manual, Volume 3, Kitchen Equipment and Materials. National Kitchen and Bath Association and University of Illinois Small Homes Council, 1993.

■ Cheever, Ellen M.; McDonald, Marylee; Geragi, Nick. Bathroom Industry Technical Manual, Volume 3, Bathroom Equipment and Materials. National Kitchen and Bath Association and University of Illinois Small Homes Council, 1992.

■ Cheever, Ellen M.; McDonald, Marylee; Geragi, Nick. Bathroom Industry Technical Manual, Volume 4, Bathroom Planning Standards and Safety Criteria. National Kitchen and Bath Association and University of Illinois Small Homes Council, 1992.

■ Christiansen, M. Aging in the Designed Environment. Haworth Press, 1990.

■ Cochran, W., Restrooms. Paralyzed Veterans of America, 1981.

■ Cullinan, Gould, Silver, Irvine. "Visual Disability and Home Lighting." Lancet March, 1979.

■ Cullinan, T.R. "Visual Disability and Home Lighting." Journal of Rehabilitation Research 3, 1980.

■ Dietsch, Deborah K. "Improve Gray Architecture." Architecture, October, 1994.

■ Eastern Paralyzed Veterans Association. Barrier-Free Design: The Law - Connecticut, March, 1992.

■ Federal Register - Volume 56, no. 144 ADA Accessibility Guidelines for Buildings and Facilities, 1991.

■ Federal Register - Volume 56, no. 44 Final Fair Housing Accessibility Guidelines, 1991.

■ General Services Administration, Department of Defense, US Department of Housing and Urban Development, and US Postal Service. Uniform Federal Accessibility Guidelines, 1988.

■ Grosslight, Jane. Lighting Kitchens and Baths. Durwood Publishers, 1993.

■ Hart, Leslie. "Design for Special Needs." Kitchen and Bath Business, December 1992.

■ Hiatt, Lorraine. "Effective Trends in Interior Designing". Provider, April, 1986.

■ Hiatt, Lorraine. "The Color and Use of Color in Environments for Older People." Nursing Homes, 1980.

■ Hiatt, Lorraine. "Touchy about Touching". Nursing Homes, 1980.

■ Hiatt-Snyder, Lorraine. "Environmental Changes for Socialization." Jounal of Nursing Administration, January, 1978.

■ Horton, Jules, lighting designer, Horton-Lees, 200 Park Avenue South, Suite 1401, New York, New York. Interview.

■ Jerome, Jeffrey, Director, and David Ward, Curator. Future Home. Tour and interviews, Phoenix, MD, June 1994.

■ Kiewel, Harold Dean, AIA, 4770 White Bear Parkway, White Bear Lake, MN, 55110. Interview - January, 1995.

■ Kira, Alexander, The Bathroom. Penguin Books, 1976.

■ Lehman, Betsy. "Making a House Livable for Elderly." Boston Globe, July 22, 1985.

■ Leibrock, C., & Behar, S. Beautiful Barrier-Free: A Visual Guide to Accessibility Van Nostrand Reinhold, 1993.

■ Leibrock, Cynthia. Easy Home Access, 1985.

■ Mace, Ronald L., Graeme J. Hardie and Jaine P. Place. Accessible Environments: Toward Universal Design. Center for Accessible Housing.

■ McKay, Hayden, lighting architect, Hayden McKay Lighting Design, 31 West 21st St., New York, NY. Interview - November, 1994.

■ Miller, Katie and Elizabeth Hite. Accessibilities for Everybody. University of Kansas.

■ Moore, Lois J. and Edward R. Ostrander, In Support of Mobility: Kitchen Design for Older Adults, Cornell University, 1992.

■ Mullick, Abir, Benches and Seats. Suny, Buffalo,

■ Mullick, Abir, Bath Lifts. Suny, Buffalo,

■ National Center for Health Statistics. (statistics), 1994.

■ National Council on Aging. (statistics), 1993.

■ National Council on Disability, ADA Watch - Year One, 1993.

■ New York State Rural Housing Coalition, Inc. "Designing Housing to Meet Special Needs." Rural Delivery, June 17, 1993.

■ Nissen, LuAnn, Ray Faulkner and Sarah Faulkner. Inside Today's Home. Harcourt Brace College Publishers, 1992.

Nolan, William and Joseph Boehm. "Forever Young." Better Homes and Gardens, October, 1994.

Null, Roberta. "Environmental Design for the Low Vision Elderly." Journal of Home Economics, Fall, 1988.

Paskin, Nancy and Lisa-Anne Soucy-Maloney, Whatever Works - Confident Living for People with Impaired Vision. Lighthouse, Inc., 1992.

Raisch, Marsha. "A Kitchen for All Seasons." Better Homes and Gardens Kitchen and Bath Ideas, Fall, 1994.

Rascho, B. Housing Interiors for the Disabled and Elderly. Van Nostrand Reinhold, 1982.

Research and Training Center on Independent Living, University of Kansas. Guidelines for Reporting and Writing About People with Disabilities. National Institute of Disability and Rehabilitation Research, 1987.

Rosenberg, Robert, O.D., Lighting and the Aging Eye, Lighthouse Low Vision Services, 1994.

Shapiro, Joseph. No Pity, Times Books, 1994.

Sit, Mary. "Home Sweet Home." Exceptional Parent's Guide for Active Adults with Disabilities, Spring, 1992.

Tetlow, Karin. "Contrasting Colors". Interiors, September, 1993.

Understanding Developmental Disabilities. Indiana Governor's Council on Development Disabilities.

United States Department of Labor, Bureau of Labor Statistics, Occupational Outlook Handbook, Beran Press, 1994.

White, Betty Jo; Mary H. Yearns; Glenda Pifer; Robert Null. "Future Environments: Forecasts and Issues." Journal of Home Economics, Spring, 1989.

Wrightson, William and Campbell Pope. From Barrier Free to Safe Environments: The New Zealand Experience World Rehabilitation Fund, Inc., 1989.

Wylde, M., Adrian Barron-Robbins and Sam Clark, Building for a Lifetime, Tanton Press, Inc., 1994.

Wylde, Margaret. Enabling Products II - A Sourcebook. National Kitchen and Bath Association, 1995.

Yepsen, Roger. "A Home for Life." Practical Homeowner, 1987.

Zola, Irving Kenneth, Ph.D. Living at Home - The Policy Convergence of Aging and Disability.

Index

Becoming one

WORKBOOK

D1463525

WORKBOOK

Exercises in
Intimacy

JOE BEAM

HOWARD
PUBLISHING CO.

Our purpose at Howard Publishing is to:
• *Increase faith* in the hearts of growing Christians
• *Inspire holiness* in the lives of believers
• *Instill hope* in the hearts of struggling people everywhere
Because He's coming again!

Becoming ONE Workbook © 1999 by Joe Beam
All rights reserved. Printed in the United States of America

Published by Howard Publishing Co., Inc.,
3117 North 7th Street, West Monroe, Louisiana 71291-2227

99 00 01 02 03 04 05 06 07 08   10 9 8 7 6 5 4 3 2 1

No part of this publication may be reproduced in any form without the prior written permission of the publisher except in the case of brief quotations within critical articles and reviews.

Library of Congress Cataloging-in-Publication Data
Beam, Joe.
    Becoming one : study guide : exercises in intimacy / Joe Beam.
      p. cm.
    ISBN 1-58229-079-2
       1. Marriage—Religious aspects—Christianity—Problems, exercises, etc. 2. Intimacy (Psychology)—Religious aspects—Christianity—Problems, exercises, etc. I. Title.

    BV835 .B365 1999
    248.8'44—dc21

                                                         99-047710

Managing editor, Philis Boultinghouse
Manuscript editor, Jennifer Stair
Interior design by Stephanie Denney
Cover design by LinDee Loveland

Author's Note: Because everyone's particular situation is unique, the ideas and suggestions contained in this book should not be considered a substitute for consultation with a psychiatrist or trained therapist.

Scripture quotations not otherwise marked are from the Holy Bible, New International Version. Copyright © 1973, 1978, 1984 International Bible Society. Used by permission of Zondervan Bible Publishers.

Contents

Intentional Intimacy

Intimacy.

If ever a word meant different things to different people, this is the one. Some see intimacy as sharing, bonding, and closeness. Others see it as a sexual encounter or some other special action involving two people. So what is intimacy? A feeling? A state of mind? A state of relationship? A specific set of actions? Or is it a combination of all these things and more?

If you want a clearer definition of intimacy, we suggest you read *Becoming ONE*, the book we designed this workbook to complement. In it we develop a detailed study of how two people become one spiritually, emotionally, and sexually. This workbook is most helpful when used in conjunction with *Becoming ONE*, but if you wish, you may work through just these exercises.

We've designed these exercises to help a man and woman learn how to develop the greatest level of intimacy possible for them. We anticipate that most people who take the time and expend the emotional energy to work through these exercises will be husband and wife teams, but the levels of intimacy of the couples who participate will be quite varied. Some may be very much in love but want to discover if there's anything more they haven't yet attained. Others may have mediocre marriages—at best—but are willing to work to make their marriages better if only someone will show them how. And finally, based on our experience at Family Dynamics Institute, we know that as many as a third of those who work through these exercises will be people who have given up hope. They come to this study not with anticipation but with resignation. "Let's try this one last thing before we call it quits. At least then we can walk away saying we've done all we could to save the marriage."

We strongly believe that people in all three categories will find this study a blessing, and many, if not most, will reach levels of intimacy in their relationship that they didn't know could exist. The only criteria is that a couple be able to communicate openly and honestly without getting into intense and painful arguments. If you can't communicate without rancor, we recommend you first complete Family Dynamics Institute's *A New Beginning* seminar to learn how to be "friends" before attempting to learn intimacy.[1] But for every couple who can be open and honest with each other, this workbook should take them to fulfilling levels of intimacy.

Does this claim seem a bit too bold? If we didn't have the track record we do, perhaps it would be. But thousands upon thousands of people have gone through our marriage seminars, and the number of participants continues to grow exponentially.[2] That not only gives us a lot of experience; it also gives us a great deal of insight and understanding. And it gives us a lot of confidence in the potential for increased love between husband and wife, no matter where they are in their relationship as they begin this study.

For those who work through these exercises as part of a *Becoming ONE* eight-week interactive course, the increased intimacy will be much greater. These couples will work through the appropriate exercises together and then spend two and a half hours each week in a fun, educational, and fast-paced class setting with eleven other couples. We've trained facilitators across the United States and Canada to conduct these eight-week seminars, and these facilitator couples know just what to do to make the class effective and powerful.[3]

A Disclaimer

Because most people will not be using this workbook as part of marital therapy, we, of necessity, only use tools that don't require professional interpretation. The simple tools we use are designed to help couples learn about God and each other and about how to increase intimacy in their relationship. Therefore, you shouldn't use any questionnaire, model, or exercise in this book to make an absolute determination about your relationship or future. We give you these exercises as suggestions to help you grow and learn, not as definitive, surgical tools for the removal of all that's bad in your relationship or implantation of all the good that should be there. We believe that the exercises in this book are good and helpful. But they are only tools, not the final authority or the be-all and end-all for your marriage.

Unless you are working through this material under the direction of a licensed marital therapist, don't view it as therapy. Even if you are enrolled in the eight-week *Becoming ONE* course—unless one of the facilitators *is* a licensed therapist and is *also* seeing you professionally—don't view the words or advice of your facilitator couple as the views or directions of a therapist. Your facilitator couple is interested in helping others grow and has a lot to offer you, but we didn't train them to be therapists, and you should not to view them as such.

Now, with that clear, it's time to begin.

Directions

1. Complete one chapter each week. If you follow that schedule, in just ten short weeks you'll have worked through this entire workbook. Why stay with so strict a regimen? Because some of these exercises will really make you think, and some of them will lead to sessions of unmasked sharing with each other. That can be emotionally draining at times, just as it can be emotionally exhilarating at times. If you take too long or don't follow a specific schedule, you'll never finish. Therefore, to gain the most from the exercises, make yourselves stay on schedule. If you're in the *Becoming ONE* class, the facilitators and other class members will help you stay motivated and on track.

2. Don't skip any exercises or chapters. Take things in order. Even when the reason for the order isn't apparent to you, be assured that we've designed these exercises to flow from one to the other. If you skip one, you may discover a few exercises down the line that ask you to incorporate information you wrote in a previous exercise. Obviously, if you've skipped the called-for exercise, you won't be able to complete the one you're currently working on. So please stay on track and stay in order.

3. Always write down your answers to the questions. It isn't good enough just to tell your spouse what your answer is. Good teachers and trainers understand this basic truth: You can talk without thinking, but you cannot write without thinking. The very act of writing your answers will take you to deeper levels of understanding of yourself, your spouse, and the principles for developing a more intimate relationship. This workbook provides lines for answering specific questions and a wide margin for taking notes as you think and work through the exercises.

In some chapters you'll notice that the exercises call for you to answer questions that are similar to questions you've answered in earlier chapters. Don't despair; that's by design. We know from our work with marriages that you will evolve in your view of these questions as you work through the ten chapters. As you grow in understanding each other, you should be sharing that growth and those evolving thoughts. The occasionally repetitive nature of questions about specific, important marital matters not only allows but also creates the right scenario for you to share your personal growth—whether gradual or rapid.

Have fun, and learn a lot. In just a few weeks you will have a greater level of love, devotion, and intimacy.

The Craving for Intimacy
God Created Us for ONEness

Everyone wants intimacy, even if our awareness of the wanting is weak. We all want intimacy with another human, and many of the things we do in life stem from that basic, unyielding desire. God made us to want intimacy, to need it. When He placed Adam on this planet by himself, He said that it was not good that the man should be alone.[1] He made Eve as the completion of Adam, which in turn made Adam the completion of Eve. Both the man and the woman had been formed "just so" as the Creator made them to join perfectly together into one flesh, one person.[2] He made us to want intimacy—ONEness—with another, and He designed us so that we could fulfill that craving in marriage.

Too bad that it doesn't always work out that way.

Any husband and wife can develop the intimacy God intended if they go about it correctly. But the truth of the matter is that only about one in four do. The other 75 percent of married couples want intimacy but don't know how to make it happen. Some of them remain married a whole lifetime, hoping that one day intimacy will come. Others just resign themselves to accepting what they have and being happy for the security of having a home and mate. But more and more people are leaving their marriages, refusing to accept the lack of intimacy and hoping to find it in the next relationship...or maybe the relationship after that.

At Family Dynamics Institute, we regularly hear from people who married with the anticipation of an intimate immersion into each other but, unfortunately, instead found themselves continuing to exist as two very separate people, protected and shielded from each other. They exist in a marital paradox of physical proximity and emotional detachment.

"I love him like a brother...but who wants to be married to her brother?"

"She's a wonderful woman, and she deserves the best in life. But that must mean being with someone besides me. We just don't 'click.' We should just admit our mistake and move on with our lives."

Sometimes it isn't quite that bad. Sometimes people tell us that they used to feel the ecstasy of intimacy in their relationship, but somehow, over the years, the fire has grown cold. These folks don't come with the defeatist attitude of those who've nearly given up; they come hoping we can show them how to regain what they've lost.

And happily, a large percentage of those who come to our seminars do so because they love each other and are relatively happy in their relationships. They don't come in desperation; they come for preservation. "What can you do to help us always love each other as long as we live? To grow even closer, if possible, than we are now so that we can have all that there is to have in a marriage?"

No matter which category you begin in—desperate, resigned, or relatively happy—we offer you a tool to learn to love each other more. A tool to develop more intimacy. A way to delve deeper into each other and explore the nuances of what it really means to be one flesh.

To get the most out of this experience, you each need to complete the exercises in separate workbooks as you simultaneously read the book *Becoming ONE*. We designed the two books to be used together. The exercises in this workbook are based on lengthier explanations and illustrations in the accompanying book. Even better, we hope that you work through these exercises as part of a *Becoming ONE* eight-week seminar. If so, you'll have eleven other couples working through these materials with you. You'll have fun in your two-and-a-half hour class session each week, and you'll learn greater levels of intimacy as you do your "homework" in the *Becoming ONE* book and this workbook.

Are you ready? Let's begin!

EXERCISE 1:
ESTIMATING YOUR
SATISFACTION LEVEL

Researchers into marital relationships sometimes use the Kansas Marital Satisfaction Survey, a tool that has been validated many times over. If you're enrolled in the *Becoming ONE* seminar, you completed that survey before your class session, and you will be asked to complete it again at the end of the course. Right now we want to use it a little differently. Rather than asking you to complete the survey in its entirety, we believe you may gain insight into your own relationship by answering just the last question. This isn't an "official" test, and you shouldn't view the results that way. This exercise is simply intended to give you a quick "checkup" or "snapshot" of where you *may* be in your relationship with each other.

Using the following scale, answer the following question with the appropriate number:

How satisfied are you with your relationship with your spouse?_____

1	=	extremely dissatisfied
2	=	very dissatisfied
3	=	somewhat dissatisfied
4	=	mixed
5	=	somewhat satisfied
6	=	very satisfied
7	=	extremely satisfied

In just a minute, we'll ask you to chart your answer on a four-quadrant scale like the samples below. But first, take a look at these samples and notice the relationship between the satisfaction levels of husband and wife and the quadrant in which their lines intersect.

In the sample charts below, the husband's score is 6 and his wife's score is 5. When we draw intersecting lines from each score on the husband's chart, they meet in the right upper quadrant—the "fulfilled" quadrant. When this couple plots their scores on the wife's chart, the lines will intersect in the same quadrant. When one is fulfilled, the other is fulfilled.

Sample Husband's Chart   Sample Wife's Chart

If, on the other hand, the husband scored a 6 and the wife a 3, he would fall in the "blind" category and she would fall in the "frustrated" category as illustrated on the next page.

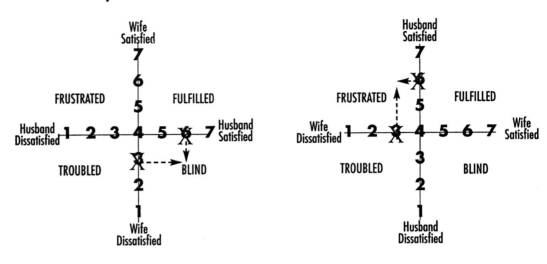

Sample Husband's Chart

Sample Wife's Chart

Any time one spouse charts into either the "blind" or "frustrated" areas, the other will naturally fall into the exact *opposite* area. If either spouse charts a "troubled" or "fulfilled" quadrant, the other spouse will chart in the *same* quadrant.

Share your satisfaction level with your spouse. Now, to get a picture of the "state of affairs" in your marriage, chart your satisfaction level and your mate's satisfaction level on the following four-quadrant scales.

Husband's Chart

Wife's Chart

Our chart might not be such an eyeopener to those in the "troubled" or "fulfilled" quadrants. Both husband and wife have an awareness of what's going on in the marriage. On the other hand, this chart may really be a shock to someone in the "blind" area. He or she *thinks* that things are going well in the marital relationship, but things are likely not going well if his or her spouse is "frustrated" in the marriage.

Why put you through this exercise?

So you can know your starting point. No one should live in ignorance of what is really happening in his or her marriage. If a problem exists—if intimacy isn't present—*both* of you should be aware of that, not just one of you. The "frustrated" spouse needs for the "blind" spouse to gain his or her "sight."

As you end this exercise, learn from it. If one of you scored in the "blind" quadrant, please don't show any hostility or anger toward your spouse. You will never know the truth about your relationship—or anything else of consequence, for that matter—if you make your spouse afraid to tell you the truth. Ask *why* your spouse is unfulfilled. Spend as much time as you need to ask questions of your spouse and to learn why he or she feels this lack of satisfaction. You may not like the answers, but you need to hear them.

After you've had plenty of time to talk with each other, answer all of the following questions that are applicable to you.

1. What did you learn that you needed to know about your spouse's satisfaction with your relationship?_____

_____

_____

_____

_____

_____

2. What areas, if any, did your spouse identify where you are failing to fulfill him or her?_____

_____

_____

_____

_____

_____

3. What specific things will you do to make your relationship the most fulfilling it can be?_____

_____

_____

_____

_____

EXERCISE 2:
THE NEED FOR INTIMACY WITH GOD

In the accompanying book *Becoming ONE*, we make the statement that to be close to each other you must first each be close to God. Let's see how that works. Please answer the questions below and share your answers with each other.

1. In the first exercise of this chapter, you each rated your satisfaction with your relationship with each other. In what ways do you believe your current personal relationship with God affected your spouse's satisfaction score? Be as specific in your answer as you possibly can._____
_____
_____
_____
_____

2. In what ways do you believe your spouse's current personal relationship with God affected your satisfaction score? Be as specific in your answer as you possibly can._____
_____
_____
_____

3. Being extremely honest, write a description of what you want your relationship with God to be like._____
_____
_____
_____
_____

4. Now, being just as honest, write a description of what you want your spouse's relationship with God to be like._____
_____
_____
_____
_____

5. Describe what you think would happen to your relationship if you and your spouse were to develop a deeper intimacy with God than you have now. Be as specific as you can._____
_____
_____
_____
_____

Now, share your answers with each other. It makes no difference who goes first—flip a coin if necessary—but one of you share your answers to question 1.

The other spouse may ask questions for clarification and understanding, but no arguing, debating, or disagreement is allowed. After all, when a person tells how he or she feels about a matter, that feeling is true, whether the other person wants it to be or not. Allow your relationship to grow by allowing true feelings to be shared without editing or hedging to avoid conflict.

When the first spouse finishes question 1, the second spouse should then share his or her answer. Follow this pattern until each of you shares your answers to all five questions.

EXERCISE 3: THE TRIANGULATION OF LOVE

In *The Psychology of Love*, one of the most enlightening books about the nature of love available today, Dr. Robert J. Sternberg presents a clear and helpful description of the three components of love between a husband and wife:

- *Decision/Commitment.* The short-term dimension of this component is the decision that you love someone. The long-term dimension is that you commit yourself to maintain that love. Interestingly, sometimes people get to the long-term dimension without experiencing the short-term. Without ever consciously making any decision to do so, they evolve into a relationship with strong commitment.

- *Intimacy.* Intimacy to Sternberg means closeness, connectedness, warmth, and bondedness. It has to do with understanding each other, accepting each other, and having open and intimate communication with each other. Obviously, intimacy carries emotion, but not the intense emotion of the next component.

- *Passion.* Sternberg defines passion as physical attraction, sexual desire, and other strong emotional attraction to another person.

To illustrate the three components, Sternberg placed them on his "Triangulation of Love" model.

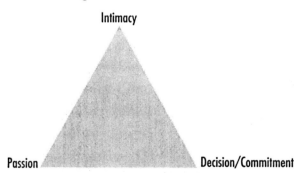

Triangulation of Love

Intimacy

Passion   Decision/Commitment

Dr. Sternberg also developed a scale to measure each of the three components of love and to help you learn which components of love you currently have for your spouse and how strong each component is.[3]

Begin this exercise by finding the answer charts labeled "Answers" (page 10) and tearing them out of your books (or copy them if you prefer). Then use the answer charts, (not the "statements" section) to rate each statement (from pages 8 and 9) on a 1 to 9 scale. Note that the blanks represent your spouse's name.

Each of you will rate each statement twice, with a different perspective each time. (Each answer page has special instructions to tell you the perspective you should use as you rate the statements.)

Rating the Intimacy, Passion, and Commitment You Feel

1	2	3	4	5	6	7	8	9

not at all   moderately   extremely

Statements

1. I am willing to share myself and my possessions with _____.
2. I idealize _____.
3. I plan to continue in my relationship with _____.
4. I value _____ greatly in my life.
5. My relationship with _____ is very romantic.
6. I view my commitment to _____ as a solid one.
7. I feel that _____ really understands me.
8. Just seeing _____ excites me.
9. I view my relationship with _____ as permanent.
10. I have a comfortable relationship with _____.
11. I find _____ to be very personally attractive.
12. I could not let anything get in the way of my commitment to _____.
13. I am actively supportive of _____'s well-being.
14. I cannot imagine another person making me as happy as _____ does.
15. Because of my commitment to _____, I would not let other people come between us.
16. I am able to count on _____ in times of need.
17. I would rather be with _____ than with anyone else.
18. I expect my love for _____ to last for the rest of my life.
19. I share deeply personal information about myself with _____.
20. I especially like physical contact with _____.
21. I cannot imagine ending my relationship with _____.
22. _____ is able to count on me in times of need.
23. I adore _____.

24. I feel a sense of responsibility toward _____.

25. I feel that I really can trust _____.

26. There is something almost "magical" about my relationship with _____.

27. I view my relationship with _____ as a good decision.

28. I receive considerable emotional support from _____.

29. I find myself thinking about _____ frequently during the day.

30. I am certain of my love for _____.

31. I feel that I really understand _____.

32. I cannot imagine life without _____.

33. I am committed to maintaining my relationship with _____.

34. I have a warm relationship with _____.

35. I fantasize about _____.

36. I know that I care about _____.

37. I communicate well with _____.

38. My relationship with _____ is passionate.

39. I have confidence in the stability of my relationship with _____.

40. I give considerable emotional support to _____.

41. Nothing is more important to me than my relationship with _____.

42. I will always feel a strong responsibility for _____.

43. I feel close to _____.

44. When I see romantic movies and read romantic books I think of _____

45. Even when _____ is hard to deal with, I remain committed to our relationship.

(See next page.)

If you would like to help us in a national study, please put your initials and number code on the following page. (See endnote 4 on page 109.)

Code_____
(initials + last 3 digits of
social security number)

Answers—Part 1 (*What You Feel Is Characteristic*)

Rate the statements from the previous section as to how *characteristic* they are of your relationship. In other words, to what extent does each statement reflect how you currently feel in your relationship? Write your answers using the 1 to 9 scale (on page 8) here:

1.	2.	3.
4.	5.	6.
7.	8.	9.
10.	11.	12.
13.	14.	15.
16.	17.	18.
19.	20.	21.
22.	23.	24.
25.	26.	27.
28.	29.	30.
31.	32.	33.
34.	35.	36.
37.	38.	39.
40.	41.	42.
43.	44.	45.
Total Column	Total Column	Total Column
Average	Average	Average

Answers—Part 2 (*What You Think Is Important*)

Now rate the statements as to how *important* they are to your relationship. In other words, to what extent do you feel it is important that you should feel this way, regardless of how you actually feel? Write your answers using the 1 to 9 scale here:

1.	2.	3.
4.	5.	6.
7.	8.	9.
10.	11.	12.
13.	14.	15.
16.	17.	18.
19.	20.	21.
22.	23.	24.
25.	26.	27.
28.	29.	30.
31.	32.	33.
34.	35.	36.
37.	38.	39.
40.	41.	42.
43.	44.	45.
Total Column	Total Column	Total Column
Average	Average	Average

Understanding Your Scores

As you may have guessed from the answer charts, at the bottom of each column you should total the score for *that* column and then divide by 15 to get the average rating for that category. The first column (the one to your left) measured *intimacy*. The middle column measured *passion*. And the third column (the one to your right) measured *commitment*. Each of you, both husband and wife, now has an average rating for how you actually *feel* in each category and an average rating for what you think is *important* to feel in that category. Your part 1 answers reflect how you feel; your part 2 scores reflect what you think is important to feel.

Jot your averages here:

Part 1 (what you feel is characteristic)   Part 2 (what you think is important)

   ____ intimacy average   ____ intimacy average

   ____ passion average   ____ passion average

   ____ commitment average   ____ commitment average

Four Levels of Insight

First Insight

The first insight this exercise may give you into your relationship can come from examining your own average scores. Ideally each person should discover that his or her average scores on parts 1 and 2 are roughly the same in each category. In other words, it is generally better if your *intimacy* score on how you really feel is fairly close to the *intimacy* score on what you think it is important to feel. The same is true for *passion* and *commitment*. Dr. Sternberg writes, "The greater the discrepancy, the greater the potential for distress."

Let's illustrate. If a person thinks it is important to have a 9 in intimacy but averages only a 6.5, that person may feel some distress. The distress comes from having a craving for more intimacy than he or she actually feels. On the other hand, if a person wants an 8 in passion and scored a 7.8, he or she may feel fairly well satisfied with the level of passion in the relationship.

What about you? Are your average scores for how you feel in each category roughly the same as what you think it is important to feel?

Second Insight

The next level of insight comes from viewing your spouse's scores. As each of you allows the other to see your average scores from part 1 (what you feel is characteristic) and part 2 (what you think is important), you will gain insight just by seeing how similar your spouse's scores are. For example, if your spouse averaged an 8.8 in *intimacy* on his or her part 2 (what he/she thinks is important) but only a 6.2 on part 1 (what he/she feels is characteristic), you may infer that he or she isn't satisfied with the current level of intimacy. That gives a clear warning signal that the two of you need to talk carefully, yet openly, about intimacy.

Also, if you see that your part 2 score on a particular category is dramatically different from your spouse's (for example, she has a 9 for what she thinks is important in *intimacy* and he only has a 7), you might view that as a warning flag. Why? Because if your spouse wants a higher level of a particular category than you, you may be unconsciously sabotaging your relationship by not being aware of that need or desire within your mate. You may be concentrating on one component while your spouse very much wants you to concentrate on another.

Third Insight

Dr. Sternberg surveyed 101 people in his initial validation process for this survey. Their scores follow so that you may compare your scores to theirs in terms of what ratings Dr. Sternberg considers high, average, or low.

If you are willing, you can help us survey many more people to validate high, average, and low scores. If you help us, we'll send you more information to help you understand the love in your own marriage. Check this endnote for details.[4]

Here are Dr. Sternberg's conclusions. The first table may give you insight into your part 1 answers—what you feel is characteristic.

Characteristic			
"How characteristic is the description in each statement of your relationship?"			
	Intimacy	Passion	Commitment
High	8.6	8.2	8.7
Average	7.4	6.5	7.2
Low	6.2	4.9	5.7

The second table may give insight into your part 2 answers—what you think is important.

Importance			
"How important is the description in each statement to your relationship?"			
	Intimacy	Passion	Commitment
High	9.0	8.0	8.8
Average	8.2	6.8	7.6
Low	7.4	5.4	6.5

The high scores represent approximately the top 15 percent of scores, and the low scores, the bottom 15 percent.

If you compare your score on intimacy with the high, average, and low scores on intimacy listed by Dr. Sternberg above, you get an idea of what level of intimacy you feel in comparison to the general population. Again, since this is not intended to be a definitive diagnostic tool, don't let your score lead you into any kind of panic or major life decision. Just look at it as another "checkup" to give you another way to gauge your relationship.

Fourth Insight

If you have internet access, go to our Web site (www.familydynamics.net) and complete the same questionnaire there. The Web site will draw three sets of triangles from your scores to give you a visual interpretation of insights 1 and 2 listed above. The way the triangles overlap may give you a clearer vision of where you are in your relationship and the areas that need the most work.

Sharing with Your Spouse

As you share your scores with your spouse, listen, as always, carefully and without censure or criticism. You may want to talk in depth about what each of you expects in terms of intimacy, passion, or commitment. Don't be afraid to say out loud what you want, as long as you don't do it in a critical or condemning manner. Attacking won't do any good. You'll never get to where you want to go if you can't accept where each of you is starting from. So get started. Sit down with no distractions (no TV, no kids, phone off the hook) and share your scores, your desires, and your needs with each other. Answer all questions the other asks as honestly as you can. If you feel that a question is too specific and will lead to a fight or argument, either of you may answer with, "I'll answer that specifically before we finish this workbook, but not now. Now I just want to learn how to be in love with you the way God wants us to be, you want us to be, and I want us to be. So for the time being, I'll answer in general terms instead of specific terms."

Whenever one of you invokes this defense, the other must accept and move on.

EXERCISE 4:
WHERE DO WE GO
FROM HERE?

Our experience with thousands of marriages tells us that *all* marriages have room for growth. If you averaged 9.00 for every component in the previous exercises, chances are you've not been totally honest with yourself. If you have been, we at Family Dynamics Institute would like to study you to see how you've attained perfection!

Any component you don't rate a 9.00 in is a place for concentration and improvement. Whether you start with a 1.00 or with an 8.75, there is room to grow. Of course, the person who scored a 1.00 has a longer way and a tougher route, but he or she can shoot for a 9.00 with complete hope that love *will* increase. The key is to learn how to grow one step at a time.

The exercise with which we end this chapter is relatively simple but should have profound impact on your life and your marriage.

In this concluding exercise, you and your spouse will write a plan on how to start moving toward a 9.00 in each component. You've likely already had discussions with your spouse in other exercises in this chapter, but you *must* interact with each other in this exercise.

Begin by completing each of the following three sets of questions by yourself. You may use the provided pages in this workbook or several pages of clean paper that you can later place in a file. Then share your answers to the *intimacy* questions with your spouse and discuss them until you have agreement.

Using the "characteristic" scores rather than the "importance" scores, work first on the plan of the spouse who has the lower average score in a component (from exercise 3). Once you have completed the plan for the spouse with the lower score, then work on the plan of the spouse with the higher score on that component.

Continue working through the exercise with the sets of questions about *passion*, and then discuss your answers to the questions about *commitment*. When you finish answering these questions, you'll be well on your way to making a wonderful marriage.

Intimacy Component Average Score_____._____

1. What do I/we already do that creates intimacy in our relationship?

_____
_____
_____
_____
_____
_____
_____
_____

2. What do I/we fail to do that would create more intimacy in our relationship?

_____
_____
_____
_____
_____
_____
_____

3. What do I need to start doing right away to move from the level of intimacy that I now feel to the level that I desire to feel?_____

_____

_____

_____

_____

_____

Passion Component Average Score_____._____

1. What do I/we already do that creates passion in our relationship?

_____

_____

_____

_____

_____

_____

2. What do I/we fail to do that would create more passion in our relationship?

_____

_____

_____

_____

_____

_____

3. What do I need to start doing right away to move from the level of passion that I now feel to the level that I desire to feel?_____

_____

_____

_____

_____

Commitment Component Average Score_____._____

1. What do I/we already do that creates commitment in our relationship?

_____

_____

_____

_____

_____

2. What do I/we fail to do that would create more commitment in our relationship? _____

_____

_____

_____

_____

3. What do I need to start doing right away to move from the level of commitment that I now feel to the level that I desire to feel?_____

_____

_____

_____

_____

_____

Chapter 2

The Triune Nature of Intimacy
Learning How to Love—Sexually, Emotionally, and Spiritually

"I want more! I want to experience him in every way possible, knowing every nuance of him, understanding him like no other. I love him with all my heart and he loves me, but I want that next level. I want us to be what some call 'soul mates.' Is it possible? Can I know him and love him even more deeply than I do now? Just show me how, and I'll do it."

Are these the words of an enamored wife?

They certainly could be; I've heard wives say similar things. Husbands too. But actually they are my paraphrase of the sentiment the apostle Paul expressed about Jesus. The Scripture says it this way: "I want to know Christ…becoming like him…. Not that I have already obtained all this…but I press on to take hold of that for which Christ Jesus took hold of me."[1]

That word *know* in this passage is the Greek word *ginosko* (ghin-oce'-ko), which is a prolonged form of the verb that means to know absolutely. It has been translated into such English phrases as "be aware of," "feel," "have knowledge of," "be sure," and "understand." He wanted to absolutely know, understand, and be aware of Jesus. He wanted to feel Him in his inner being.

So what do Paul's cravings about his relationship with Jesus have to do with your intimacy with your mate?

When each person in a marriage develops a similar sense of longing for his or her mate, that marriage will move to a different place. Paul loved Jesus and had given his body as a "living sacrifice" to Him (Romans 12:1). In every way possible, he made himself one with his Lord.

While we should never put our mates in the place God should hold in our lives, we should strongly crave ONEness with them. God made us to find one type of completeness in Him. He made us to find another type of completeness in our spouse. Both require a giving of emotions, body, and spirit.

17

Why?

As explained in *Becoming ONE*, complete intimacy has three dimensions—physical, emotional, and spiritual. If you want a wonderful relationship with God, you must join Him in all three ways. It works in a similar way in marriage.

Physical union alone is unsatisfying, at best.

Emotional union alone is friendship, sometimes amazingly deep friendship, but it still falls short of the complete ONEness God intends for husband and wife.

Spiritual union alone is what we feel when we first meet a Christian brother or sister, but it is not the fullness of the intimacy God intends in marriage.

The deepest levels of intimacy with your mate begin with a craving to know him or her spiritually, as Paul longed to know Christ. Couple that with a craving for deeper physical and emotional intimacy, and you're well on your way to reaching a dimension in your relationship with each other that few suspect exists and even fewer find.

EXERCISE 1: THE DIFFERENT DIMENSIONS OF INTIMACY

In chapter 2 of the book *Becoming ONE*, we showed you the "complete ONEness model" and discussed seven types of intimacy. Below we briefly review those types of intimacy.

- Body only = Sexual Intimacy
- Spirit only = Spiritual Intimacy
- Emotions only = Emotional Intimacy
- Spirit and body but not emotion = Heartless Intimacy
- Emotions and body but not spirit = Romantic Intimacy
- Spirit and emotions but not body = Celibate Intimacy
- Intimacy in spirit, emotions, and body = ONEness Intimacy

To help you understand how this works in human relationships, in this exercise you will read a few Bible stories and decide which kinds of intimacy the couple in each story shares. We begin by giving two examples:

Example 1

When Samson visited the prostitute at Gaza,[2] he had only sexual relations with her. There is no indication of any kind of emotional or spiritual intimacy. Therefore, the kind of intimacy he experienced with her was Sexual Intimacy.

Example 2

David met Abigail, "an intelligent and beautiful woman,"[3] who gave glory and praise to God[4] as did David.[5] When her husband died abruptly, David wasted no time in proposing marriage. She immediately accepted and became his wife.[6]

Since David viewed her as intelligent and beautiful, we can assume that they shared a friendship that included emotional attraction. Her relationship with God and his relationship with God provided the basis for a spiritual union. As soon as they married, they shared the physical intimacy of marital sex. Therefore, we conclude that they shared ONEness Intimacy. We believe that one of the closest relationships David ever developed was with Abigail.

Now, it's time for you to share what you think. Answer the following questions together as an exercise in learning about the various dimensions of intimacy. We give our conclusions as noted in the endnote for each question.

1. Read the story of Jacob and Leah in Genesis 29:31–35 and 30:16–21. Which, if any, of the three dimensions of themselves did they share? (Ask yourself questions like: Did they share bodies in sexual activity? Did they share emotional closeness? Did they share spiritual closeness?) Based on your interpretation of these passages, what kind of intimacy did they experience? Be sure to talk out your answer with each other. _____

_____

_____

Check the endnotes for our answer.[7]

2. Read the story of the woman washing Jesus' feet in Luke 7:36–50. Using the same kind of process you did in the last question, write here the kind of intimacy you believe she shared with Jesus. _____

_____

_____

Check the endnotes for our answer.[8]

3. Read the story of David and Bathsheba in 2 Samuel 11. What kind of intimacy did they share in this story? _____

_____

_____

Check the endnotes for our answer.[9]

4. Think of what you know about the Bible and write below the names of a biblical couple that you believe had ONEness Intimacy (other than David and Abigail!). If you just can't think of one, you may write the names of a couple you personally know who you believe experiences this kind of intimacy.

_____

_____

_____

_____

EXERCISE 2:
WHICH INTIMACY DO YOU SHARE?

Perhaps by now you are ready to explore how much intimacy you have with your mate in the areas of body, emotions, and spirit. That's exactly what we ask you to do in this next exercise.

As you and your spouse schedule your week, be sure to give yourselves at least a couple of hours to complete this exercise.

Using the following fifteen statements, we ask you first to rate what you think *should* exist in your relationship and then to rate what you think *actually* exists in your relationship right now. We give five questions in each area. Some of the questions are similar to the ones in the preceding chapter, but it is important that you answer them again here in this context.

The blanks represent your spouse. Rate your agreement to each statement on a 1 to 9 scale. Rate all fifteen statements before sharing your answers.

1	2	3	4	5	6	7	8	9
not at all				moderately				extremely

Sexual Intimacy

1. I am satisfied with the frequency with which _____ and I have sex.
   I think this should be _____. It actually is _____.
2. I am satisfied with _____'s involvement/participation when we have sex.
   I think this should be _____. It actually is _____.
3. I am satisfied with _____'s skill/technique as a sexual partner.
   I think this should be _____. It actually is _____.
4. I am satisfied with the level of sexual passion I feel for _____.
   I think this should be _____. It actually is _____.
5. I am sexually satisfied with _____.
   I think this should be _____. It actually is _____.

Emotional Intimacy

6. _____ and I agree on what I consider to be basic principles and values.
   I think this should be _____ . It actually is _____.
7. _____ and I agree on routine matters and decisions.
   I think this should be _____. It actually is _____.
8. _____ and I are emotionally close to each other.
   I think this should be _____. It actually is _____.

9. _____ understands my deepest thoughts and feelings.

    I think this should be _____. It actually is _____.

10. _____ demonstrates acceptance for what I think and feel.

    I think this should be _____. It actually is _____.

Spiritual Intimacy

11. _____ and I agree on what I consider to be foundational religious beliefs, principles, and values.

    I think this should be _____. It actually is _____.

12. _____ and I each have a close relationship with God.

    I think this should be _____. It actually is _____.

13. _____ and I agree on how religious beliefs, principles, and values apply to daily life.

    I think this should be _____. It actually is _____.

14. _____ and I feel a spiritual closeness to each other.

    I think this should be _____. It actually is _____.

15. _____ and I share spiritual activities that bring us closer to God and to each other.

    I think this should be _____. It actually is _____.

After you've completed all fifteen statements, decide who will go first in sharing his or her *should be* rating to statement number 1. (Be sure not to share your *actual* rating just yet.) After the first spouse shares, the other spouse shares his or her *should be* rating to statement 1. If you rated the *should be* scores differently, share why you gave the statement that rating. Be sure to discuss what each of you understands the statement to mean before sharing your *actual* ratings.

Next, the first spouse shares his or her *actual* rating for statement 1. Then the other spouse shares his or her *actual* rating for statement 1. Again, talk about any discrepancies in rating, and answer every question asked by either spouse.

We say this again because it is so important: If either of you has a question about the *should be* rating or the *actual* rating, discuss the matter to your mutual satisfaction before moving to the next question. As always, don't argue, pout, or punish. You're not trying to convince your spouse but to understand your spouse.

Follow the same pattern until you've discussed all fifteen questions.

EXERCISE 3:
LOOKING AHEAD TO GREATER INTIMACY

Complete intimacy—ONEness intimacy—comes when two people share their emotions, bodies, and spirits. While the questions in the previous exercise certainly weren't exhaustive, we designed them to give you a starting place to learn how to share these three parts of yourselves with each other.

As you shared your answers to those questions, you may have discovered that you are sexually satisfied, emotionally agreed, and spiritually sharing with each other. If so, that's wonderful! But it may also be that you discovered that there were some areas where you can already start planning ways to become more intimate with each other. For example, if your spouse scored you an 8 in his or her satisfaction with your sexual skills and techniques, you know that you can learn to be a better lover by striving to be a 9. If he or she rated you a 2 or 3, the same holds true; you still strive for a 9. Wherever you are now, there is always a way to become better, to grow closer, and to fulfill each other more.

Of course, no one can do that if he or she spends time pouting over not being scored as highly as he or she wished. *Pouters* don't grow, nor do they develop deeper, more intimate relationships. *Doers* are the people who make those kinds of things happen. Whatever scores you received from your spouse in the last exercise, you can now begin to make plans as to how to increase those ratings and develop more intimacy in every part of your relationship—physically, emotionally, and spiritually.

So here is the place for you to make that plan.

Begin by working through the following questions alone. When you both finish, share your answers with each other.

Be aware that when you share your answers, you, in essence, are making a commitment to do these things for each other. Don't make a commitment you don't intend to keep. In describing the kind of person who dwells in the Lord's sanctuary and lives on His holy hill, the psalmist gave several descriptors including this one: a person "who keeps his oath even when it hurts."[10] God expects you to do what you say you will do.

Sexual Intimacy

1. When your spouse gave *actual* ratings in questions 6 through 10 in exercise 2, which questions did he or she score you lowest in? Why?_____

_____

_____

_____

_____

2. What is it that your spouse wants from/with you sexually that he or she feels isn't occurring? _____

_____

_____

_____

_____

3. If you didn't rate each other with perfect scores, what do you think the "real problem" is that keeps you from being as close to each other and/or fulfilled sexually as you want to be?_____

_____

_____

_____

4. Carefully consider what you've written for the questions just above and then answer the following question: What specific things can *you* do to help the two of you develop the deepest level of sexual intimacy possible?_____

_____

_____

_____

_____

Emotional Intimacy

1. When your spouse gave *actual* ratings in questions 1 through 5 in exercise 2, which questions did he or she score you lowest in? Why? _____

_____

_____

_____

_____

2. What is it that your spouse wants from/with you that he or she feels isn't occurring?_____

_____

_____

_____

_____

3. If you didn't rate each other with perfect scores, what do you think the "real problem" is that keeps you from being as close to each other emotionally as you want to be?_____

_____

_____

_____

_____

4. Carefully consider what you've written for the questions just above and then answer the following question: What specific things can *you* do to help the two of you develop the deepest level of emotional intimacy possible?_____

_____

_____

_____

_____

Spiritual Intimacy

1. When your spouse gave *actual* ratings in questions 11 through 15 in exercise 2, which questions did he or she score you lowest in? Why? _____

_____

_____

_____

_____

2. What is it that your spouse wants from/with you spiritually that he or she feels isn't occurring?_____

_____

_____

_____

_____

3. If you didn't rate each other with perfect scores, what do you think the "real problem" is that keeps you from being as close to each other spiritually as you want to be?_____

_____

_____

_____

4. Carefully consider what you've written for the questions just above and then answer the following question: What specific things can *you* do to help the two of you develop the deepest level of spiritual intimacy possible?_____

_____

_____

_____

_____

Repairing Intimacy Diversions and Drains
Understanding How Intimacy Is Generated

"It's hard to understand," she sighed.

It didn't appear that she expected us to have the explanation, only that she wanted to share her perplexity. Jean had just told us of a friend whose life had taken a strange twist. Sue had been a loving wife and mother, a volunteer in several charitable organizations, and a leader in her church. If Broadway were developing a play whose leading character was Harriet Homemaker, they would have cast Sue in the role without a moment's hesitation. But now things were different, and that difference had seemed to happen almost overnight.

A couple of years earlier, Sue had decided to enter the business world for the first time since the birth of her children. Her children were grown, and Sue wanted to fill her life with new adventures. Finding a job wasn't the easiest task because of her lack of employment history, but she finally succeeded in landing a position that offered her immediate challenge and a chance to advance as she proved herself. She soon showed her employers that being a homemaker for the past several years hadn't made her any less intelligent or less aggressive than those who had been in the job market all along. She quickly learned the ropes and showed an innate talent for the job. Within two years, she had skyrocketed to a position of responsibility and prestige.

Good news?

That depends on one's perspective.

Within months of attaining her new position, she moved out of her home, filed for a divorce from her husband of twenty-three years, and started sporting a handsome young man as her companion at company social events. It was when Jean reached that point in her story that she shared her bafflement: "It's hard to understand."

Though I don't know Sue and, therefore, don't know all the particulars of her life, I had an educated guess as to what had happened. If, indeed, she had been a loving wife—meaning that hadn't been a facade disguising a bad relationship—the reason for her change was likely caused by an intimacy diversion.

Intimacy Diversions

As we explain in the accompanying book, *Becoming ONE*, intimacy with our mates is generated when *communication*, *time*, and *actions* are invested in them, much like electricity is generated when water flows through turbines. If the water flow through a turbine is somehow diverted, that turbine produces no electricity. In a similar way, if our communication, time, and actions are diverted to someone or something other than our spouses, our hearts will produce no intimacy toward our mates.

If Sue lost the love she had previously felt for her husband, she obviously redirected the communication, time, and action that she had been directing toward him to either something or someone else. Maybe both.

We believe that a person's primary concentration of intimacy-producing elements (communication, time, action) should be directed toward God and that the secondary concentration should be toward his or her spouse. Next would come children, then other close relatives. The energy that's left should be divided between friends, work, hobbies, or other things that are important to the person. Using our turbine illustration, we picture it this way:

The Correct Flow

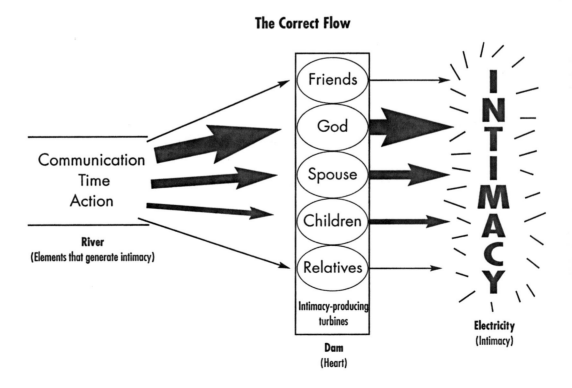

Communication
Time
Action

River
(Elements that generate intimacy)

Friends

God

Spouse

Children

Relatives

Intimacy-producing
turbines

Dam
(Heart)

INTIMACY

Electricity
(Intimacy)

If a person focused equally on all the above, he or she wouldn't develop greater levels of intimacy for one thing over another. For example, if a person focused equally on God, spouse, children, relatives, and friends, he or she would feel the same amount of intimacy for each. No person would stand out; none would have a special place in his or her life. Therefore, we believe that focusing equally on everyone and everything is an incorrect flow of energy, as illustrated here:

The Incorrect Flow

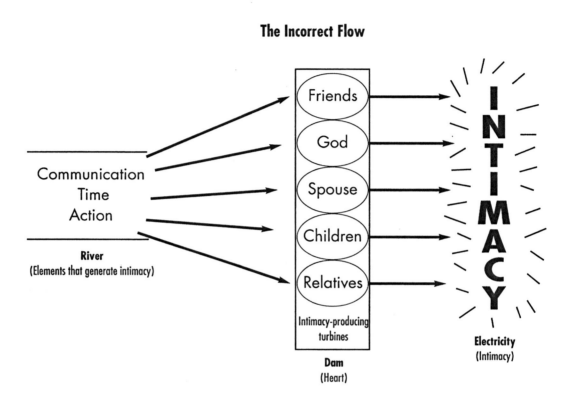

While the scenario illustrated above is not good, there's another that's even worse. When the flow of communication, time, and action that should be directed toward God or one's spouse is diverted to some other person or thing, we call that an intimacy *diversion*. For example, if a person focused more communication, time, and action toward becoming rich or powerful than toward developing a close relationship with God, that would divert his or her intimacy away from God. In the same way, if a person focused more communication, time, and action toward a person other than his or her spouse, feelings of intimacy for the spouse would fade as feelings of intimacy for the other person grew. Still using our turbine illustration, we show that here:

The Diverted Flow

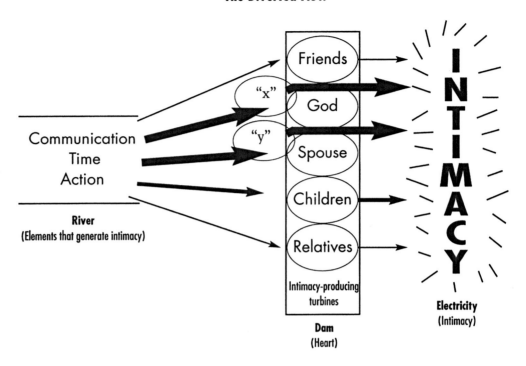

Now that we've explained the model, are you ready to find where you focus your communication, time, and action? This exercise could reveal much about *why* you feel as you do about God, your spouse, your children, and others.

EXERCISE 1:
WHERE IS YOUR FOCUS?

In this exercise, you will have to use as much honest judgment as you can. You will create a list of all the people, things, and emotional needs in your life that get any of your communication, time, and actions. (We've already put a couple of people and things on your list.) Once you've completed your list, we'll explain how to use it as an evaluation tool. *For now, just put the people, things, and emotional needs in the column at the left without worrying about the blank spaces to the right.*

As you list people, you can write them as a group if you wish. For example, you can write "children" or "friends" or "coworkers" rather than writing individual names. *But* if you give special attention to one person within that group, you must list that person by name. For example, you may use "friends" to represent everyone who is your friend, but if one of your friends gets more attention than the others—your best friend, for example—then list his or her name separately. The same would be true for a child you focus more energy on or a coworker you interact with differently than others.

Okay, get started on your list. Remember, every *person, thing,* and *emotional need* that gets some of your communication, time, and action should be included. Don't leave anyone or anything out. Use a separate piece of paper if necessary.

God   _____

Spouse   _____

Children   _____

_____   _____

_____   _____

Relatives   _____

_____   _____

_____   _____

Friends   _____

_____   _____

_____   _____

_____   _____

Coworkers   _____

_____   _____

Other people   _____

_____   _____

_____   _____

_____   _____

_____   _____

Church   _____

Hobbies   _____

_____   _____

Work/Career   _____

Desires/Goals   _____

_____   _____

Emotional needs   _____

_____   _____

Obsession/Addiction   _____

_____   _____

Recurring temptation   _____

_____   _____

TOTAL   __100__

Figuring the Focus

You may notice that we wrote the word "Total" at the bottom of the list on the left and the number "100" on the right. That's because you have 100 points to represent *all* communication, time, and action you give to people or things. Those 100 points have to be distributed between all the entries you made.

We ask you to honestly write the percentage of focus you expend on each of the entries. Of course, any space in which you wrote something must receive a score. Any of those *we* included that have meaning to you should also receive a score. For example, if you have children, place a "focus score" in the blank next to where we listed children. If you don't have children, you would leave that space blank.

It may take you a time or two to get this right. When you finish, all of your scores must total 100. So think through this as you place your scores.

One last word: Don't put a score that you think *ought* to be your focus. We're asking you to place a score that you think *really* reflects the focus you currently give.

When you finish scoring, go to the next part of this exercise.

Interpreting Your Scores

Look carefully at the scores you listed. Does anyone or anything stand out? Or are they about even down the line? Where is God in the equation? Where is your spouse?

If everything and everyone you listed are about even, you likely feel no greater intimacy for one person or thing than you do for another. While you may feel that your life is balanced, your spouse may see it very differently. He or she may feel neglected. He or she may even feel that you are distant and hard to get close to. One thing is sure: If your spouse doesn't stand out with a greater score than other people or things in your life, you aren't yet developing the kind of intimacy God intended you to have with him or her.

Most people will discover that a handful of people or things will have higher scores than the rest of the items or people in their lives. If that is so for you, those things are the focus of your life and are likely the people or things that you feel the greatest levels of intimacy for. They get the most of your communication, time, and action—the elements that generate intimacy.

Because you'll use them in the next exercise, list here any people or things that stand out from your list. Rate them in order, highest score to lowest. (Don't feel compelled to fill in all five blanks. Just list those things that had scores that stood out.)

Highest Scored Items

1. _____   2. _____   3. _____

4. _____   5. _____

EXERCISE 2:
DISCOVERING YOUR ntimacy DIVERSIONS

Based on your highest scoring items from exercise 1, you should be able to identify your intimacy diversions to fill in the turbine model below. In the circles, write the names of the people or things that you rated with the highest scores. Draw the appropriate thickness for each line, making lines thicker for higher scores and thinner for lower scores. If you have any questions, just look back at the beginning of this chapter to the diagram we call "The Correct Flow."

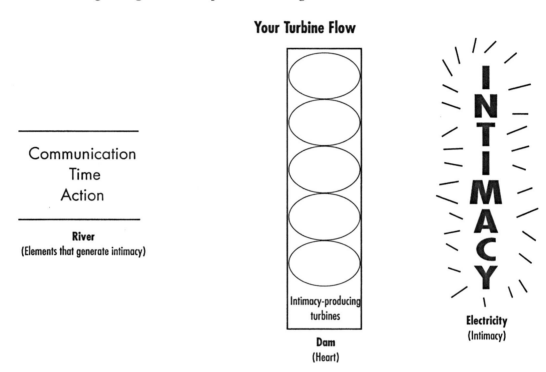

Look at what you've drawn above. Where do God and your spouse fit? Do they have the largest, thickest lines? Or are their lines about the same or even smaller than others?

If God has the heaviest line and your spouse has a line that is slightly smaller, wonderful. If you've done the exercise honestly, that says you are heading in the right direction.

If, on the other hand, the lines you've drawn for each circle are about equal, see that as a visual representation of how you need to change your focus. If you want to increase your intimacy either with God, your spouse, or both, you will have to *do* things differently than you do now. You *must* concentrate more on in-depth communication, quality time in great quantities, and intentional actions that fulfill your spouse's needs if you want to grow in intimacy with him or her. You *must* concentrate more on in-depth Bible study and prayer, taking the time to really commune with God and serve Him in *actions* rather than just *words* if you want deeper intimacy with Him.

Let's take this one step farther. Now we ask you to draw another diagram with a slightly different twist. If you scored anything or anyone (even your spouse) higher than you did God, place that person or thing in the circle that is just to the left of the circle with "God" in it. If you scored anyone or anything higher than you did your spouse (other than God, of course), place that person or thing in the circle that is just to the left of the circle with "Spouse" in it. If there are several people or things you scored higher than "God" or "Spouse," write them *all* in the appropriate circle.

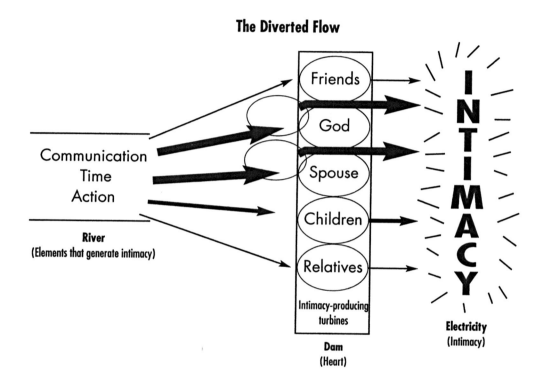

The Diverted Flow

Communication
Time
Action

River
(Elements that generate intimacy)

Friends

God

Spouse

Children

Relatives

Intimacy-producing turbines

Dam
(Heart)

INTIMACY

Electricity
(Intimacy)

Look at the above chart very carefully. Those two circles just to the left of the circles for God and spouse give a clear picture of why you feel the levels of intimacy that you do. If you wrote anything in the circle just to the left of the circle for God, you probably have before you a clear, graphic representation of why you aren't any closer to Him at this point in your life. The same holds true for the feelings you have for your spouse if you wrote anything in that circle.

If you've been honest and accurate, when you examine the above drawing you may be looking at the person or thing in your life that is the diversion that stands between you and the intimacy you need with God or your spouse.

EXERCISE 3:
DISCOVERING YOUR INTIMACY DRAINS

Sometimes a lack of intimacy in a marriage is caused by an intimacy *drain* rather than a diversion. Drains keep the intimacy generated by the "turbine" from being *felt* by the person it's intended for. This occurs when a person does the right things but those right actions are negated by other, wrong actions.

Intimacy drains are any behaviors that you do or fail to do that keep your spouse from feeling intimacy for you.

We diagram that concept this way:

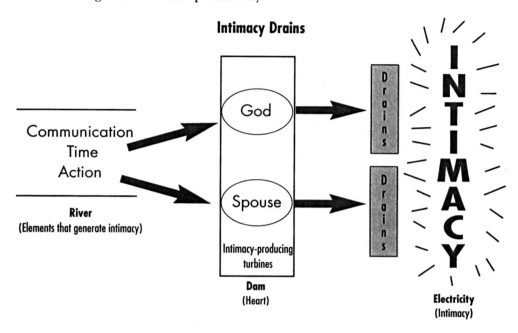

Intimacy drains are barriers that soak up any and all positive behavior, rendering it powerless to create intimacy in the spouse it is aimed at.

1. We know of only one way to discover any intimacy drains in your relationship, and that is to ask. So go ahead, ask your spouse the following question, then write his or her answers in the space provided below. And remember, as always, don't disagree or argue. If you do, you'll likely just commit another intimacy drain. "What, if anything, do I do or fail to do that prevents you from feeling the deepest levels of intimacy for me?"_____

_____

_____

_____

2. Now, ask yourself if you know of any behavior in you that serves as an intimacy drain between you and God. "What, if anything, do I do or fail to do that may prevent God from having the level of intimacy He wants with me?"_____

_____

_____

_____

3. Before you leave this exercise, go back to the intimacy drain diagram above and write in the corresponding rectangle on the diagram any drains you discovered. This will serve as a visual reminder of what may be hindering your relationship with God or with your spouse.

EXERCISE 4: MAKING NEEDED REPAIRS

Completing exercises 2 and 3 may have caused any one of several feelings within you. You may look back at the diagrams you drew and think, "Hey, I'm doing pretty good at this intimacy thing!" Or you may look at them and feel, "It's no use; I don't love my spouse like I should, and that diagram shows me that I never will." Maybe some people reading this even feel a third possibility: "Okay! Now I see what I'm doing wrong. If I want to grow closer to God and to my spouse, I see what must be changed in my life, what has to be reprioritized or replaced."

Whatever your current feeling, we have one last exercise in this chapter that will help you know where to go from here. It has four simple steps, and we urge you to complete each one.

Step 1: Ask God

In the New Testament, a young man approached Jesus to ask Him what he "lacked" in his relationship with God.[1] Jesus looked into the young man's heart and saw the "intimacy diversion" that stood between him and his completeness in God. Jesus answered, "If you want to be perfect, go, sell your possessions and give to the poor, and you will have treasure in heaven. Then come, follow me." In this verse the word *perfect* refers to completeness or wholeness—ONEness, if you will.

If you know the story, you know that the young man "went away sad, because he had great wealth." He wanted ONEness with God but wasn't willing to give up the intimacy diversion that kept him from achieving it.

What about you?

You may have written one or more intimacy diversions between you and God or between you and your spouse in the diagrams in the previous exercises. You may have also listed some intimacy drains. If so, you already have a very good idea of what is keeping your relationship from being what it ought to be. But we ask you not to stop there. You may have neglected to list something of importance, not necessarily because you aren't being honest with yourself but because of an inner "blindness" that keeps you from seeing all you need to see. To overcome that, we ask you to consult God. If you want ONEness with God and ONEness with your spouse, you would be extremely wise to ask God to tell you what, if anything, stands between you and the intimacy you desire.

In just a moment we'll ask you to actually write that prayer in your workbook so you can think it through before you pray it and can revisit it regularly until you get God's answer. He may show you an existing intimacy diversion between you and Him in any number of ways. Maybe your preacher will talk about it in his sermon. Maybe your Bible study class will discuss it. Maybe your own reading of the Scripture will suddenly open your eyes. It could even be that God will answer in an article you read, a program you watch, or a conversation you have with a friend.

Or maybe you know even before you ask. Maybe it's what you put on the diagrams in the earlier exercises or that thing you're thinking about right now. But don't trust just your thoughts when God will make things even clearer to you.

1.   In the space below write a heartfelt prayer to God, asking Him to reveal anything that stands as an intimacy diversion to your relationship to Him. Ask Him if there is any intimacy drain. Use your own phrasing, but make sure your point is clear and that God knows exactly what you are asking of Him. _____

_____

_____

_____

_____

_____

2.   Now, in the following space write a second prayer. This time ask God to reveal to you anything that stands as an intimacy diversion or drain to your relationship with your spouse. Again, phrase it your way, but be specific in your prayer. _____

_____

_____

_____

_____

3.   Stop right now and read both of these prayers to God. Say them out loud and include them as part of a greater prayer to God. Praise Him for who He is and what He can do. Thank Him in advance for answering your requests. Ask Him for courage to hear and believe the answer when it comes. Ask Him for courage to repair any intimacy diversion or drain you discover.

Step 2: Ask Your Spouse

It's very possible that God will answer your prayers through the mouth of your husband or wife. As a matter of fact, it could be that he or she has been trying to tell you about intimacy diversions or drains for some time now, but for some reason, you haven't heard it correctly.

You may have noticed that we asked you to do only one thing with your spouse so far in this chapter. We didn't ask you to share your diagrams or your lists or even your prayers, though we did request that you ask your spouse about any potential intimacy drains. Now it's time to bring the two of you together to finish this chapter. Your spouse has been doing the same exercises you have, so each of you should be ready to answer some questions.

The following questions are similar to the ones you used in exercise 3 to discover your intimacy drains, but the questions here also include intimacy diversions, and having the answers repeated here will help you plan how to repair your diversions and drains.

Begin by asking your spouse the following questions. Write what you hear from your spouse in the provided space.

Be very honest with each other as you answer the following questions, but do not use this as an opportunity to attack each other for something you aren't happy about. This should be a sharing, learning experience that can deepen your relationship for the rest of your lives. Don't spoil it with pettiness or bitterness. Look deep within your hearts and share as God would have you share.

1. What intimacy diversions or drains do I have that keep me from having the deepest level of intimacy with God?_____

_____

_____

_____

2. What intimacy diversions or drains do I have that keep me from having the deepest level of intimacy with you?_____

_____

_____

_____

3. What (or how) do you think I need to change? What do I need to do differently?_____

_____

_____

Step 3: Reprioritize or Replace

Complete this step and the next when you feel that you know all the intimacy diversions and drains, if any, that exist in your relationship with God or your relationship with your spouse.

Once you identify an intimacy *diversion*, you must decide if you will repair it by *reprioritization* or *replacement*. For example, if you're spending too much time at work, perhaps you can reprioritize and find ways to spend more time with your spouse. But if you are developing an improper relationship with another person besides your spouse, that can't be reprioritized. The communication, time, and action focused on that person must be stopped; the intimacy diversion must be removed and replaced.

Jesus apparently saw that the rich young man loved his wealth so much that he couldn't reprioritize it in his life. To find true intimacy with God, the young man had no choice but to remove the diversion altogether.

You do not have the same choice in repairing intimacy *drains*. You can't *reprioritize* habits that drain the affects of the intimacy you focus on your mate, keeping him or her from reciprocally feeling intimacy for you. Intimacy drains must be removed. Things like manipulating your spouse or attacking with repeated angry outbursts must be completely eliminated and replaced with positive behavior.

Just before you do this exercise, ask God again for courage to do what should be done. Also ask Him for the wisdom to know what to do.

Below, list briefly any intimacy diversions you've identified. Then *circle* the appropriate action that you must take to repair it.

Intimacy Diversions or Drains to My Relationship with God

- An intimacy diversion or drain in my life is _____
_____.

To repair it, I must reprioritize / remove it.
- An intimacy diversion or drain in my life is _____
_____.

To repair it, I must reprioritize / remove it.
- An intimacy diversion or drain in my life is _____
_____.

To repair it, I must reprioritize / remove it.

Intimacy Diversions or Drains to My Relationship with My Spouse

- An intimacy diversion or drain in my life is _____
_____.

To repair it, I must reprioritize / remove it.
- An intimacy diversion or drain in my life is _____
_____.

To repair it, I must reprioritize / remove it.
- An intimacy diversion or drain in my life is _____
_____.

To repair it, I must reprioritize / remove it.

Step 4: Make a Plan of Action

The last step in this exercise is crucial. How many times has a person known that he or she *should* do something and then not done it? To keep that from happening to you, you need to make a plan of action, including goal dates for accomplishment, and then follow that plan intently. Unless there is something in the plan that you just can't let your spouse see right now, share your plan with him or her and ask for assistance in making each step happen.

Look at what you wrote above and then complete the following. Include all diversions or drains to your intimacy with God and to your intimacy with your spouse. If necessary, use extra pages. We give you space to deal with as many as five diversions or drains.

Intimacy Diversions/Drains

- The diversion or drain is_____

   My plan to repair/remove it is_____

   _____

   _____

   _____

   _____

   _____

   _____

   My goal date to have this repair/removal completed is_____

- The diversion or drain is_____

   My plan to repair/remove it is_____

   _____

   _____

   _____

   _____

   _____

   My goal date to have this repair/removal completed is_____

- The diversion or drain is_____

   My plan to repair/remove it is_____

   _____

   _____

   _____

   _____

   _____

My goal date to have this repair/removal completed is_____

- The diversion or drain is_____

  My plan to repair/remove it is_____

  _____ _____

  _____

  _____

  _____

  _____

  _____

My goal date to have this repair/removal completed is_____

- The diversion or drain is_____

  My plan to repair/remove it is_____

  _____

  _____

  _____

  _____

  _____

My goal date to have this repair/removal completed is_____

Chapter 4

Developing Emotional Intimacy, Part 1
Learning Intimacy from the Inside Out

Have you ever been faced with a situation where you couldn't do what you wanted to do because someone insisted you complete a prerequisite first? Skydivers won't strap a chute on you and allow you to leap through an airplane door until you've completed instruction on how to land on the earth rather than crash into it. Colleges and universities won't let you enroll in the courses that really get your attention until you successfully complete other, duller classes they've strewn in your path.

Shall we all sigh collectively at the unfairness of life?

Since you're used to this in other areas of your life, surely you won't mind being subjected to it here. By now you surely want to delve into deep, intricate conversations with your spouse that will carry you to the profound depths of love, understanding, and intimacy that poets write odes to. And we want that for you too.

But not just yet.

First, there is a crucial, initial step to emotional intimacy that we urge you to complete, even if you at first feel it is a waste of your time. From the accompanying book, *Becoming ONE*, you know that there are four steps to emotional intimacy:

- You must accept yourself as you are—loving yourself as a creation of God with worth and value.

- You must share facts—starting with nonthreatening facts and gradually sharing those you are more fearful to tell.

- You must share feelings—starting with those you feel will be accepted and gradually sharing those you think your spouse may not want to hear.

- You must accept the other—accepting your spouse's intrinsic value and worth, accepting the facts of his or her life, and accepting what he or she feels.

41

These steps sound simple, but many spouses find them difficult to live out on a day-to-day basis. Some people try to rearrange the order of the steps, but that doesn't work. You can't do steps 2 through 4 until you finish the critical prerequisite of step 1.

People who don't accept themselves as they are fall into two categories: *pretenders* and *deniers*. Pretenders don't like who they are, so they play the role of a person they want to be. The Bible calls these people "hypocrites," a word that means to act a part. Deniers are those who believe that they are too sinful or that they aren't pretty or smart or that they can't do anything of value. Unlike the pretenders, they don't play a role, acting as if they are something they're not. They don't believe they can be anyone other than who they think they are, and they live well below their potential in nearly every area of their lives.

Obviously, either state is a barrier to communication. How can pretenders tell the truth, being open and honest about everything when they play a role that they think brings them rewards or acceptance? And how can deniers let anyone see deep inside when they believe that what's deep inside is too ugly to share?

To make sure that you are neither a pretender nor denier—or to find the cure if you are—work through these brief exercises.

EXERCISE 1:
ACCEPT YOUR PAST—WHAT YOU HAVE DONE OR WHAT WAS DONE TO YOU

Too many folks don't love themselves as God commands[1] because they are convinced that God doesn't love them. They fear that God finds them repulsive because of what they've done. Others believe their repulsiveness comes from things over which they had no control—terrible things done to them by others. They secretly feel that the evil occurrence was their fault, that somehow they triggered it. Either way, whether that experience resulted from their own actions or the actions of others, they think the very fact that it happened makes them unworthy and unlovable. Nothing could be farther from the truth. But before we lead you through the scriptures that will show you otherwise, make sure that you're being honest with yourself about what has happened that makes you feel so repulsive.

Making It Real

First, make it real by admitting that it happened. Keep that experience from being a morbid memory and give it a form you can deal with by writing it down. If there is anything that you feel guilt about, write it down. It may be something that was done to you (sexual abuse, rape, emotional abuse, etc.) or something that you did (pornography, adultery, murder, stealing, lying, etc.). What you struggle with may be a particular event, a period of time, or a recurring temptation. If it's a particular event, answer the following three questions for each event you feel bad about. If you feel unlovable because of what you did or what happened to you during a period of time, answer the following three questions for the time period, rather than singling out a specific event from that period. If what you're thinking of is a recurring desire, like homosexual stirrings or barely controlled lust, don't try to remember each specific event but deal with the recurring temptation. You may need extra paper but don't hesitate to answer these three questions. It's more important to do the exercise right than to scrimp on paper or time.

1. What is the event, period, or recurring temptation that makes you at times feel unlovable?_____

_____

_____

_____

_____

2. What makes you continue to hold guilt or shame or other negative emotions about this event, period, or recurring temptation?_____

_____

_____

_____

_____

3. What would God have to do to make you feel clean, healed, holy, and lovable? _____

_____

_____

_____

_____

It's possible that you answered question 2 about your feelings of guilt or shame or degradation with something like, "Because it was so bad. No one who has any good in them could have done that." Or maybe, "Because I enjoyed it, and if the right situation presented itself again, I'm not sure I could withstand the temptation." Perhaps even, "Because of the consequences. You can't imagine the harm it caused, who it affected, and how many people know. Man, nobody can ever forget what I did." And for others, "It's because I really *want* to do it again. Sometimes I think about it and find myself trying to figure out how I can find the opportunity to do it again."

If the experience is something that happened to you, you may even think, "It's my fault. If I had been different…or smarter…or where I was supposed to be…or a better person, it wouldn't have happened." We've heard these responses and many, many more during the years we've helped people find the forgiveness of God. We can't take time here to tell you all that you should think about if you wrote answers like those we've listed above, but we can recommend you get and read the book *Forgiven Forever*,[2] which deals with all these and more in greater detail. Suffice it to say that your answers likely aren't unique; many of us feel the same way about ourselves.

That leads to the answer you may have given for question 3. Maybe you wrote something like, "I wish God would snap His fingers and take me back in time to before that event or time period. Then, maybe, I could keep it from happening." Or perhaps, "If God could just make everyone forget that it ever happened, then I could feel clean." Maybe you were even so bold as to write, "I need God to change me, to make me different, to put a new heart within me."

If you wrote anything like those statements, you aren't alone. Read Psalm 51, and you'll see the same sentiments expressed by David after he committed adultery and murder.

Why do we ask you to write those things down? As we said earlier, we want the event, period, or recurring temptation to be very real in your heart and mind right now. If so, it's time for the next set of questions.

Understanding Forgiveness

1. What did God mean when He said that when He forgives us, He puts our sins as far away from us as the east is from the west? (Psalm 103:12)._____

_____

_____

_____

2. What did He mean when He told us that He will remember our sins no more? (Hebrews 10:17)._____

_____

_____

3. What sin have you committed that God will not forgive? (Romans 5—read the whole chapter)._____

_____

_____

_____

4. If the thing that causes you the most difficulty in loving yourself is something that was done to you, please answer this question: What do you think God wanted you to learn when He said, "Do not take revenge, my friends, but leave room for God's wrath, for it is written: 'It is mine to avenge; I will repay,' says the Lord. On the contrary: 'If your enemy is hungry, feed him; if he is thirsty, give him something to drink. In doing this, you will heap burning coals on his head.' Do not be overcome by evil, but overcome evil with good"? (Romans 12:19–21).

_____

_____

_____

_____

_____

5. What peace would you have in your heart if you, like Jesus and Stephen, could forgive the person or people who hurt you? (Luke 23:34; Acts 7:60).

_____

_____

_____

_____

The truth of the matter is that God wants you to feel clean and forgiven and whole and lovable. If you don't, it's because you don't believe Him or because you refuse to forgive others. Doubting *yourself* is one thing, but doubting *God* is another altogether. Don't hurt Him any longer by denying His wonderful grace and mercy. He doesn't want you to hurt and is offering you forgiveness now.

Now, here are the final four questions.

Making Forgiveness Real

1. Are you a Christian? _____ (If you don't know, please contact us at 1-800-650-9995 and ask for the booklet *ABCs of the Christian Faith*.[3]) To be forgiven by God, you must be one of His children. Jesus said, "I told you that you would die in your sins; if you do not believe that I am [the one I claim to be], you will indeed die in your sins" (John 8:24).

2. Have you asked God to forgive you, confessing your sin and seeking His healing power? If not, do it right now. Write your confession and prayer for forgiveness here. It will help you to write it; then you can pray it sincerely to God.

_____

_____

_____

_____

3. If you can't feel God's healing power, find mature, loving, nonjudgmental Christians to whom you can confess further to find more of God's power. "Therefore confess your sins to each other and pray for each other so that you may be healed. The prayer of a righteous man is powerful and effective" (James 5:16). Who are godly people to whom you can confess without fear and know that they will pray for your emotional and spiritual healing? Write here whom

you will ask to help you and when you will ask them._____
_____
_____
_____

4. Have you asked God to give you a forgiving heart toward those who sinned against you, hurt you, or abused you? If not, do it now. Ask Him to replace the hurt, anger, grief, bitterness, or any other negative emotion you feel with His healing love. Write your prayer here._____
_____
_____
_____
_____
_____

EXERCISE 2: ACCEPT YOUR PHYSICAL IMPERFECTIONS

When people get past the spiritual and emotional burdens that prevent godly self-love, many still feel inferior and unlovable because they think they aren't quite as pretty, tall, handsome, or trim as others. They look at themselves and think that they're unlovable because they're ugly. Some turn to eating disorders because they feel unlovable. Others move into sinful behaviors that lead them right back into the trap we mentioned in the previous section. Either way, the emphasis is wrong.

The Bible tells us that Jesus was not anything special to look at (Isaiah 53:2). If you aren't a supermodel or a superstar, you look more like Jesus than they do! If Jesus were on the earth again today, He wouldn't make it to the evening news, much less the cover of *People* magazine, based on His looks. He'd be a "plain Jane," a "Joe Citizen"—He'd be lost in the crowd. Realizing that, answer the following six questions about your body.

1. What don't you like about yourself as far as appearance is concerned?_____
_____
_____
_____
_____

2. In the grand scheme of things—especially eternal things—what difference does your appearance make? Why is it so important to you to look different than you do now? _____
_____
_____

_____

_____

3. Think carefully about your answer to question 2. What does it tell you about your desires—especially about what is really important to you?_____

_____

_____

_____

_____

4. In what ways could your desires expressed in question 3 be fulfilled, even without your appearance changing at all. _____

_____

_____

_____

_____

5. List all the things that you need to thank God for that you *do* have physically. When you've made the list, take time to pray and thank Him for what He's given you physically._____

_____

_____

_____

_____

6. What can you change that you have the time and money and willingness to change? As you answer that question, answer these along with it: Is it important enough to you to do it? Why? What will you do about it? _____

_____

_____

_____

_____

Some aspects of your physical appearance can be changed and should be. If you're overweight, you're abusing your body, and any effort to slim down is a good effort. But if you're not as tall as you'd like to be, there isn't anything you can do from a physical standpoint, and you should learn to thank God that He made you as He did. Your worth and value isn't based on your height or the size of your nose or the number of fingers on your hand or even if you can walk without crutches or see without glasses. Your worth isn't based on how you look but on who you are.

EXERCISE 3:
ACCEPT YOUR GOD-GIVEN TALENTS AND GIFTS

Too often we think we need to be someone other than who we are. We enjoy a great singer and wonder why we don't have that talent. We are enraptured by an orator and wonder why God didn't give us that gift. We need to quit thinking about what we don't have and start thanking God for what we do have.

1. List here all the talents and gifts that God has given you. What are all the things you can do that bless this earth, the people on it, or the society in which you dwell?_____

_____

_____

_____

_____

2. Now ask your spouse to list your strengths, talents, gifts, and attributes. Write them here._____

_____

_____

_____

_____

3. Ask at least one of your friends—several if you get the chance—to help you with this exercise. Tell them what this chapter is about and ask them to list what they see as your strengths, attributes, and gifts. Transfer some of their comments to this page._____

_____

_____

_____

_____

4. Now, take stock of all you've written and make a prayer list. Write it here. Thank God for all that He's blessed you with._____

_____

_____

_____

_____

If you are enrolled in a Family Dynamics Institute *Becoming ONE* course, your facilitator will guide you in how you should share your answers with your spouse. If you are not enrolled in the FDI course, we suggest you spend at least an hour this week discussing your written answers with your spouse. Allow each to "skip" any questions he or she is not comfortable discussing. Your goal is to help each other feel better about yourselves, not to learn everything your spouse wrote.

Developing Emotional Intimacy, Part 2
Learning How to Make Intimacy Grow

Just the other day in a seminar I watched it happen again. I asked the question, "What is the number one reason that men visit prostitutes?" It usually takes the audience a few minutes to figure it out, but this time a male newlywed quickly sang out, "To talk!"—which is the right answer.

Immediately his wife spun to face him with murder in her eyes and venom on her tongue. "How do you know that?!" she spat at him, completely disregarding the fact that more than three hundred pairs of ears heard every word.

"I read it. It's in lots of articles and…"

"I'm *sure* you did!" she huffed and then spun away from him so that for the remainder of the session she held her back to him. When the session was over, she lifted her nose high and strode indignantly from the room as he followed like a dog at heel.

They didn't come back.

I was hoping they would return so I could predict their future for her. Their marriage has a structural flaw, and if they make it past the third anniversary, it will be only because she will teach him to lie effectively and smoothly.

Teach him?

Sure. That's how behavioral psychology works. Negatively reinforced behaviors tend to diminish; positively reinforced behaviors tend to repeat. She taught him that if he said anything that she didn't like, even uttering a known fact that she found displeasing, she would punish him (negatively reinforce him). It wouldn't take him long to learn his role. Either he'd leave her so that he could live in truth, or he'd learn to tell her only what she wanted to hear. I'm sure she thought she wanted a marriage based on honesty and openness, but she showed hundreds of people that she would only accept a marriage based on hearing what she wanted to hear.

In a year or so she'll likely berate him, "Why don't you talk to me? You never talk to me!" I could tell her why.

The major barrier to communication in marriage (other than time constraints and misplaced priorities) is *fear*. People don't share their lives—what they have done, are doing, or plan to do—because they fear some kind of rejection from the other.

Surely you want your marriage to be based on honesty and openness. One thing is sure: If you want true intimacy, honesty must be the basis of your relationship. To develop intimacy, you must work through each of the four steps to open communication. We repeat the four steps briefly here:

- You must accept yourself as you are.

- You must share facts—first nonthreatening facts, then potentially threatening facts.

- You must share feelings—first nonthreatening feelings, then potentially threatening feelings.

- You must accept the other.

In the last chapter, we worked on step 1. Now it's time to deal with the last three steps. If you're ready to be honest and accept honesty in your spouse, you're ready to begin. If you cannot be honest or accept honesty from your spouse, we suggest you work through the exercises in the previous chapter once more before beginning this one.

EXERCISE 1:
LEARN TO SHARE FACTS

Step 2 begins with sharing facts that we deem nonthreatening—meaning we don't fear rejection, recrimination, or reprisal in sharing these facts. Then we gradually move to sharing more threatening facts. We share at this deeper level only to the degree that we find acceptance from our listener. At the first sign of any negative emotional reaction, we pull back and start editing the information we share. When we feel a threat of real rejection or reprisal, we stop sharing the truth altogether.

In this first exercise, you'll learn to share nonthreatening facts about your life by looking back on your life and remembering those events—specific or general—that molded or shaped you in any way. For example, a general event may be visiting your grandmother's farm every summer. A specific event would be something that happened during one of those visits.

We've divided your life into time segments—beginning with your early life (before school) and continuing all the way through your eighties (if you've lived that long). As you list events under each segment, try to remember those events that molded you—for the good or bad—during those times. Concentrate on *character-molding* or *life-changing* events rather than who sat next to you in third grade. Record happenings, comments made by others, or episodes that affect the way you do things today.

Don't write long descriptions right now; write just enough to jog your memory when you reread this later, so that you'll know which event your note refers to. Because you will have many more memories than you can make time for in this exercise, please spend absolutely no more than five minutes writing about each life period. In your allotted time, write down as many events as you can remember. Make your time count.

Early Life (before school)

_____
_____
_____
_____

Grammar School

_____
_____
_____

Junior High Years

_____
_____
_____
_____

High School Years

_____
_____
_____
_____

College Years

_____
_____
_____
_____

20s

_____

_____

_____

_____

30s

_____

_____

_____

40s

_____

_____

_____

50s

_____

_____

_____

60s

_____

_____

_____

70s

_____

_____

_____

80s

_____

_____

_____

_____

Now, go back through all the notes you've written and do the following:

1. Choose three events that will tell your spouse something about you—why you are as you are, why you think as you do, why you feel as you do—and that you deem nonthreatening to share. Write a little more detail about each of those three events here._____

_____

_____

_____

_____

_____

_____

_____

2. Now, go through the list again to find three events that you feel threatened to share. Choose events that reveal something about you—why you are as you are, think as you think, or feel as you feel—and that will really help your spouse to know you. Make sure these aren't things you've revealed to him or her before, unless you now plan to reveal certain dimensions that you previously kept hidden. Write about the three events you feel threatened to share with your spouse in greater detail here._____

_____

_____

_____

_____

_____

_____

_____

3. When both of you have finished this part of the exercise, sit with each other with all distractions removed—TV off, phone off the hook, kids away or in bed, "do not disturb" sign on the door—and start to share.

   a. One person shares one nonthreatening event. If he or she feels that the other person is accepting of that event and shows no sign of rejection, emotional withdrawal, boredom, or any other negative emotion, the session continues. If he or she detects any negative reaction, he or she can call a halt to the session.

   b. If the session continues, the second spouse shares one nonthreatening event. If he or she feels that the other person is accepting of that event and shows no sign of rejection, emotional withdrawal, boredom, or any other negative emotion, the session continues. If he or she detects any negative reaction, he or she can call a halt to the session.

   c. If either spouse felt the need to halt the session, commit to try again later...and later again, if necessary...until you learn to share the facts of your lives with each other without experiencing rejection in any way.

   d. Continue taking turns until each spouse has shared three events—whether this takes one session or fifteen! Neither should share when feeling negative reactions from the other, and each should work diligently at learning to hear and accept what the other has to say.

4. When you've both shared all three nonthreatening events, move on with the same process for the potentially threatening events.

Completing this exercise may happen in one night, or it may take months. Don't push or force; rather, learn to talk to each other. Learn to listen. Learn to accept what the other says about the past, or you'll never learn how to accept the present, much less the future.

Work on this exercise as long as you need to, but be sure you've finished each step and are doing well before moving on.

EXERCISE 2:
LEARN TO SHARE FEELINGS

1. Go back through the events you shared in exercise 1. This time, concentrate on sharing:

- what you felt about the event as it happened
- how you've felt about it over the years
- what you feel about it now

2. Begin with the feelings related to the nonthreatening events, then move to feelings related to potentially threatening events.

3. Use the same process you used in exercise 1 to decide when to move forward and when each spouse takes his or her turn.

Take your time. When you do this exercise right, your relationship will grow in intimacy in very dramatic ways.

EXERCISE 3:
LEARN TO ACCEPT THE OTHER PERSON

Active Listening

There are many ways to make your spouse understand that you accept him or her as life experiences and feelings are shared. You can do it by actively listening.

You can show your interest by not looking at other things, not asking distracting questions, and not inserting disconnecting thoughts. Some of the basics of active listening are as follows:

- Look directly at the person talking and not at anything else in the room.

- Make comments or sounds that show you're listening—laugh or sigh when appropriate; say "uh-huh" or "oh" or anything else that is natural. Make sure you don't say anything that shows judgment or rejection.

- Whatever you do, *never* demonstrate criticism or contempt. Criticism isn't the same as complaint. Complaints focus on behavior; criticism focuses on the person. Contempt goes one step farther and communicates disgust.[1]

- Ask clarifying questions when appropriate. Make sure they don't seem prying or attacking in any way, just a clarification so that you are sure of what he/she is saying.

- Repeat what your spouse is saying in your own words to show that you understand. For example, you might say, "You felt anger when your grandmother told you that you weren't as smart as your brother."

- Use any physical movement or action that is appropriate—hug, hold hands, etc.

As you use the skills of active listening, your mate will be carefully watching to see if you can really accept what you hear. If your mate believes that you can and will accept—even if you don't like what you hear—he or she will gradually tell you the whole truth. People want to be honest and open; they are just afraid to be. You can lead your spouse to honesty by acceptance.

Forgiveness

Sometimes acceptance means *forgiveness*. Even if you hurt. Even if you're devastated by what you hear. Remember that your mate isn't sharing this to hurt you. (You can tell if he or she is by attitude and demeanor.) If your mate is sharing these things because he or she wants to get past a barrier, overcome a sin, or in some way grow to a newer and better level of intimacy with you, help that happen. Understand that his or her humiliation of self before you isn't for any purpose other than to develop intimacy between the two of you.

As your mate shares, you may need to say, "I forgive you." Interestingly, you may need to say that about things that happened before you ever came into his or her life. Those three words, "I forgive you," are the three most powerful words in the English language—even more powerful than "I love you."

When you've each completed the exercise of sharing both nonthreatening and threatening facts *and* feelings, it's time for an exercise in acceptance.

Write a Letter

Write your mate a letter that does three things:

- Let your mate know that you understood the things that he or she was afraid to share. Reference them in some nonpunishing, nonjudgmental way, but make it clear that you know what he or she was wanting you to understand. Focus on letting your spouse know you understand and accept how he or she *feels*.

- Forgive anything that needs forgiving. Write your forgiveness in bold and powerful words. Don't make it conditional or potential. Make your mate know that your love and forgiveness are being given with all that is within you.

- Affirm his or her worth and value. Tell your spouse why you love him or her as you do it. Express your expectations for a future together and make any promises that you can genuinely make.

You probably want to write the letter on stationery or nice paper, not in this workbook. But right here make the notes from which you will write your letter. Be sure to deliver it just as soon as you possibly can.

My Letter to My Spouse

_____
_____
_____
_____
_____
_____
_____
_____
_____
_____
_____
_____
_____
_____
_____
_____

EXERCISE 4: THE PRESENT AND FUTURE

1. Set aside at least one evening a week—from now on—to talk. Thus far, we've had you concentrate on your past; now you need to talk about your present and your future. Clear out a couple of hours. Choose a time and setting where you can share without distractions or interruptions.

2. Share the facts and feelings of your day, your week, your hobbies, your church, and everything else that is important to you. Remember to start with facts, and remember to take turns.

3. If either person feels a lack of acceptance or any negative reaction, he or she may call a halt to that sharing session. Start again the next week or the next session. Neither spouse should ever push, cajole, or make a negative remark. Remember that people want to share, but they only share when honesty is rewarded or reinforced.

4. When you talk about the future, answer questions like:

   • What do you want to be doing five years from now?

   • What have you always wanted to do that you never have?

   • What dream did you have as a kid that hasn't yet been fulfilled?

When you ask and answer these kinds of questions, you may find that you have many things to *do* together, which will make each of you very happy! As you learn to become more intimate by talking and feeling, you will find ample opportunity to give each other the kind of intimacy each wants. You'll be taking more trips together, finding more things to do together, and tackling more projects together.

Chapter
6

Developing Sexual Intimacy, Part 1
Opening the Door to Sexual Ecstasy

Sex.

Just the word grabs immediate attention. It's used to entice people to actions of every kind imaginable. Quite a few corporations use sexy advertising to get the public to buy their products. Some women use their sexual charms to attract and manipulate men. Many comedians make sex a major part of their routine because it's sure to get a laugh—especially if their punchline tiptoes on the edge of decency. Even clothes designers, cosmetic companies, and purveyors of perfumes concentrate on sexual allure.

With all that bombardment from every side, it would be easy for a husband or wife to confuse the Madison Avenue brand of sexuality with the sexual fulfillment God designed for marriage. God intends sex to be wholesome, satisfying, and thoroughly enjoyable. He never designed it to be what some people have made it—dirty, hidden, shameful, and degrading.

If you've read the chapter on sexual fulfillment in the accompanying book, *Becoming ONE*, you know that the Bible speaks very specifically about sex, without shame or embarrassment. The Bible doesn't just tell us which sexual acts are sinful and debasing, it also paints a lovely picture of complete sexual fulfillment and happiness.

Unfortunately, few Christians have developed complete sexual fulfillment in their marriages.

In the weekend seminar that I conduct called *Love, Sex & Marriage*, I include a session where individuals can anonymously submit written questions about sex.

I don't think you'd like reading them.

Oh, some are okay, even amusing. Some of the questions are intentionally funny; some just ask for information on certain matters. But then there are the handfuls of sheets covered with heartbreak where the writer pours his or her misery into a few scrawled sentences on the page.

We receive the same questions over and again at each seminar—sometimes in a man's handwriting, other times in a woman's. The questions are frequently prefaced by short explanations that let me know that the writer has already passed from desperation to hopelessness. And yet they ask anyway: *Can you help? Is there an answer? Is this all I have to look forward to for the rest of my life? How can I stay faithful?*

It's true of the general populace, and my experiences in state after state make me believe it is definitely true among Christians: For all the talk and emphasis on sex in our society, many husbands and wives have no clue how to find the fulfillment God designed for the sexual union of marriage.

But the answer is there. God does want sexual happiness for us, and He told us how to find it. It's right in the Bible.

Let's look to it for our first exercise in this chapter.

EXERCISE 1: WHAT DOES THE BIBLE SAY?

God addressed this strong sexual desire and need in humans through the writings of Paul in 1 Corinthians 7:2–5:

> But since there is so much immorality, each man should have his own wife, and each woman her own husband. The husband should fulfill his marital duty to his wife, and likewise the wife to her husband. The wife's body does not belong to her alone but also to her husband. In the same way, the husband's body does not belong to him alone but also to his wife. Do not deprive each other except by mutual consent and for a time, so that you may devote yourselves to prayer. Then come together again so that Satan will not tempt you because of your lack of self-control.

Working together, answer these questions about the information in the above passage.

1. Which mate does Paul say has the need for marital fulfillment?_____
   _____
   _____
   _____
   _____

2. In the context of this passage, what is the meaning of "marital duty"?_____
   _____
   _____
   _____
   _____

3. What does Paul mean when he says the wife's body belongs to the husband and the husband's body belongs to the wife?_____

_____

_____

_____

_____

4. What is meant by "depriving" one's mate?_____

_____

_____

_____

5. What does Paul mean when he says that "depriving" may only be done by mutual consent?_____

_____

_____

6. What does Paul mean when he says that "depriving" may only be done for a time?_____

_____

_____

7. Why does Paul say that the couple should be praying during the time of "depriving"? _____

_____

_____

8. What does Paul mean when he says Satan "will...tempt you because of your lack of self-control"?_____

_____

_____

9. Now, how does this passage specifically apply to your marriage?_____

_____

_____

_____

EXERCISE 2:
BIBLICAL PROHIBITIONS

In the accompanying book, *Becoming ONE*, we listed ten biblical prohibitions concerning sex. A great deal of what the Bible teaches about sex comes in the form of prohibitions. Don't let that make you think God is against sex. He made it! But He made it to be enjoyed in His design—not in any human aberration of that design. Let's examine some of those prohibitions. By knowing what God prohibits, we can deduce what God designed to be fulfilling in sexual union.

Working together, look up each of the passages listed below and read them aloud. After reading the verses, answer the questions about each prohibition.

Incest

God strongly condemned sexual relations with a "close relative." (For the sake of time, you may wish to skip looking up all the verses below and just read one or two.) Relatives listed include:

- Mother (Leviticus 18:7)

- Father's wife or stepmother (Leviticus 18:8; under penalty of death, Leviticus 20:11)

- Sister, half-sister, or stepsister (Leviticus 18:9, 11; penalized by being cut off from the people, Leviticus 20:17)

- Grandchild (Leviticus 18:10)

- Aunt (Leviticus 18:12–14; penalized by dying childless, Leviticus 20:19)

- Daughter-in-law (Leviticus 18:15)

- Sister-in-law (Leviticus 18:16)

- Daughter or granddaughter of woman one had sex with (Leviticus 18:17; penalized by death, Leviticus 20:14)

1. Why do you think God would make sexual relationships with these relatives a sin?_____

_____

_____

_____

2. Which relatives did you expect to find in the laws against incest that you don't see listed above?_____

_____

_____

_____

3. What should people in our day learn from these Old Testament passages?

_____

_____

_____

_____

Homosexuality

God strongly condemns sexual relations with a person of the same gender in the Old Testament (Leviticus 18:22; penalized by death, Leviticus 20:13). He condemns it just as strongly in the New Testament (Romans 1:24–28; penalized by spiritual death, Romans 1:27; 6:23).

1. What is God's view on homosexual activities?_____

_____

_____

2. Sometimes people who would never actually be involved in same-sex situations will fantasize about it. What would these passages lead you to understand about those kinds of fantasies?_____

_____

_____

3. Read 1 Corinthians 6:9–11. What do these verses tell us about a homosexual's ability to live a life free from homosexual activity?_____

_____

_____

4. What application, if any, does that have to your marriage?_____

_____

_____

_____

Rape

If a man raped a married or engaged woman, he was to be executed while the woman was held to be innocent and worthy of no punishment. If the woman could have summoned help but didn't, she was also to be executed (Deuteronomy 22:23–27).

In the Old Testament, if a man raped a single, unengaged woman, he was not put to death. The penalty was to marry her with no possibility of divorce, ever (Deuteronomy 22:28–29).

1. The New Testament doesn't specifically mention rape. From your reading of the passages above, what do you believe God's view of rape is in our day? _____

_____

_____

2. In our era, if a man forces his wife to have sex with him by threatening physical harm or by physically overpowering her, is that a sin before God?_____

_____

_____

_____

3. What other ways could a person "rape" his or her spouse, bringing harm either physically, emotionally, or spiritually?_____

_____

_____

_____

Consensual Sex Outside of Marriage

In the Old Testament, if a man slept with a woman who consensually engaged in sex with him, his penalty was to marry her (if her father wished) with no possibility of divorce (Exodus 22:16–17).

The New Testament made it clear that God expected sex to take place only in the boundaries of marriage (1 Corinthians 7:2–5). Anyone guilty of sexual sin—called "fornication" in some versions and "sexual immorality" in others—would suffer spiritual death unless he or she found God's forgiveness (Galatians 5:19–21).

1. If a couple not yet married—even if they are engaged—participates in oral sex with each other, is that a sin before God?_____

_____

_____

_____

2. What sexual limits exist for any couple not yet married—even if they are engaged?_____

_____

_____

3. What, if anything, about your activities together before marriage do you need to confess before God and have Him cleanse your conscience of?_____

_____

_____

_____

Adultery

In the Old Testament adultery only occurred if a married woman was involved. A man who slept with a single woman (see above) didn't commit adultery since men could, by law, have more than one wife. Since women couldn't, by law, have more than one husband, any sexual encounter with another man—married or single—was adultery. God vehemently condemns it (Leviticus 20:10) and listed the punishment as death (Deuteronomy 22:22).

In the New Testament anyone married to one person but sleeping with another committed adultery. "Marriage should be honored by all, and the marriage bed kept pure, for God will judge the adulterer and all the sexually immoral" (Hebrews 13:4).

1. What is God's view of a person who commits adultery?_____
_____
_____
_____
_____

2. Why do you think so many people are guilty of the sin of adultery?_____
_____
_____
_____
_____

3. How could you make your sex life together so fulfilling that adultery's temptation would have little drawing power to either of you?_____
_____
_____
_____
_____

Lust

In the Old Testament God phrased it this way: "You shall not covet your neighbor's wife" (Exodus 20:17). In the New Testament Jesus said, "You have heard that it was said, 'Do not commit adultery.' But I tell you that anyone who looks at a woman lustfully has already committed adultery with her in his heart" (Matthew 5:27–28).

1. At what point does attraction become lust?_____
_____
_____
_____

2. How is it possible for a woman to commit the sin of lust?_____
_____
_____
_____
_____

3. If a person fantasized about another while having sex with his or her spouse, would that be lust that God condemns?_____
_____
_____

Prostitution

God stated He detests prostitution (Deuteronomy 23:17–18). In the New Testament He said through Paul, "Do you not know that your bodies are members of Christ himself? Shall I then take the members of Christ and unite them with a prostitute? Never!" (1 Corinthians 6:15).

1. Why do you think a man or woman would engage the services of a prostitute?

_____

_____

_____

2. How could a married couple develop the kind of relationship—spiritually, sexually, emotionally—that would prevent either of them from ever being tempted by a prostitute?_____

_____

Bestiality

Any person, male or female, who participated in sexual activity with any animal was to be put to death under the Old Testament law (Leviticus 20:15–16).

1. Read the Old Testament passage about bestiality. What is God's view about a person who has sex with an animal in our day?_____

_____

_____

2. How would God view a person or couple who fantasized about bestiality or who read about it or watched it in pornographic material?_____

_____

_____

Sex during the Menstrual Period

A basic principle of Scripture is "the life of a creature is in the blood" (Leviticus 17:11). Therefore, blood is always treated as holy—even in the New Testament (Acts 15:29).

Understanding that principle helps us understand God's law listed in the Old Testament about sexual relations during the wife's menstrual period. He said that it shouldn't happen (Leviticus 15:24; 18:19) and listed the penalty as being "cut off" from the people (Leviticus 20:18). Many today believe that particular part of the "blood" law was given primarily for health reasons—the people of the Old Testament did not have access to our modern hygiene or medicines—and that particular law has no application to Christians. Others feel that it lists God's view of the sanctity of blood and should still be observed by Christians who respect God's feelings.

1. What do you understand God's view of sex during the menstrual period to be for people today?_____

_____

_____

_____

Harm the Body

While this isn't specifically mentioned as I will describe it, the principle applies to anything that affects a person's body. Remember, the context in which the following passage is found is one that discusses sexual activity. In 1 Corinthians 6:19–20, Paul wrote, "Do you not know that your body is a temple of the Holy Spirit, who is in you, whom you have received from God? You are not your own; you were bought at a price. Therefore, honor God with your body." While our spirits belong to God, so do our bodies. We are not to do anything that desecrates the temple of God that our body is. Sexual activity that harms the body should not occur.

1. What sexual practices can you think of that would violate this principle?

_____

_____

2. Which sexual practices, if any, should you discontinue in your relationship because they harm at least one of you physically, emotionally, or spiritually?

_____

_____

EXERCISE 3:
ACCEPTABLE SEXUAL PRACTICES

If we summarize everything from exercise 2, the following limitations are the only ones that exist for sex to be everything that God intended.

- Sex must only take place in the confines of marriage.
- Sex may never involve: (1) another person besides your mate, (2) any animal, or (3) anything that causes harm to either person's body.

1. List as many activities and practices you can think of or imagine that a couple could employ in their sex lives without violating Scripture. First, each of you make a list by yourself. Then combine your lists here._____

_____

_____

_____

_____

_____

_____

EXERCISE 4:
ACHIEVING SEXUAL FULFILLMENT

This is the same exercise listed at the end of chapter 6 in *Becoming ONE*. In this workbook the difference is that we ask you to write answers to the questions listed.

Discussing Sexual Fulfillment

1. Discuss in detail what brings each of you to the greatest levels of arousal and desire. Take turns. Listen carefully. Take your time. Try to learn more about your spouse than you know now.

2. Write here what you learned about your spouse's arousal and desire._____
_____
_____
_____
_____
_____

Exploring Bodies

1. Give your spouse a detailed exploration of your body. For example, the wife can guide her husband's hand to help him understand why and when and where the swelling of arousal takes place in her breasts and genitals and to explain how her body lubricates itself for intercourse. Remember, go very slowly and explain things in detail—especially your emotions and physical sensations.

2. When the husband has fully explored his wife's body (only as she guides him!), he then takes her hand and gives a similar explanation of his body's reactions. He, too, concentrates on explaining his emotions and physical sensations.

3. Write here what you learned about your spouse's body and his or her reactions to various physical stimuli._____
_____
_____
_____
_____
_____

Removing Barriers

1. Discuss inhibitions or guilts that have prevented you from being completely open sexually with your spouse. Take turns. Be understanding and avoid any criticism or contempt. Discuss how what you learned in this chapter could help you get past these inhibitions or guilt.

2. What did you learn about your spouse that will give you insight into helping him or her become more open sexually?_____

_____

_____

_____

_____

_____

Developing Sexual Intimacy, Part 2
Becoming Consummate Lovers

In the previous chapter you began a process to become a better lover. Don't take offense; you may be the best lover on the planet, but any person can become more skilled at anything he or she wishes to concentrate on.

We started in the last chapter by exploring God's plan for sexual fulfillment, including various restrictions He placed on sex. Those restrictions weren't to make sex less enjoyable. Just the opposite. They actually enhance the relationship between husband and wife. They keep the sexual union between them pure and ultimately intimate.

But God did more than tell us He made sex a vital part of our relationship. He did more than give us the parameters of what is and isn't acceptable in human sexuality. He also included in His Bible a description of what great lovemaking is. As He often did throughout the Bible, He taught this to us not through legalistic directions but through a wonderful story. All we have to do is read the story carefully, and we'll learn marvelous methods of consummate lovemaking.

We find the story in Solomon's Song of Songs. In this beautiful and poetic book, Solomon and his bride each give us glimpses into fulfilling lovemaking as they describe each other and their reactions to each other.

Some read this story and see only symbolism of the love Jesus would one day have for His church, ignoring the sexual dimension altogether. Don't make that mistake. While this beautiful picture of love certainly can be used as an analogy of the deep, intense love that Jesus feels for His bride—His church—and that the church in return should feel for Him, its original message was explicitly sexual. Just as Jesus and His church become one as each person in His church gives him- or herself to Him in body, heart, and spirit—so do husband and wife become one flesh when they sexually unite—bringing body, heart, and spirit together. That isn't dirty or shameful. It's just the way it is. Our uniting completely with our spouses whom we deeply love is a vivid representation of uniting ourselves with Jesus as we give ourselves to Him.

That said, let's leave the deep theological implications to another study and get back to our purpose at hand. Since Song of Songs is so sexually explicit, there is much to learn about becoming consummate lovers.

Before we begin a few exercises to learn from Solomon's song, allow us to point out that it is written in the idiom of Solomon's day. We, for example, use many idioms to refer to sex. We talk of people "sleeping together." Because you understand the idioms of our day, you have no difficulty understanding that "sleeping together" refers to sexual intercourse.

We have other idioms to refer to the sex act, women's breasts, male and female genitalia, and the like. We quickly interpret their meaning because we've heard those or similar phrases in conversations about sex. But imagine what it would be like for a person a couple of thousand years from now who was trying to interpret a man's love letter to his wife. You can probably pick out five or ten words in a just a couple of minutes that the husband might use that wouldn't be so easy to interpret by a person from a different time and place.

So it is with Solomon and his bride.

They speak the vernacular of their day, not ours. So to understand them, we must do some interpreting of our own. How? By reading carefully the context and doing the best we can to figure what he or she is referring to.

Not only is this great interpretative fun, it actually is quite educational. It tells a lot about the techniques of a great lover.

We strongly urge you to read the accompanying book, *Becoming ONE*, to get the full impact of the verses that follow in our exercises.

As you read Song of Songs, be aware that the person speaking (Solomon or his wife) changes rapidly—sometimes without a clear indication of the change. It's important that you know who's speaking, or you won't understand what is being said. We'll tell you who is speaking in each of the following verses. We give an endnote reference on each passage to tell you what we think the verse means. We put our interpretations in the endnotes instead of in this text because we believe you will gain greater knowledge by working through the verses on your own.

EXERCISE 1:
SOLOMON ON SEX

In the book, *Becoming ONE*, we shared one scripture from Song of Songs and asked you to try to figure out what it was describing. Here, we repeat that verse and give you space to write out your answer. (We've also repeated the hints so you won't have to refer back to the book.) Then, we ask you to read and try to interpret a few more verses. By understanding what these verses mean, you'll get a wonderful picture of what fulfilling sex between a husband and wife should be.

Read the scriptures together, discuss them with each other, then each write your interpretation of the following verses in your own study guides.

Song of Songs 4:6

"Until the day breaks and the shadows flee, I will go to the mountain of myrrh and to the hill of incense."

Note: Solomon is speaking to his wife in this passage.

1. How long does he anticipate the lovemaking session will last? _____

2. What is he referring to when he speaks of "the mountain of myrrh and the hill of incense?" We've provided you with some hints below._____

_____

Hints: As you answer this question, notice that his use of the words *mountain* and *hill* are singular, not plural. Also, remember that myrrh and incense are unique and special aromas or fragrances. And notice that it doesn't appear that the mountain of myrrh and the hill of incense are different places but two ways to refer to the same place. Does your answer to question 2 consider all those factors?

If you wish, you may see our interpretation by checking this endnote.[1]

Song of Songs 4:15

"You are a garden fountain, a well of flowing water streaming down from Lebanon."

Note: Solomon is addressing his wife in this passage.

1. What is he describing?_____

_____

Hint: He describes his wife's reaction to his lovemaking. As you interpret this verse describing how she reacts to him, remember that your words should explain the image that he uses, *flowing* and *streaming.*

2. What does this reaction on her part tell you about Solomon's lovemaking skills and techniques?_____

_____

_____

_____

If you wish, you may see our interpretation by checking this endnote.[2]

Song of Songs 4:16

"Awake, north wind, and come, south wind! Blow on my garden, that its fragrance may spread abroad. Let my lover come into his garden and taste its choice fruits."

Note: Solomon's wife is responding to Solomon's statement in the previous passage.

1. What is she asking him to do?_____

_____

Hint: Whatever Solomon meant by a "flowing" garden stream in the preceding verse is the same body part that she refers to. She says that it has fragrance. Remember that as you interpret this verse, you should clearly delineate what she wanted from him—what he was to do and where he was to do it.

2. How enthusiastic is she about wanting him to do that for her?_____

_____

_____

If you wish to see our interpretation, check this endnote.[3]

Song of Songs 7:7–9

"Your stature is like that of the palm, and your breasts like clusters of fruit. I said, 'I will climb the palm tree; I will take hold of its fruit.' May your breasts be like the clusters of the vine, the fragrance of your breath like apples, and your mouth like the best wine."

Note: Again, Solomon is addressing his wife.

1. What do you think Solomon meant when he said, "I will climb the palm"?

_____

_____

2. What does this verse tell you about Solomon's lovemaking skills and techniques?_____

_____

Hint: To understand what Solomon is telling her, concentrate on what he means when he compares her body to the stately palm tree. What would she understand him to be telling her when he says that he will "climb the palm tree"? What image does that draw in your mind? What action do you see him doing that fits that description?

If you wish to see our interpretation, you may find it in this endnote.[4]

Song of Songs 7:9–10

"May the wine go straight to my lover, flowing gently over lips and teeth. I belong to my lover, and his desire is for me."

Note: This is Solomon's wife responding to him.

1. What is she describing?_____

_____

_____

_____

2. What does her language tell you about her involvement and enjoyment of their sexual encounter?_____

_____

_____

_____

Hint: This time Solomon's wife speaks to him, replying to his statement that he would climb the palm. She graphically tells him her response to his action. What is she saying will occur? Remember, your interpretation should be supported by the image she paints with her words. She's poetically describing something.

If you would like to see our interpretation, you may find it in this endnote.[5]

EXERCISE 2: LEARNING "TECHNIQUE" FROM SOLOMON

In the book, *Becoming ONE*, we pointed out several insights from Solomon's Song of Songs for both husband and wife on how to be greater lovers.

Solomon's Insights—Techniques for Husbands

Working together as husband and wife, answer the following questions, combining what you learned in the book with what you learned from our discussion of the various references from Song of Songs. Remember, if a husband learns to love his wife like Solomon loved his, he should receive the same kind of response from his wife that Solomon received from his. Be sure to write your answers in your workbooks.

1. Describe what foreplay, plateau, orgasm, and afterglow would be like for the two of you if each of you could have each stage in the way that you would most enjoy it.

Foreplay: Actions and words that prepare each person's body for intercourse. The man's penis fills with blood and becomes erect. The woman's breasts and genitals swell and become more sensitive. She also begins to lubricate. _____

_____

_____

_____

_____

Plateau: The period of sustained physical, emotional, and mental pleasure. _____

_____

_____

_____

_____

_____

Orgasm: The culmination of the plateau stage by a few seconds of extremely pleasurable physical sensation. The male typically ejaculates. The female typically has strong vaginal contractions. _____

_____

_____

_____

_____

_____

Afterglow: The period during which each person's body relaxes to its natural state. Men usually prepare quickly during foreplay and relax quickly in afterglow. Women usually prepare more slowly during foreplay and relax more slowly during afterglow. _____

_____

_____

_____

_____

_____

1. What would you need to do different from what you are doing now to make each of the four stages more pleasurable for each of you? (Think of everything you need to say here. Talk about it openly and honestly.) _____

_____

_____

_____

_____

2. How much time would you have to have available to achieve this special lovemaking you just described?_____

_____

_____

_____

_____

3. When can you make time for this to happen (including all the arrangements such as children, work schedules, etc.)?_____

_____

_____

_____

_____

_____

_____

_____

4. Make a "date" right now for when you will enjoy a lovemaking session like you've described above. When is that specific date?_____

EXERCISE 3:
LEARNING TO
COMPROMISE

In *Becoming ONE*, we explain that sometimes each mate has to learn to compromise to meet the needs or desires of the other. It isn't unusual for one to want something sexually that the other doesn't feel comfortable doing for some reason. In the book we listed the following steps to compromise:

- Each should understand and accept either the desire or the hesitation of the other.

- Pray for God to solve the problem. Ask Him to give each of you understanding of the other. Ask Him to get each of you past whatever memories, misconceptions, misunderstandings, or hang-ups that you have. Ask Him to give you a wonderful, totally uninhibited sex life within the parameters of His boundaries.

- Each of you should make it your unalterable goal to fulfill the other as best you can within the parameters of God's will.

If either of you wants something that the other has refused or is refusing to grant, please use this exercise to find a compromise. If that situation doesn't exist in your marriage, skip to exercise 4.

Understand Each Other

Whether you are the hesitant or requesting spouse, answer all the following questions to the best of your understanding.

1. Write what the desire of the requesting spouse is: _____
_____
_____

2. Write why he or she desires it: _____
_____
_____
_____
_____
_____
_____

3. Write why the hesitant spouse feels hesitation or resistance: _____
_____
_____
_____
_____
_____
_____

4. Each of you should write a statement accepting what the other feels. Be sure to make it kind and warm and loving. Rewrite the statement as many times as you need to until your spouse says, "Yes, that's exactly how I feel. You really understand."

Your statement of understanding: _____
_____
_____
_____
_____
_____

Make a Prayer Guide

1. Write a statement that you will use when you pray to God asking Him for more understanding and acceptance of your spouse's feelings on this matter.

Your first prayer statement: _____
_____
_____
_____
_____

2.   Write a statement that you will use when you pray to God asking Him to get you over any bad memories, misconceptions, misunderstandings, or hang-ups.

Your second prayer statement:_____

_____

_____

_____

_____

_____

3.   Write a statement that you will use when you pray to God asking Him to give you a wonderful, totally uninhibited sex life within the parameters of His boundaries.

Your third prayer statement:_____

_____

_____

_____

_____

_____

4.   Now, using what you've each written in your workbooks, bow together and pray aloud to God all that you've written. Add anything your heart desires to praise Him or petition Him for. Each should pray in turn. The hesitant partner will pray his or her first prayer statement, then the other prays. The hesitant partner will then pray his or her second prayer statement, and the other follows again. Follow this pattern until you are done.

A Plan for Compromise

Now each of you write what you will do to reach a compromise on this matter. The one who desires the action should write how he or she will remove all pressure from the other and demonstrate patience and acceptance, as long as it takes. The one who is reticent should write how he or she will make a plan to do—at least on some level and schedule—the thing that the other wants. Make sure to include goal dates as to when you can achieve this.

1.   The "requesting person's" statement of compromise:_____

_____

_____

_____

_____

_____

_____

2. The "hesitant person's" statement of compromise:_____

_____

_____

_____

_____

_____

_____

Be sure to live by what you've written here. Don't promise anything that you won't commit to fulfilling, whether it's removing all pressure from the other or satisfying the desire of the other.

EXERCISE 4:
MAKING SEX FUN

This exercise consists of a game that you will play with each other. The rules are simple.

1. Each of you will write three sexual scenarios that you would enjoy. You may make each as romantic or as fanciful as you like. You may choose location, time of day, apparel, activities (especially sexual activities), and anything else that appeals to you. As you write each scenario, do so in detail, as if you were describing what has already happened.

2. When you have finished, you will give your three scenarios to your mate. He or she will read them to make sure that you haven't included anything outside his or her "comfort zone." If something is uncomfortable, rewrite the scenario as many times as it takes to make it exciting and pleasing to you while also comfortable for your mate.

3. Once your mate agrees to the three scenarios, he or she has six weeks to complete all three of them. Exactly when each scenario is to be completed is to be kept a secret. You know that each of the scenarios will happen, but you don't know in what order or on what days. Of course, at the same time you will be planning the surprise fulfillment of the three scenarios given to you by your spouse. You, too, will have read them and given approval.

Each of you will complete each scenario just as written and approved. Make it fun. Make it as much of a surprise as you can, even though you know that your mate is simmering in anticipation.

4. Just remember, the scenario must abide by the following prohibitions:

    • It cannot involve any person—even in fantasy—other than the two of you.

    • It cannot involve any animal.

    • It cannot involve anything that does harm to either of you.

Commitment Statement

Can you imagine how frustrating it would be if each of you wrote the scenarios and then one refused to complete the exercises in six weeks? We know one couple who experienced this frustration. He fulfilled her three scenarios, but she became distracted by her work and never did complete his. She didn't mean to hurt him, but the result was the same as if she did. He was devastated.

To keep either of you from making that mistake, we ask you to read, date, and sign the following commitment. Each person signs it in his or her workbook and in the spouse's workbook! That way each of you has an agreement that you may use, if necessary, to gently nudge your spouse to complete the exercise.

Husband's Agreement

I, _____, agree to participate in and complete the three sexual scenarios for my wife, _____. I agree to the following conditions:

- I have the right to compromise with my spouse until all exercises meet approval from each of us.

- I will work with my spouse to come to agreement on every scenario within one week of signing this agreement.

- I will complete all three of my spouse's sexual scenarios within six weeks of the date we come to agreement about those exercises.

- If sickness or unexpected crisis keeps me from fulfilling this agreement within the specified time, I will allow my spouse to pick a new time limit and to add one more scenario to the original three. (Of course, I continue to have the right to compromise until we find a mutually acceptable version of the scenario if I have objections to the original.)

I completely agree with all the statements above and agree that I will abide by all conditions of this agreement.

Date _____

Signed_____

Wife's Agreement

I, _____, agree to participate in and complete the three sexual scenarios for my husband, _____. I agree to the following conditions:

- I have the right to compromise with my spouse until all exercises meet approval from each of us.

- I will work with my spouse to come to agreement on every scenario within one week of signing this agreement.

- I will complete all three of my spouse's sexual scenarios within six weeks of the date we come to agreement about those exercises.

- If sickness or unexpected crisis keeps me from fulfilling this agreement within the specified time, I will allow my spouse to pick a new time limit and to add one more scenario to the original three. (Of course, I continue to have the right to compromise until we find a mutually acceptable version of the scenario if I have objections to the original.)

I completely agree with all the statements above and agree that I will abide by all conditions of this agreement.

Date_____

Signed_____

Make this a game that each of you can enjoy to the fullest. Since it isn't likely that you want your scenarios to be written forever in this workbook, we ask you to use your own paper rather than supplying space here.

If you agree to do this game, exchange the first drafts of your scenarios within a week. Have fun!

Developing Spiritual Intimacy
—As a Couple

Removing Barriers and Finding Intimacy through Acceptance

"My wife has really been pushin' me, but I keep resistin'. She wants me to pray with her and read the Bible with her and stuff like that. You know that's not my thing. I'm kind of a private guy, and my prayin' is just between me and God, you know? And I'm no Bible scholar. Maggie knows a whole lot more 'bout that than I do. Why would she want to study the Bible with me? You think she's tryin' to embarrass me or somethin'? She keeps on pushin', and I keep on avoidin'."

I liked Billy and knew that he was stretching his comfort zone to tell me something as personal as this. We had become friends at church, and as a result of our friendship, I gave him any remodeling jobs I needed done. We were standing in the backyard guzzling Coca-Colas® in the shade of a southern yellow pine as he took a break from some minor carpentry work on the outside of our home. I was honored that he was telling me his concern and figured that *the* question had to come next.

It did.

"You think I'm doin' wrong by refusin' her?"

I took a long draw on the sweet nectar, emptying the can with practiced ease. After wiping my mouth with the back of my hand as Southern sharing-a-Coke®-in-the-backyard tradition required, I answered in a way I knew he'd appreciate.

"Yeah."

He sighed and pushed his Atlanta Braves hat back so far that I glimpsed the pale portion of his usually protected forehead. He moved us quickly into serious discussion territory by saying next what I hoped he'd say: "Why?"

Why, indeed.

If you've read the accompanying book, *Becoming ONE*, you've seen our arguments as to why. We cite Scripture and show without doubt that God expects both husband and wife to grow in their relationship with Him—not just as individuals but as a family. We won't take the time to repeat those arguments and cite those scriptures here. We'll use simple logic.

We assume that you are working through this workbook because you desire the deepest, most intimate relationship possible in your marriage. Wonderful. There is no better goal in a marriage. But we've reminded you from the very beginning that the craving for intimacy inherent in humankind isn't just for intimacy with another human—even as strong as that drive is. We also carry an even stronger need for intimacy with God. Because of our triune nature—body, mind, and spirit—we only experience the truest form of intimacy with another person when we are intimate with that person in all three areas. We find complete ONEness only when we have sexual intimacy, emotional intimacy, *and* spiritual intimacy.

Since the logic of that is so simple, why do so many people have trouble developing spiritual intimacy? Why would Billy have such resistance to praying or studying Scripture with Maggie? If you and your spouse aren't sharing spiritual activities that lead to spiritual harmony, why aren't you doing those things?

In our experience with thousands of couples, we've discovered that the reason most of them don't share spiritual activities is one of the following three: (1) spiritual lethargy, (2) misplaced priorities, or (3) fear of openness.

Spiritual lethargy refers to not making the effort to spend time together in spiritual activities. For example, the reason that a couple doesn't pray together is that one or both of them have too many other things they prefer to do. They may watch too much TV, play too much golf, or go to every game played by the local semi-pro hockey team. Nothing urgent pulls them to these events or activities. They're just too spiritually lazy to give up their pleasures, relaxations, and hobbies to make a regular time to pray or study or do Christian acts of service.

Misplaced priorities refers to the tendency of some to put work or ministry before important relationships. They overtax themselves with matters they consider urgent, working long hours or giving themselves to charitable work until late at night or on the weekends. They might even be so dedicated to a ministry that it prevents them from ministering to their own spouse or children. Saying that scheduling problems prevent a couple from making the time to regularly pray or study is a polite way of saying that they have their priorities wrong.

Fear of openness prevents people from praying with their spouses because they either fear rejection or ridicule from their spouse or they feel embarrassment and shame within themselves. They usually feel inadequate in their Bible knowledge or hypocritical in their lives because they fail to live up to the standards they believe to be right. Sometimes they compare themselves to others and see themselves as lacking or unholy by comparison. They can't pray openly in the presence of their spouses because they could never focus on the prayer. They'd be too worried about their own inadequacies.

Fear of rejection was the cause of Billy's hesitation. He struggled with feeling embarrassed about his lack of Bible knowledge and his feelings of spiritual inadequacy when he compared himself to his perception of his wife.

Do you think any of these three—or maybe even a combination—could be behind your lack of praying and studying Scripture with your spouse? Are you willing to be honest enough to find out?

⌒〜〜〜〜〜⌒

EXERCISE 1:
DISCOVERING WHY SPIRITUAL INTIMACY DOESN'T EXIST IN YOUR MARRIAGE

Here's a simple exercise to help you figure out whether any or all of the three hindrances we just listed apply to you.

Spiritual Lethargy

Answer the following questions honestly. When you've finished, share your answers with each other.

1. Are there times you could pray or study Scripture with your spouse or children if you simply turned off the television earlier? If so, when? _____
_____
_____
_____

2. Are there times you could pray or study Scripture with your spouse or children if you curtailed your involvement in some hobby or interest you are involved in? If so, which hobbies and activities? How often do you participate in these outside interests?_____
_____
_____
_____

3. Are there times you could pray or study Scripture with your spouse or children if you decided that it would be important to you to do that? If so, when can you make time for these spiritual activities?_____
_____
_____
_____

4. After you share your answers to the above questions with each other, please answer the next question together. Is spiritual lethargy a factor in your lack of praying and studying Scripture together? If so, how much of a factor is it? _____
_____
_____
_____

Misplaced Priorities

As we examine misplaced priorities, you will probably find it more difficult to face the answers to these questions than to those under the spiritual lethargy section. It's one thing to give up things you feel are optional. It's quite another to change things you feel are more obligatory. With all honesty, answer the following questions:

1. What is there in your life (job, special responsibility, project to which you are committed, or anything else) that is so important that it justifies neglecting the spiritual life of your family? How does it justify that?_____

_____

_____

_____

_____

_____

_____

2. Examine those things that keep you from sharing spiritual activities with your spouse or children. Look deep within yourself and answer this question: What do you personally gain from that thing (job, special responsibility, project to which you are committed, or anything else) that is so beneficial to you that it justifies neglecting the spiritual life of your family? How does it justify it?_____

_____

_____

_____

_____

_____

3. If any person in your family were to suffer a spiritual defeat—such as never becoming a child of God or ruining his or her life by ungodly actions—because you were seldom home to lead your family, would it be worth it? Would you be willing to pay that price to continue in the activities or job or ministry that now causes you to neglect the spiritual life of your family? If so, why is it worth that cost?_____

_____

_____

_____

_____

_____

_____

4. After you share your answers to the above questions with each other, please answer the next question together. Are misplaced priorities a factor in your lack of praying and studying Scripture together? If so, how much of a factor is it?____

_____

_____

_____

_____

Fear of Openness

From our experience at Family Dynamics Institute, we've concluded that fear of openness is the most common barrier to spiritual sharing. While it may seem at first glance that this would be easier to overcome than misplaced priorities, our experience teaches us that isn't necessarily so. Fear of rejection, ridicule, embarrassment, or shame is a powerful factor. We vigorously avoid any activity that has the potential to embarrass or shame us. Please answer the following questions. When you've finished, share your answers with each other.

1. Do you think that you might be embarrassed if you were to pray or study Scripture with your spouse or children? If so, why? Please make your answer as specific as you can._____

_____

_____

_____

_____

2. Do you think that your spouse may either think derogatory thoughts or say negative things to you or about you if you were to pray or study Scripture with him or her? If so, why do you think he or she would do that?_____

_____

_____

_____

_____

3. How much fear, if any, do you have of being totally open in prayer to God if your spouse could hear your prayer? Why do you fear that?_____

_____

_____

_____

_____

4. After you share your answers to the above questions with each other, please answer the next question together. Is fear of openness a factor in your lack of praying and studying Scripture together? If so, how much of a factor is it?_____

_____

_____

_____

_____

EXERCISE 2:
REMOVING BARRIERS TO SPIRITUAL INTIMACY

Now that you've identified the barriers that might be preventing you from sharing spiritually with your spouse or children, the next step is to remove those barriers. I know that you will only remove them if you feel that the blessings you gain are worth the changes that you will have to make. I urge you to trust God to bring that blessing, and I urge you to make needed changes with the full expectation that you will consequently reach deeper levels of intimacy with your spouse than you've ever known.

Removing Spiritual Lethargy

If spiritual lethargy is a barrier to spiritual intimacy, take steps to remove it. What will you have to give up? What schedule will you have to make and faithfully keep? What can you do to call each other to accountability to ensure that you regularly study Scripture and pray together?

1. As you talk about what you need to do and will do, write your plans and commitments here._____

_____

_____

_____

Rearranging Misplaced Priorities

If misplaced priorities are keeping you from sharing spiritually, you may be faced with some very tough choices. You may remember that in Chapter 3 we discussed how "intimacy diversions" can sometimes be corrected by reprioritizing. We also pointed out that some of them must be removed altogether.

Several years ago, a wonderful Christian couple, Lee and Becky Fouts, did just that. Lee was progressing through the ranks of his company and doing quite well financially. If anyone needed the money, he and Becky did. They had a house full of children, and anyone who has children knows how expensive *one* can be. Imagine raising five with hardly any spacing in their ages! But Lee realized that he would be spending more and more time at work and less and less time with his children if he continued making headway in the corporate rat race. One day he walked into my office and told me he'd taken a demotion and was moving his family to Searcy, Arkansas. He had researched a Christian school there and wanted his children to have that type of education. A lesser ranking position in his company was open in that region, and he took it, reversing every paradigm of his peers. He *willingly* moved down the corporate ladder and let his company know that he would *stay* in that position for years and years to come. He wanted to raise his children right and give them all the spiritual education he felt they deserved.

Care to guess about the spiritual intimacy in that family?

Not only do Lee and Becky love each other deeply, sharing themselves in every dimension, including spiritually, but their children are all dedicated Christians. Not long ago I was speaking for a church in Texas when the brother making announcements beamed to the congregation that their missionary in Africa would be making a visit soon. I had a chance to beam myself when they announced the missionary's name: Nick Fouts, Lee and Becky's oldest son.

Lee made the sacrifice to rearrange his priorities and open the door for spiritual intimacy with his wife and his children.

Do you need to do something similar?

Do you have the faith and courage to do it?

Discuss with your spouse any misplaced priorities that are negatively affecting your spiritual intimacy. Figure out how you can either reprioritize or remove the barrier. If removing the barrier will cause hardship for a time, plan how you can handle the hardship.

1. When you've agreed on a plan, write your plan here. _____

_____

_____

_____

_____

_____

_____

Dispelling the Fear of Openness

If fear of openness is negatively affecting your spiritual intimacy, please do all that is necessary to heal this problem.

Overcoming Feelings of Inadequacy

To remove any feelings of inadequacy, we ask that the two of you spend several minutes talking about any embarrassment or fear of ridicule or rejection that causes you to hesitate to pray. Discuss the following questions together and then write out your answers.

1. What rejection, ridicule, or potential embarrassment do you fear might happen if you pray or study Scripture together?_____

_____

_____

2. When you told your spouse these fears, what encouragement did he or she give you? Write that encouragement here. _____

_____

_____

_____

_____

_____

_____

Overcoming Shame and Embarrassment

In the accompanying book, *Becoming ONE*, we explained several steps to overcoming the barrier of feeling shame or embarrassment for sins and shortcomings. The following questions correspond to the six steps in chapter 8 in the book. Answer them as honestly and openly as you can.

1. What lingering guilt do you feel over events or actions from your past? What will you do to find the help to overcome this lingering guilt?_____

_____

_____

_____

_____

_____

_____

2. If there is any current sin in your life—angry outbursts, pornography, mistreatment of your spouse, lying, stealing, an unconfessed affair, or whatever—write it here as you confess it to your spouse. _____

_____

_____

_____

_____

_____

_____

_____

_____

3. If there is any physical dimension to the sin, destroy it or return it. For example, destroy pornography, cancel your Internet service, or return something you stole. What will you do to remove the physical dimension of the sin?

_____

_____

_____

_____

_____

_____

_____

4. If you confessed a sin or sins to your spouse, what words of forgiveness did he or she offer you? (The words of forgiveness may not come immediately; be patient as your spouse adjusts to your revelation.) _____

_____

_____

_____

_____

_____

_____

5. Write a commitment to your spouse that you will answer all his or her questions without hesitation or complaint. Show your spouse the statement and assure him or her that you will live up to this commitment. _____

_____

_____

_____

_____

_____

_____

6. Make a vow to your spouse that you will live from this point on as a faithful Christian. Show your spouse this vow and tell him or her that you will live up to your commitment. _____

_____

_____

_____

_____

_____

_____

EXERCISE 3:
PUTTING YOUR PLAN FOR SPIRITUAL INTIMACY INTO ACTION

Now that you are removing barriers to spiritual intimacy, you need to act immediately to develop habits of spiritual sharing. Right now make a commitment to each other to pray and study Scripture together. Decide the time during the week that you will do this, and protect that scheduled time as if it were the most important appointment that you have.

It very well may be.

As you grow together, you will want to include acts of Christian service, but begin now with Bible study and prayer.

Where do you start?

Bible Study

We suggest that a good place to start your Bible study is with the exercises in chapter 9, working through those Bible studies together. Those studies take you completely through the Gospel of John and the Book of Acts. Take your time. If it takes you a month or a year to work through those books, that's perfectly all right. It's better to take the time to learn than to rush through on some artificial schedule.

You may prefer to begin your study together with the book we recommend in chapter 9 by Fee and Stuart, *How to Read the Bible for All Its Worth*. It's an excellent study that will prepare you for many more studies in the future.

Of course, there may be a good small group Bible study you could join at your church. If you don't have a church home but are attending our *Becoming ONE* course at a church in your city, ask the facilitator couple if they know of a good Bible study. Often our facilitator couples begin a special Bible study class at the end of the eight-week classes just for the couples who attended. Ask your facilitators if they plan one. If so, you and your spouse can study together during the week and then share what you learn with the other couples you've already learned to trust and love. That gives you a way to keep developing your new friendships while also growing in spiritual intimacy as a couple.

Prayer

If you don't know how to pray together, you may enjoy using a pattern that many Christian use and that is shared in the book, *Becoming ONE*. It's called the ACTS pattern for praying.

1. *A–Adoration*. Write as many phrases as you can think of that praise God, exalting Him above all. Aim your emotions of awe and admiration at Him, and let them flow from you. If you want a clue as to how to do this, read through

Psalms, and you'll find many examples. As a matter of fact, you can read those psalms of praise to God as part of your prayer. Write your phrases here._____

_____

_____

_____

_____

_____

_____

2. *C–Confession.* Write down the things you need to confess to God—any failures, foibles, or wrong acts you've done. Be specific, and don't leave out anything, no matter how trivial it may seem to you. It's true that He sees everything, but praying specifically and openly is helpful to you and pleasing to Him. Learn to be open with Him about everything while at the same time learning to be sensitive about every wrong you do, no matter how slight. Don't hold anything back. Write those things here._____

_____

_____

_____

_____

_____

_____

3. *T–Thanksgiving.* List everything you can think of that you're thankful for. Start with those things most important to you and move in ever increasing circles until you include a wide list of appreciation. Thank God for everything that's good and wonderful in your life, in the lives of your relatives and friends, in the nation, and in the world. Learn to be thankful for everything. As you grow spiritually, you'll learn to thank Him for things that you wouldn't have thought to be thankful about earlier in your life. Write your thanksgivings here._____

_____

_____

_____

_____

_____

_____

_____

4. *S–Solicitation.* List all the things you want to ask of God—things you need and things you want but don't necessarily need. Don't be hesitant or shy. Just

make sure your requests aren't selfish. Nothing is impossible for God. Write your
requests here._____

_____

_____

_____

_____

_____

Now, take these notes with you to your place of prayer and use them to guide
you and your spouse as you pray together. You may pray by any method you wish,
but one method is for each of you to take turns praying sentences or paragraphs.
This means that one of you prays in adoration and then pauses while the other
prays in adoration. Take turns until one of you decides to move to confession.
Continue to pray alternately, for as long or as short a time as you wish, until the
prayer concludes. Whoever prays last gives some kind of closing salutation to
God.

You can see from what you wrote in this exercise that your prayer life will be
much more than some superficial ritual. You'll soon be branching out and praying
about all kinds of things. Always make sure that you have plenty of time to pray
and never feel rushed to "jump in" with words when your spouse pauses. Periods
of silence and reflection are certainly allowable. Just keep focused on God, and
you'll be a prayer warrior before you know it.

Chapter
9

Developing Intimacy with God
—Personally
Becoming His in Mind, Body, and Spirit

If you want your relationship with your spouse to be all it can be, you must first develop a deeply intimate relationship with God. To help you do this, we offer scriptures for you to peruse on your own time and in your own way.

Just in case you're wondering, this *is* crucial to your study of marriage and intimacy. But because of the very personal nature of this study, you and your spouse may not be able to work through these exercises in one week.

The exercises in this chapter walk you through scriptures to help you determine if, indeed, you are in union with God as one of His children. Before you think, "Well, I can just skip this one! I've been a Christian since…" we urge you to avoid that temptation and do the exercises anyway. What have you to lose in spending quality time in the Word of God?

We simply list various scriptures, without commentary or explanation, and ask you to read them. You will decide from your study what those scriptures mean and how you should respond to them.

In order to help you in your study, try to buy or borrow a good Bible handbook. You can find such a book in a Christian bookstore, or you can borrow one from a church. Bible handbooks explain the circumstances under which each book of the Bible was written and to whom it was written. They also tell you something about the situation the Bible author addresses. These things are crucial to understanding what a particular book of the Bible is saying. Some Bibles even have in-depth introductions to each book. Studying the Bible this way allows you to figure out for yourself what the Bible is saying rather than blindly accepting what some person—even a good person—tells you that it means. It's always better to let the Scripture speak for itself when you can.

If you want to get *really* serious about your study, pick up a copy of *How to Read the Bible for All Its Worth: A Guide to Understanding the Bible*, published by

Zondervan and written by Gordon Fee and Douglas Stuart. If you work through the exercises in that book, you'll be a better Bible student than most of the people in the world, even better than most longstanding church members! Fee and Stuart will teach you how to understand a Bible passage's historical context as well as its literary context.

The most important thing for your study is a good Bible, preferably one that is relatively easy to understand *and* an accurate translation of the original languages the Bible was written in. I prefer the New International Version, published by Zondervan, but you can get a knowledgeable clerk in any Christian bookstore to show you the translations available and the relative strengths and weaknesses of each. Just choose one that is recognized as accurate and that has a language style comfortable for you.

Finally, get a spiral notebook or binder to write in as you study. Actually writing things down will help you process the information and make it real.

So, are you ready?

EXERCISE 1:
WHO IS THIS JESUS?

Your first exercise begins with your reading an introduction to the Gospel of John either from a Bible handbook or a good study Bible. Make sure you understand to whom the book is written and why it was written. Understand the culture of the people John writes to and what he was trying to teach them. When you've done that, you're ready for the essential step.

Read the entire Gospel of John.

Yes, all twenty-one chapters.

And read it in one sitting. Don't allow yourself to be distracted or stymied. Just keep reading until you've read the whole book. Most people can read it easily in less than an hour. When you've finished, answer these questions in your notebook.

1. What is this book about?

2. Why did God have John write it?

3. What is it that God wants me to know, think, and feel when I have finished reading it?

When you can answer these questions, you are ready to begin the real Bible study. Start again by reading chapter 1. When you finish, answer the questions and do the exercises below. When you complete both steps, move to chapter 2 and do the same thing with that chapter. Then move to chapter 3, then chapter 4, and so on until you finish the book. As we said, this will take time, but it's worth it.

Step 1: Outline Each Chapter

Outlining isn't as difficult as you may think. The following simple questions will get you started: What is the main thought of this chapter? Where are the natural paragraphs? Where do thoughts change?

Using those thought changes as your points, outline the chapter in a way that makes it easy for you to understand. Each thought change is a major point. The explanations and statements about that thought become the minor points.

Take your time and make this chapter come alive for you.

Step 2: Questions

1. What did I learn about Jesus?

2. What does He expect from me? What does He want me to do?

3. Have I done it?

4. If not, when will I do it?

EXERCISE 2: HAVE I OBEYED HIS WILL FOR ME?

Exercise 2 is very easy to explain. We ask you to do everything you did for the Gospel of John with the Book of Acts, except that the questions in step 2 will be different. Acts is longer than John and so will take more time. But there's no need to rush. Enjoy yourself and take your time. Begin with step 1 of the previous exercise. Then answer the following questions.

1. What did I learn about becoming a Christian? What did the people who were being converted in the Book of Acts do to respond in faith to the call of Jesus?

2. Have I done those things like they did?

3. If not, when will I do them?

4. What did I learn about commitment and service as a child of God?

5. Am I living like those committed Christians lived?

6. If not, when will I commit myself to Jesus like that?

EXERCISE 3: RATING MY SURRENDER TO GOD

Based on all you've learned from studying the Gospel of John and the Book of Acts, will you now compare yourself to the standard of faith and submission you read in those books? Rate yourself for the following three questions on a scale of 1 to 9. 1 means not at all, and 9 means completely. 5 means you aren't sure. The other numbers represent graduations on that scale.

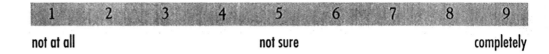

not at all   not sure   completely

Evaluate Yourself

1. As directed in Romans 12:1, I have offered my body as a living sacrifice, holy and pleasing to God. _____

2. I love God with all my heart, soul, and mind just as Jesus commanded in Matthew 22:37. _____

3. As Galatians 5:16 says, I live by the Spirit and no longer gratify the desires of the sinful nature. _____

Examine your answers to the three questions above. Be sure that you are comfortable that your answers are accurate.

Evaluate Your Spouse

Now, rate your spouse on the same three questions, using the scale above, while he or she rates you in his or her book.

1. As directed in Romans 12:1, my spouse has offered his or her body as a living sacrifice, holy and pleasing to God. _____

2. My spouse loves God with all his or her heart, soul, and mind just as Jesus commanded in Matthew 22:37. _____

3. As Galatians 5:16 says, my spouse lives by the Spirit and no longer gratifies the desires of his or her sinful nature. _____

As we've instructed you before, set aside some time to discuss your evaluations with each other. If you and your spouse are in relatively close agreement about your ratings to these three questions, you should have a fairly accurate view of your intimacy with God. If you and your spouse are in disagreement about your ratings, you now have a wonderful chance to discuss spiritual matters.

The goal isn't to convince one or the other who is right. The goal is to find a way for each of you to develop the deepest level of intimacy with God possible. If one of you cannot confirm the other's view of his or her surrender to God, something is missing in your spiritual relationship with each other. Listen carefully to discover what that is, and then do whatever it takes to develop that shared intimacy.

See How You've Changed

Congratulations! You've worked for several weeks through exercise after exercise designed to help you develop more intimacy with each other. Some exercises were easy. Some, as you discovered, weren't easy at all.

Was it worth it?

Before you answer yes or no, allow us to tell you something we learned from a dermatologist friend of ours, Dr. Barry Thompson. When treating patients who want smoother skin but don't want a surgical facelift, Dr. Thompson takes extreme closeup pictures of the patient's face before therapy begins. Later in the therapy, he takes more closeups and asks the patient to carefully examine the "before" and "after" shots. Rather than deciding subjectively if the creams and ointments worked, the patient actually gets a way to measure the effectiveness of the treatment. "It's amazing how many patients think little good occurred until they see the pictures. The changes happen so gradually that they adjust to the new face and think it hasn't changed at all. They used to complain to me that they spent all that money and got very little in return. The pictures removed that incorrect perception. When seeing the 'evidence' clearly presented in the before and after picture, my patients find themselves very pleased with the results of the treatment."

How does that apply to you?

We asked you to take a "closeup picture" of your relationship early in this workbook. In chapter 1, exercise 3 (pages 7–10) you completed Dr. Sternberg's questionnaire to help you measure the levels of Decision/Commitment, Intimacy, and Passion in your marriage. On page 11 you wrote your average scores for each component. Now we ask you to take the "after picture." We give the same questionnaire and ask you to complete it again. When you finish, you can compare your scores and see how much you've grown in *intimacy*. Similarly, you can see how you've changed in levels of *commitment* and *passion*.

EXERCISE 1:
RATING THE INTIMACY, PASSION, AND COMMITMENT YOU FEEL

1	2	3	4	5	6	7	8	9
not at all				moderately				extremely

Statements

1. I am willing to share myself and my possessions with _____.
2. I idealize _____.
3. I plan to continue in my relationship with _____.
4. I value _____ greatly in my life.
5. My relationship with _____ is very romantic.
6. I view my commitment to _____ as a solid one.
7. I feel that _____ really understands me.
8. Just seeing _____ excites me.
9. I view my relationship with _____ as permanent.
10. I have a comfortable relationship with _____.
11. I find _____ to be very personally attractive.
12. I could not let anything get in the way of my commitment to _____.
13. I am actively supportive of _____'s well-being.
14. I cannot imagine another person making me as happy as _____ does.
15. Because of my commitment to _____, I would not let other people come between us.
16. I am able to count on _____ in times of need.
17. I would rather be with _____ than with anyone else.
18. I expect my love for _____ to last for the rest of my life.
19. I share deeply personal information about myself with _____.
20. I especially like physical contact with _____.
21. I cannot imagine ending my relationship with _____.
22. _____ is able to count on me in times of need.
23. I adore _____.
24. I feel a sense of responsibility toward _____.
25. I feel that I really can trust _____.
26. There is something almost "magical" about my relationship with _____.

27.   I view my relationship with _____ as a good decision.

28.   I receive considerable emotional support from _____.

29.   I find myself thinking about _____ frequently during the day.

30.   I am certain of my love for _____.

31.   I feel that I really understand _____.

32.   I cannot imagine life without _____.

33.   I am committed to maintaining my relationship with _____.

34.   I have a warm relationship with _____.

35.   I fantasize about _____.

36.   I know that I care about _____.

37.   I communicate well with _____.

38.   My relationship with _____ is passionate.

39.   I have confidence in the stability of my relationship with _____.

40.   I give considerable emotional support to _____.

41.   Nothing is more important to me than my relationship with _____.

42.   I will always feel a strong responsibility for _____.

43.   I feel close to _____.

44.   When I see romantic movies and read romantic books I think of _____

45.   Even when _____ is hard to deal with, I remain committed to our relationship.

Code_____

(initials + last 3 digits of
social security number)[1]

Answers—Part 1(What You Feel Is Characteristic)

Rate the statements from the previous section as to how *characteristic* they are of your relationship. In other words, to what extent does each statement reflect how you currently feel in your relationship? Write your answers using the 1 to 9 scale (on page 100) here:

1.	2.	3.
4.	5.	6.
7.	8.	9.
10.	11.	12.
13.	14.	15.
16.	17.	18.
19.	20.	21.
22.	23.	24.
25.	26.	27.
28.	29.	30.
31.	32.	33.
34.	35.	36.
37.	38.	39.
40.	41.	42.
43.	44.	45.
Total Column	Total Column	Total Column
Average	Average	Average

Answers—Part 2 (What You Think Is Important)

Now rate the statements as to how *important* they are to your relationship. In other words, to what extent do you think it is important that you should feel this way, regardless of how you actually feel? Write your answers using the 1 to 9 scale here:

1.	2.	3.
4.	5.	6.
7.	8.	9.
10.	11.	12.
13.	14.	15.
16.	17.	18.
19.	20.	21.
22.	23.	24.
25.	26.	27.
28.	29.	30.
31.	32.	33.
34.	35.	36.
37.	38.	39.
40.	41.	42.
43.	44.	45.
Total Column	Total Column	Total Column
Average	Average	Average

Understanding Your Scores

As you may have guessed from the answer charts, at the bottom of each column you should total the score for *that* column and then divide by 15 to get the average rating for that category. The first column (the one to your left) measured *intimacy*. The middle column measured *passion*. And the third column (the one to your right) measured *commitment*. Each of you, both husband and wife, now has an average rating for how you actually *feel* in each category and an average rating for what you think is *important* to feel in that category. Your part 1 answers reflect how you feel; your part 2 scores reflect what you think is important to feel.

Jot your averages here:

Part 1 (what you feel is characteristic)
_____ intimacy average
_____ passion average
_____ commitment average

Part 2 (what you think is important)
_____ intimacy average
_____ passion average
_____ commitment average

Compare Your Scores to See What You Feel Is Characteristic

To get the clearest visual interpretation of how your feelings have changed, use the chart on the following page to draw a bar graph like the one below. Like the imaginary person we've charted below, you'll draw a bar representing your "before" score (from page 11) on the left and a bar representing your "after" score (from this page) on the right.

Let us illustrate with our imaginary person.

Scores from chapter 1
Part 1 (how _____ felt then)
6.2 intimacy average
4.9 passion average
5.7 commitment average

Scores from this exercise
Part 1 (how _____ feels now)
7.4 intimacy average
7.2 passion average
8.7 commitment average

Before

After

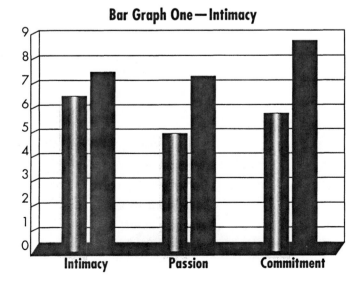

Bar Graph One — Intimacy

Our imaginary person grew from a low score in intimacy to an average score, from a low score in passion to an average score, and from a low score in commitment to a high score. (Low, average, and high are explained on page 107.) Obviously this person benefited from working through the exercises but just as obviously still has room for growth.

Jot your scores here before making your graph for what you feel is *characteristic* in your relationship.

Graph—Part 1 (What You Feel Is Characteristic)

Scores from chapter 1	Scores from this exercise
Part 1 (how you felt then)	Part 1 (how you feel now)
_____ intimacy average	_____ intimacy average
_____ passion average	_____ passion average
_____ commitment average	_____ commitment average

Now, fill in the chart with your before and after scores.

9
8
7
6
5
4
3
2
1
0

Intimacy   **Passion**   **Commitment**

Compare Your Scores to See What You Think Is Important

Graph—Part 2 (What You Think Is Important)

Scores from chapter 1	Scores from this exercise
Part 2 (what you thought important then)	Part 2 (what you think important now)
_____ intimacy average	_____ intimacy average
_____ passion average	_____ passion average
_____ commitment average	_____ commitment average

Now, plot your scores on the graph below.

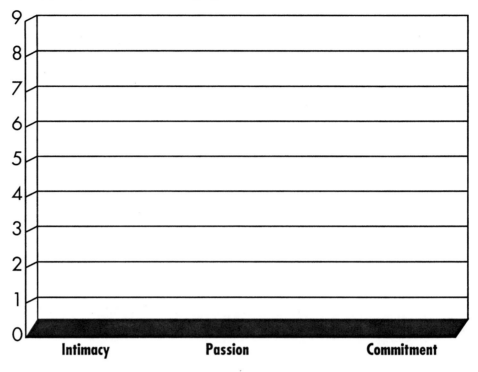

Four Levels of Insight

First Insight

The first insight this exercise may give you into your relationship can come from examining how your scores changed. If your *intimacy* score for what you feel is characteristic of your relationship is higher now than it was before, you've grown in intimacy! The greater the difference in the scores, the more growth you've likely experienced. The same holds true for *commitment* and *passion*. Our prediction is that if you had low scores at the outset, they've shown dramatic improvement. If they were high to begin with, they show less dramatic improvement, though they did improve some. Even if you only moved up slightly, that's still growth, and you should find joy in knowing that your relationship is moving the right direction!

If so, working through this workbook has been good for you.

Second Insight

The next level of insight comes from viewing your spouse's scores. As each of you allows the other to see your bar graphs, you will gain insight just by seeing how similar your spouse's scores are. If you wish to put your "after" scores next to your spouse's "after" scores, we give you two bar graphs to do that.

Use the first bar graph to compare your "after" scores on what you feel is *characteristic* of your relationship.

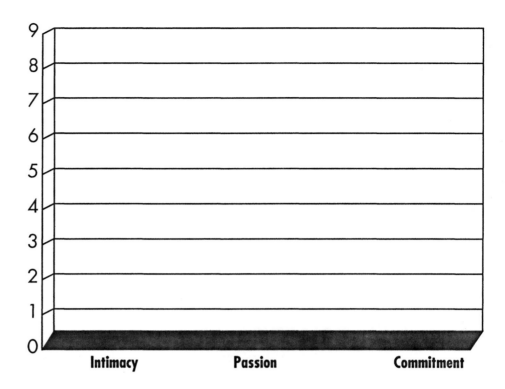

Use the next bar graph to compare your "after" scores on what you think is *important* for your relationship.

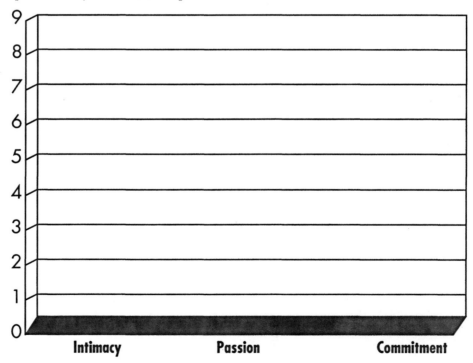

If you see that your score on a particular category is dramatically different from your spouse's (for example, she has a 9 for what she thinks important in intimacy and he only a 7), you might view that as a guide to *what* you should continue to concentrate on in your relationship. Why? Because if your spouse wants a higher level of a particular category than you, you may be unconsciously sabotaging your relationship by not being aware of that need or desire within your mate. You may be concentrating on one component while he or she very much wants you to concentrate on another.

Third Insight

Remember the high, average, and low chart from chapter 1. Those scores follow so that you may compare your scores to those in terms of what ratings Dr. Sternberg considers high, average, or low.

Compare your "after" scores to see how you've grown in your relationship. If you've only moved from low to average, that's still significant growth, in our estimation.

Characteristic "How characteristic is the description in each statement of your relationship?"			
	Intimacy	Passion	Commitment
High	8.6	8.2	8.7
Average	7.4	6.5	7.2
Low	6.2	4.9	5.7

Importance "How important is the description in each statement to your relationship?"			
	Intimacy	Passion	Commitment
High	9.0	8.0	8.8
Average	8.2	6.8	7.6
Low	7.4	5.4	6.5

The high scores represent approximately the top 15 percent of scores, and the low scores, the bottom 15 percent.

If you compare your score on intimacy with the high, average, and low scores on intimacy listed by Dr. Sternberg above, you get an idea of what level of intimacy you feel in comparison to the general population. Again, since this is not intended to be a definitive diagnostic tool, don't let your score lead you into any kind of panic or major life decision. Just look at it as another "checkup" (like the one in chapter 1) to give you another way to gauge your relationship.

Fourth Insight

Again we offer you the opportunity to go to our Web site (www.familydy-namics.net) to take the questionnaire there. When you do, your scores will be calculated and shown in overlapping triangles. More graphic than the bar charts you made in this chapter, these triangles can be quite clear on where growth has taken place and where you need to concentrate to grow more.

Sharing with Your Spouse

As you share your graphs together, listen, as always, carefully and without censure or criticism. You may want to talk in depth about what each of you expects in terms of intimacy, passion, or commitment. Don't be afraid to say out loud what you want as long as you don't do it in a critical or condemning manner. Attacking won't do any good. You'll never get to where you want to go if you can't accept where each of you is starting from. So get started. Sit down with no distractions (no TV, no kids, phone off the hook) and share your scores, your desires, and your needs with each other. Use all the skills you've learned about how to communicate with each other.

Talk specifically about every area of growth each of you has made. Talk about how you've grown, how that has affected your relationship, and what your relationship will be like if you both keep growing.

Talk openly about where growth is still needed, what should come next, and what you can do to make your marriage be all that it can be.

If we can help, just give us a call.

That's our business, you know.

Notes

INTRODUCTION—INTENTIONAL INTIMACY

1. For information about available *A New Beginning* seminars in your area, call 1-800-650-9995. If you prefer, register online (www.familydynamics.net).

2. At the time of this writing, approximately 35,000 people have enrolled in our seminars, and the number increases every day.

3. For information about facilitator couples near you, call 1-800-650-9995. If you are interested in becoming a facilitator couple, please tell us that when you call, and we'll send you a full explanation of how the classes work. If you prefer, visit our Web site (www.familydynamics.net).

CHAPTER 1—THE CRAVING FOR INTIMACY

1. Genesis 2:18.

2. Genesis 2:24.

3. The survey and normative information that follows is found on pages 45 through 48 of Robert J. Sternberg, *Cupid's Arrow* (Cambridge University Press, 1998). Used by permission.

4. If you are willing to help us in our national survey so that we can better help families, please send us a copy of your answers for this exercise. To help us put the answers into the computer for "before" and "after" scores, we ask you to use a code that consists of your initials (of your first, middle, and last names) and last three numbers of your social security number. That gives you complete anonymity while giving us a way to compare actual before and after scores. For example, the code for the author of this book would be JLB416—his initials plus the last three numbers from his social security number. (See how safe it is while also making it very unlikely that another person's code would be confused with

his?) To participate, send a copy of your response sheet to Family Dynamics, P.O. Box 211668, Augusta, GA 30917-1668.

CHAPTER 2—THE TRIUNE NATURE OF INTIMACY

1. Philippians 3:10–12.
2. Judges 16:1.
3. 1 Samuel 25:3.
4. 1 Samuel 25:26–31.
5. 1 Samuel 25:32–34.
6. 1 Samuel 25:39–42.
7. We believe these passages make it clear that Jacob and Leah had no emotional involvement. The Genesis 30 passage indicates that Leah had a relationship with God, as did Jacob, but the language seems to imply that they didn't share their spiritual lives with each other. He "dishonored" her, according to her language. Therefore, we think that they didn't really share spiritual intimacy with each other. We conclude that their intimacy was in body only, *Sexual Intimacy*.
8. Because of the great spiritual awakening taking place in this woman's life, we believe that she and Jesus shared spiritual intimacy. Also, it is very clear that she opened her heart to Him and He to her. Therefore, they shared a level of emotional intimacy. But it is just as clear that sexuality had no part in their relationship. Therefore, we conclude that they shared *Celibate Intimacy*.
9. Obviously, they shared their bodies. Just as obviously, they shared no spirituality in their coupling since the very act of adultery was a crime before God and punishable by death. The only real question is whether they shared any emotional intimacy. Was it simply lust that drew them together, or were there more factors involved? Was she drawn to "the soul of a poet" that he was? Did he find himself attracted to the intelligence and cunning she would show in later events? If all they shared was their bodies, they shared *Sexual Intimacy*. If there was also an emotional attachment where they felt real attraction and understanding of each other, then it was *Romantic Intimacy*. We opt for this choice since it seems to explain so much more about how David, the man after God's own heart, could involve himself in such a sin.
10. Psalm 15:4.

CHAPTER 3—REPAIRING INTIMACY DIVERSIONS AND DRAINS

1. Matthew 19:16–31.

CHAPTER 4—DEVELOPING EMOTIONAL INTIMACY, PART 1

1. In Matthew 19:19, Jesus commanded, "Love your neighbor as yourself." Obviously, you can't do the first half of that command until you do the last half. We can't love others until we first love ourselves.

2. Joe Beam, *Forgiven Forever* (West Monroe, La.: Howard Publishing, 1998).

3. An invoice for a modest amount for the book and shipping cost comes with the book. If you cannot afford to pay the invoice for any reason, instead of sending money, send us a letter telling us if you indeed found a relationship with Jesus.

CHAPTER 5—DEVELOPING EMOTIONAL INTIMACY, PART 2

1. For a detailed discussion of these and other practices that prevent clear communication, see John M. Gottman, Ph.D., *Seven Principles for Making a Marriage Work* (n.p.: Crown Publishers, 1999).

CHAPTER 7—DEVELOPING SEXUAL INTIMACY, PART 2

1. We understand Solomon's reference to the mountain of myrrh and hill of incense as reference to his attention to his wife's genitalia during their lovemaking. Even in medical books the area at the top of the woman's genital area is called *mons* or *mount*. He knew that while all the other parts of her body need kissing and caressing, her orgasms emanate from her clitoris. He intended to pay attention to that part of her body all night long, revisiting it again.

2. In verse 11 he says her lips drop sweetness as he refers to the delights of kissing her. Then he says of her in verse 12, "You are a garden locked up...a spring enclosed, a sealed fountain." As he continues comparing her to a garden, he begins to refer to her alluring fragrances finally coming back to the theme of myrrh that he described back in verse 6. As he revisits that part of her body, he now notes that it is no longer "locked up" or "enclosed." Now he says the part of her he calls her "mountain of myrrh" (see above endnote) is "flowing" and "streaming." We believe he's referring to her coming to complete arousal—moving from "locked up" to "flowing"—and that her genitalia has become extremely lubricated. As we discuss in *Becoming ONE*, that means he is a slow and skilled lover.

3. Her "garden" is her genitalia that Solomon had just referred to as extremely lubricated. She references its unique fragrance and asks Solomon to "blow" on it and "taste" it. In other words, she is asking him to perform oral sex on her.

4. Solomon obviously understood the woman's different approach to sex. He didn't rush her, instead taking all night long, "until the day breaks and the shadows flee," when he had opportunity. He knew that women build to a sexual crescendo slowly, and he took his time to execute what we today call foreplay. He "climbed the palm" rather than taking it abruptly. That image he painted makes one think that he started by kissing her feet—maybe even her toes or the erogenous zone of the soles of her feet—and worked his way up. Since he repeatedly

said throughout the book that he wasn't concerned with time, we picture him kissing and caressing any part of her body as long as she continued to find it pleasurable. He wasn't in a hurry to get anywhere or complete anything. He obviously kissed her calves, the backs of her knees, her thighs. This man was a consummate lover.

5.   Her statement about her wine flowing over his lips and teeth seems to be a specific reference to deep kissing and an implied reference to what he would experience as he kissed her genital area.

CHAPTER 10—SEE HOW YOU'VE CHANGED

1.   If you are willing to help us in our national survey so that we can better help families, we asked you in chapter one to send us a copy of your answers for this exercise. To help us put the answers into the computer for "before" and "after" scores, we asked you to use a code that consists of your initials (of your first, middle, and last names) and last three numbers of your social security number. That gives you complete anonymity while giving us a way to compare actual before and after scores. For example, the code for the author of this book would be JLB416—his initials plus the last three numbers from his social security number. (See how safe it is while also making it very unlikely that another person's code would be confused with his?) To participate, send a copy of your response sheet to Family Dynamics, P.O. Box 211668, Augusta, GA 30917-1668.

LaVergne, TN USA
27 March 2010
177285LV00001B/3/A

9 781582 290799